Politik und Religion:
Eigenlogik oder Verzahnung?

HISTORISCHE ZEITSCHRIFT

Beihefte
(Neue Folge)

Herausgegeben von Lothar Gall

Band 45

R. Oldenbourg Verlag München 2007

Robert von Friedeburg/Luise Schorn-Schütte
(Hrsg.)

Politik und Religion: Eigenlogik oder Verzahnung?

Europa im 16. Jahrhundert

R. Oldenbourg Verlag München 2007

Bibliografische Information Der Deutschen Bibliothek
Die Deutsche Bibliothek verzeichnet diese Publikation in der Deutschen Nationalbibliografie; detaillierte bibliografische Daten sind im Internet über <http://www.dnb-d-nb.de> abrufbar.

© 2007 Oldenbourg Wissenschaftsverlag GmbH, München
Rosenheimer Straße 145, D-81671 München
Internet: oldenbourg.de

Das Werk einschließlich aller Abbildungen ist urheberrechtlich geschützt. Jede Verwertung außerhalb der Grenzen des Urheberrechtsgesetzes ist ohne Zustimmung des Verlages unzulässig und strafbar. Dies gilt insbesondere für Vervielfältigungen, Übersetzungen, Mikroverfilmungen und die Einspeicherung und Bearbeitung in elektronischen Systemen.

Umschlagentwurf: Dieter Vollendorf
Gedruckt auf säurefreiem, alterungsbeständigem Papier (chlorfrei gebleicht).

Satz: Typodata GmbH, München
Druck: Memminger MedienCentrum, Memmingen
Bindung: Thomas Buchbinderei, Augsburg

ISBN: 978-3-486-64455-5

Inhalt

Einleitung. Politik und Religion: Eigenlogik oder Verzahnung?
Von *Robert von Friedeburg* und *Luise Schorn-Schütte* 1

Eigenlogik oder Verzahnung? Religion und Politik im lutherischen
Protestantismus des Alten Reiches (16. Jahrhundert).
Von *Luise Schorn-Schütte* 13

„Officium in rempublicam". Fürstliche Herrschaft und Territorialstaat
in politischen und rechtlichen Reflektionen und Projektionen im
Jahrhundert der Reformation. Von *Robert von Friedeburg* 33

„Le Grande Cassure": Violence and the French Reformation.
By *Mark Greengrass* 71

Traditional Politics and Visionary Theology: The English
Reformation. By *Ralph Houlbrooke* 93

The English Reformation in the Sixteenth Century: Major Themes
and New Viewpoints. By *Martin Ingram* 129

Bibliographical Update. By *Ralph Houlbrooke* and *Martin Ingram* .. 163

Autorenverzeichnis 165

Einleitung

Politik und Religion:
Eigenlogik oder Verzahnung?

Von

Robert von Friedeburg und *Luise Schorn-Schütte*

I. Europäische Grundfragen

1. Traditionen – Visionen: unter dieser Thematik stand der 44. Deutsche Historikertag, der 2002 in Halle an der Saale stattfand.[1] Und unter dieser Thematik wurde in frühneuzeitspezifischer Konzentration auch die Sektion verhandelt, deren Ergebnisse hier vorgelegt werden.

Im Blick auf das Europa des 16. Jahrhunderts lautete die Frage: Gab es eine visionäre Theologie, die einer traditionalen Politik gegenüberstand? Kann man davon sprechen, daß es wechselseitige Verzahnungen gegeben hat, und wie veränderte das die Beziehungen zwischen Kirche und Welt, Politik und Religion?

Indem die stets aktuelle Frage nach dem Verhältnis zwischen Religion und Politik mit derjenigen nach Tradition und Vision/Innovation verbunden wurde, veränderte sich deren Richtung. Anliegen der Referate und Diskussionen war es deshalb vor allem, einen Beitrag zur Klärung der Begrifflichkeiten zu leisten: was ist Tradition, was Innovation in der Frühen Neuzeit? Ist die Entflechtung von Religion und Politik, die viel diskutierte „Desakralisierung" also, innovativ, so wie dies in der Forschung stets betont wird?[2] Wie aber verträgt sich mit einer solchen Aussage das frühneuzeitliche Selbstverständnis, wonach Legitimität von Herrschaft, von Teilhabeforde-

---

[1] Im Jahre 1893 waren erstmals Hochschullehrer, Gymnasiallehrer und Archivare in München zusammengetroffen, um einen Gründungsaufruf für einen Verband der Historiker und Archivare zu verabschieden, ein Jahr später nahm Karl Lamprecht diese Anregung auf und berief den 2. Historikertag nach Leipzig ein. Erstmals in Halle fand das Historikertreffen 1900 zum sechsten Mal statt.

[2] Der entwicklungsgeschichtliche Blick der Geschichtsschreibung hat natürlich zu Recht herausgestellt, daß die im 19. Jahrhundert allmählich erreichte Auflösung der Verzahnung von Religion und Politik das Krisenpotential politischer Konflikte um das Moment der Religion entschärft hat. Dessen Charakterisierung als „Moderner Werden" von Konfliktlösungen ist aber nur eine unter mehreren Möglichkeiten, es ist die Sicht des Historikers ex post.

rung stets nur in deren Einbindung in Traditionen oder in deren Wiederbelebung gegeben war? Offensichtlich war es in der Frühen Neuzeit selbstverständlich, von einer *innovativen Kraft der Tradition* auszugehen. Wie ist mit diesem Selbstverständnis das Verhältnis von Religion und Politik zu verbinden, von dem nicht zu Unrecht betont wird, daß deren *Verzahnung* als das Charakteristikum des 16. und 17. Jahrhunderts gilt? Heißt das dann, daß die reformatorische Bewegung, weil in ihrer Konsequenz eine neuerliche Verzahnung von Religion und Politik stattfand, eine traditionale Bewegung war? Wie ist mit dieser Aussage dann aber die lang beschriebene Charakterisierung der Reformation als Umbruch zu vereinbaren?

2. Der Blick auf die Forschungstraditionen zeigt einmal mehr, wie sehr der zeitgenössische Blick die Fragen an die Geschichte und dementsprechende Antworten vorstrukturiert. Für England, Frankreich und die Territorien des Alten Reiches[3] konstruierten die Historiker des 19. Jahrhunderts jeweils nationale Befreiungsbewegungen, die je nach regionaler Zugehörigkeit in die protestantischen oder katholischen Traditionen eingebunden wurden.[4] In den Forschungen der späten 60er bis 80er Jahre des 20. Jahrhunderts dominierte die Frage nach dem Charakter der Reformation als „Volksbewegung" oder „Fürstenreformation", um die Schlagworte jener intensiven Debatten noch einmal aufzunehmen; damit wurde gestritten darüber, ob die Potentiale des Widerstandes und der Teilhabe in der reformatorischen Bewegung stärker waren als diejenigen der Treue zur Obrigkeit. Diese Debatte war zumindest in den deutschen Varianten Teil jener „Fragen an die Geschichte", die in den siebziger Jahren in beiden deutschen Staaten wenn auch mit unterschiedlichen Vorzeichen gestellt wurden, und mit deren Hilfe nach den demokratischen Spuren auch und gerade in der deutschen Vergangenheit gesucht wurde.[5] Daß dieses Verfahren dem politisch argumentierenden Historismus des 19. Jahrhunderts im Sinne eines Droysen, Ranke und

---

[3] Das Alte Reich insgesamt stand nie im Blick der Reformationsforschung des 19. und frühen 20. Jahrhunderts, dieses verbot sich aufgrund der politisch-nationalen Blickrichtung.

[4] Eine vergleichende Darstellung dieser europäischen Traditionen der Reformationsgeschichtsschreibung fehlt erstaunlicherweise, siehe aber *Olaf Mörke*, Die Reformation. Voraussetzungen und Durchsetzung. München 2005, der in seinem Forschungsüberblick die internationale Debatte konsequent mit berücksichtigt; zum Stand der Forschung jetzt auch *Luise Schorn-Schütte*, Reformationsgeschichtsschreibung – wozu? Eine Standortbestimmung, in: Dieter Hein/Klaus Hildebrand/Andreas Schulz (Hrsg.), Historie und Leben. Der Historiker als Wissenschaftler und Zeitgenosse. Festschrift für Lothar Gall zum 70. Geburtstag. München 2006, 137–150.

[5] Selbstverständlich wird hier nicht die Identität der Fragestellung von marxistischer und nichtmarxistischer Reformationsgeschichtsschreibung behauptet; das Bemühen aber, die als verschüttet charakterisierten Traditionen deutscher Geschichte, seien sie nun als sozialistische oder als demokratische markiert, wieder zu entdecken, war durchaus ein paralleles.

Burckhardt[6] sehr verwandt war, wird aus der Distanz von dreißig Jahren deutlicher, als es den an den Debatten Beteiligten seinerzeit möglich war.

Läßt sich vor diesem Hintergrund, der zu sehr unterschiedlichen Forschungstraditionen geführt hat, Gemeinsames, Verbindendes für die mitteleuropäische Landkarte artikulieren?

3. Wichtig ist für alle drei Regionen die Frage: wie konstituiert sich der Raum des Politischen? Gibt es überhaupt die Vorstellung einer Trennung des Religiösen und des Politischen im Sinne von Sektoren, wie sie für das 19. Jahrhundert konstatiert und ebenso für die Bereiche Staat und Gesellschaft angenommen werden? Otto Brunners Nachweis, daß es derartige Trennungen in der Frühen Neuzeit nicht gegeben habe, ist trotz der berechtigten Kritik an der starken Zeitbindung der Brunnerschen Forschungen nicht zu bestreiten.[7] Reinhard Blänkner hat diese Feststellung differenzierend bestätigt, indem er anerkennt, daß sich am Ende des 16. Jahrhunderts zwar ein neuer Raum des Politischen jenseits der konfessionellen Fundamentalismen etablierte, dieser Prozeß aber nicht als „Autonomisierung" bezeichnet werden könne. Denn eine „grundsätzliche Ablösung des Politischen vom Religiösen" fand nicht statt, selbst wenn in akuten Konflikten theologisch-konfessionelle Dominanzansprüche zugunsten weltlicher (auch militärisch geübter) Macht zurückgenommen wurden.[8]

Die Autonomie des Politischen ist eine Projektion der zeitgebundenen Fragestellungen der Historiker des 19. ebenso wie des 20. Jahrhunderts. Diese gewiß pointierte Feststellung erhält auch durch die erneuerte Intensität Gewicht, mit der sich die jüngere politikwissenschaftliche Forschung dem Verhältnis von Religion und Politik zuwendet. Sie identifiziert Religion als einen Grundbegriff politischer Theorie: „Tatsächlich zeigt jedoch [...] die aktuelle Debatte über Religion und Politik, daß Religion auch unter dem modernen Vorzeichen einer weltanschaulichen Neutralität des Staates ein wesentlicher Faktor der Politik und somit grundlegend für ihr Verständnis bleibt."[9]

---

[6] Zur politischen Geschichtsschreibung des 19. und frühen 20. Jahrhunderts, die sich methodisch im Rahmen der Historismusdebatten bewegte, gibt es eine ausufernde Literatur, die allerdings überwiegend aus den 80er/90er Jahren des 20. Jahrhunderts stammt, so daß stets die innovativen Potentiale der beteiligten Historiker (z. B. Jacob Burckhardts) herausgearbeitet wurden. Aus einem anderen Blickwinkel *Luise Schorn-Schütte*, Historische Politikforschung. Eine Einführung. München 2006.
[7] Wolfgang Reinhard allerdings bewertet die Interpretation Brunners ausschließlich als Ergebnis seiner zeitgenössischen nationalsozialistischen Bindungen; dem wird hier widersprochen. Siehe *Wolfgang Reinhard*, Probleme deutscher Geschichte: Reichsreform und Reformation 1495–1555. Stuttgart 2002, 35–42.
[8] *Robert Blänkner*, Historizität, Institutionalität, Symbolizität. Grundbegriffliche Aspekte einer Kulturgeschichte des Politischen, in: Barbara Stollberg-Rilinger (Hrsg.), Was heißt Kulturgeschichte des Politischen? Berlin 2005, 71–96, hier 83.
[9] *Tine Stein*, Religion, in: Gerhard Göhler/Matthias Iser/Ina Kerner (Hrsg.), Politische Theorie. 22 umkämpfte Begriffe zur Einführung. Wiesbaden 2004, 315–331, hier 316.

Nicht zuletzt deshalb ist es dringliche Aufgabe der *Historiker* zu beschreiben, worin die Eigenart jener politischen Theologie bzw. theologisierten Politik in solchen historischen Zeiten besteht, in der eine weltanschauliche Neutralität der politischen Herrschaft gerade nicht existierte. Zu fragen ist deshalb an dieser Stelle, worin sich die politische Theologie im 16. Jahrhundert von den Vorläufern im 15. und den Entwicklungen im späten 17. Jahrhundert unterscheidet. Und damit treffen wir auf erstaunlich ausgeprägte europäische Gemeinsamkeiten, die sich auf vielerlei Ebenen beschreiben lassen.

4. Der Vorschlag von Barbara Stollberg-Rilinger, das Politische nicht zu definieren, dürfte nicht weiter führen.[10] Als Ergebnis der hier dokumentierten Diskussionen ist es vielmehr durchaus möglich, den europäischen Raum des Politischen im 16. Jahrhundert zu benennen, allerdings in einer regionalen und chronologischen Differenzierung, die bislang nicht geleistet wurde. Dazu tragen die hier vorgelegten Beiträge bei.

In jedem Fall war es nicht der Raum „*des* Staates". Denn nicht allein auf der Ebene der „hohen Politik" fanden jene Debatten über den Vorrang von Glauben oder pragmatischer Politik statt, die die Forschung seit Generationen beschreibt. Für die deutschen Verhältnisse der dreißiger bis frühen sechziger Jahre dieses Jahrhunderts ebenso gewichtig ist es, den Charakter der Verzahnung zwischen beiden Faktoren wahrzunehmen, der sich als enge Kooperation zwischen jenen protestantischen Theologen und Juristen darstellt, die im Umkreis des schmalkaldischen Krieges als politische Berater der protestierenden Stände fungierten. Sie entstammten zumeist dem städtischen Bürgertum, nur selten traten adelige Mitglieder in diese Kooperation ein; in der Forschung ist die Gruppe treffend als „territoriales, gelehrtes Bürgertum" bezeichnet worden.[11]

In England zeigten sich andere Koalitionen, der niedere Adel war in diesen Prozeß sehr wohl mit eingebunden[12], entsprechendes gilt für Frankreich. Hier allerdings hatte sich die Verzahnung von Religion und Politik zu einem seit den ausgehenden 1550er Jahren gewalttätig geführten Konfessionskampf unter Beteiligung des Adels und des städtischen Bürgertums zugespitzt.[13] Die Etablierung eines politisch-theologischen Raumes jenseits sol-

---

[10] *Barbara Stollberg-Rilinger*, Einleitung: Was heißt Kulturgeschichte des Politischen?, in: dies. (Hrsg.), Was heißt Kulturgeschichte des Politischen? (wie Anm. 8), 9-24.
[11] Siehe u. a. *Luise Schorn-Schütte*, Prediger an protestantischen Höfen der Frühneuzeit. Zur politischen und sozialen Stellung einer neuen bürgerlichen Führungsgruppe in der höfischen Gesellschaft des 17. Jahrhunderts, dargestellt am Beispiel von Hessen-Kassel, Hessen-Darmstadt und Braunschweig-Wolfenbüttel, in: Heinz Schilling/Herman Diederiks (Hrsg.), Bürgerliche Eliten in den Niederlanden und in Nordwestdeutschland. Studien zur Sozialgeschichte des europäischen Bürgertums im Mittelalter und in der Neuzeit. (Städteforschung, Rh. A, Bd. 23.) Köln/Wien 1985, 275-336.
[12] Siehe dazu die Beiträge von Houlbrooke und Ingram in diesem Band.
[13] Siehe dazu den Beitrag von Greengrass in diesem Band, zudem die anregenden Überlegungen zur Möglichkeit einer Trennung von Glauben und politischem Opportunismus

cher Gewaltanwendung setzte deshalb zu einem Zeitpunkt ein, in dem in England und Deutschland die Verzahnung von Politik und Religion auf jener mittleren Expertenebene soeben erst zur selbstverständlichen Praxis geworden war.

5. Die hier interessierenden Parallelen und Unterschiede lassen sich einerseits greifen in den theoretischen Reflexionen der Zeitgenossen, in der Eigenart also der politica-Literatur; andererseits finden sie sich in den ganz konkreten Konflikten vor Ort artikuliert, in Gestalt also einer „politischen Sprache", die sich zeit- und regionenspezifisch identifizieren läßt.[14] Daß die konfessions- und herrschaftspolitischen Unterschiede zwischen den europäischen Regionen damit nicht belanglos wurden, ist nachdrücklich festzuhalten (siehe unten II.).

In allen drei Regionen erwies sich die Einbindung einer *neuen Sozialgruppe protestantischer Geistlichkeit* als soziale und konfessionspolitische Herausforderung. Denn obgleich der sakrale Charakter des geistlichen Amtes aufgegeben war, beanspruchten die protestantischen Pfarrer einen Gestaltungsspielraum, der sich in einem spezifisch geistlichen Amtsverständnis artikulierte und in den Debatten um das Verhältnis zwischen Kirche und Welt als Zündstoff wirken konnte.

Für das *Alte Reich* läßt sich dieser Vorgang in der Wiederbelebung der Drei-Stände-Lehre nachweisen; zahlreiche gelehrte Theologen und etliche gelehrte Juristen verstanden sie als Modell einer sozialen und politischen Ordnung, die Gleichgewicht durch Herrschaftsverteilung sicherte.[15] Dem lag die Vorstellung einer Ordnung zugrunde, die durch klar voneinander getrennte Amtssphären gekennzeichnet war, weltliche Obrigkeit (status politicus) war nur einer unter anderen, die Kirche (status ecclesiasticus) ein weiterer.

---

im französischen Adel des ausgehenden 16. Jahrhunderts bei *Ronald G. Asch*, Religiöse Selbstinszenierung im Zeitalter der Glaubenskriege, in : Historisches Jahrbuch 125, 2005, 67–100, hier bes. 71: „daß man sich eines Anachronismus schuldig mache, wenn man im Blick auf das 16. und 17. Jahrhundert auch nur versuche, im Einzelfall exakt zwischen wahrer Glaubensüberzeugung und politischem und religiösem Opportunismus zu unterscheiden, in der vermeintlichen Hoffnung, auf diese Weise den wahren Kern einer Persönlichkeit identifizieren zu können."
14 Siehe dazu den methodischen Ansatz der Cambridge School ausgeführt und kritisiert u. a. bei *Eckhart Hellmuth/Christoph von Ehrenstein*, Intellectual History Made in Britain: Die *Cambridge School* und ihre Kritiker, in: Geschichte und Gesellschaft 27, 2001, 149–172.
15 Dazu *Luise Schorn-Schütte*, Die Drei-Stände-Lehre im reformatorischen Umbruch, in: Bernd Moeller (Hrsg.), Die Reformation als Umbruch. (Schriften des Vereins für Reformationsgeschichte, Bd. 199.) Gütersloh 1998, 435–461, und *dies.*, Politische Kommunikation in der Frühen Neuzeit. Obrigkeitskritik im Alten Reich, in: Geschichte und Gesellschaft 32, 2006, 273–314; die Bedeutung der Drei-Stände-Lehre wird allmählich auch in der englischsprachigen Literatur rezipiert, siehe dazu *John Witte*, Law and Protestantism. The Legal Teaching of the Lutheran Refromation. Cambridge 2002, 9, 150 u. ö.

Ein vergleichbares Sonderbewußtsein (self consciousness) läßt sich für die englischen protestantischen gelehrten Theologen identifizieren.[16] Allerdings war die Dreiständelehre ohne Bedeutung für die englischen Debatten; dennoch ist der Amtsanspruch der Geistlichkeit von durchaus politischem Gewicht, weil er das Recht behauptete, die Amtsführung der weltlichen Obrigkeit zu überprüfen, was für den Fall eines Mißbrauchs das Recht auf Obrigkeitskritik bis hin zum Recht auf Aufkündigung des Gehorsams einschloß. Gegenüber einer dann als unchristlich zu charakterisierenden Obrigkeit bestand das Recht des Widerstandes, eines Rechts, das in den zeitgenössischen Debatten in ganz Europa eine alles beherrschende Rolle spielte.[17]

War diese Zuspitzung auf die Frage nach der Legitimität christlicher Obrigkeit ein Ergebnis visionärer protestantischer Theologie? Wohl kaum allein, denn schon die spätmittelalterlichen Debatten über die Legitimität weltlicher Herrschaft wurden geleitet von dem Anspruch geistlicher Amtsträger, eine unchristliche Herrschaft kritisieren zu dürfen, ja zu müssen, und ihr im Extremfall zu widerstehen (correctio principis).[18] Aufgrund der konfessionsspezifischen Verzahnung politischer und geistlicher Ordnungsansprüche entstand allerdings ein sich wechselseitig ausschließender Geltungsanspruch: christliche Obrigkeit konnte immer nur diejenige sein, die die eigene theologische Wahrheit schützte. Diese politische Theologie des 16. Jahrhunderts trug dazu bei, traditionale Teilhaberechte zu stärken, die zur Verteilung von Herrschaft und damit zu deren Begrenzung führten. Das allerdings war eine nicht intendierte Wirkung, möglich aber nur aufgrund der neuerlichen Verzahnung von Politik und Religion. Unter diesem Blickwinkel erwies sich das Festhalten an der Tradition als Innovation.

II. Europäische Reformationen

„Daß es Nationen gibt, ist historisch das Europäische an Europa" (Hermann Heimpel). Daher galt wenigstens bis in die 1970er Jahre innerhalb der Geschichtswissenschaft die Einsicht J. P. Coopers, „comparisons [...] are perhaps especially useful in analysing the peculiar characteristics of a given society or

---

[16] Siehe *Luise Schorn-Schütte*, Evangelische Geistlichkeit in der Frühen Neuzeit. Deren Anteil an der Entfaltung frühmoderner Staatlichkeit und Gesellschaft. Gütersloh 1996, Kap. VII, 416–448.
[17] Zu den regionalen Besonderheiten dieser europäischen Debatte siehe die nachfolgenden Beiträge.
[18] Siehe zu dieser europäischen Tradition und ihren italienischen politiktheoretischen Wurzeln jüngst *Angela de Benedictis*, Rebellare – resistere: communicazione politica come conflitto tra norme in età moderna, in: Luise Schorn-Schütte (Hrsg.), Die Sprachen des Politischen von der Antike bis ins 20. Jahrhundert. Methodische und inhaltliche Konzepte historischer Politikforschung. Berlin 2007 (im Druck).

situation".[19] Die Besonderheit der einzelnen verglichenen Umstände und Gesellschaften stand im Vordergrund, weniger die gemeinsame europäische Dimension. Wenige Themen haben eine so tief in die nationale Geschichtsschreibung eingebettete Tradition wie gerade die Geschichte der Reformation. Was eigentlich Politik sei, insbesondere das Verhältnis von Politik und Religion, stellt sich vor diesem Hintergrund für England, das Reich und Frankreich sehr unterschiedlich dar. Das heißt auch, daß theoretische Vorannahmen, die in der deutschsprachigen Geschichtswissenschaft in der Vergangenheit oder der Gegenwart forschungsleitend waren oder sind, in England und Frankreich noch nicht einmal als bekannt vorausgesetzt werden können. Das sagt über ihre Qualität nichts aus. Es muß aber als Warnung dienen vor Übertragungen von Schlußfolgerungen aus einem Kontext in den anderen. Wer die Winkelzüge Heinrichs VIII. oder der französischen Regentschaften der zweiten Hälfte des 16. Jahrhunderts beobachtet, kann sicherlich einen spezifischen Bereich politisch-strategischen Handelns identifizieren, auch wenn die Probleme, die zu lösen waren, sich z. T. aus der Reformation ergaben. Einer der wichtigsten Berater der Königin Elisabeth, Robert Cecil, formulierte 1563 gegenüber einem renitenten Prediger, der mit der Reformation der Kirche von England unzufrieden blieb: „I will not argue with you, for my part is much stronger [...] you nor any born under this kingdom may be permitted to break the bonds of obedience and uniformity. The question is not of doctrine, but of rites and ceremonies; and this I write lamentably to you: I have found more lets and impediments in the course of the gospel here [...], by certain found singularities of some men, then the most malice the papists can show."[20] Man sieht hier, wie weit die eben gemachte Beobachtung über den Raum des Politischen führt, oder eben nicht führt. Cecil beruft sich auf die Obrigkeit im Richteramt, die Autorität der Krone, die Pflichten der Untertanen zum Gehorsam. Aber er weiß auch, daß die Legitimität der königlichen Befehlsgewalt nicht durch Häretiker ausgeübt werden kann, und sucht die Probleme als solche der Riten und Zeremonien, nicht des Bekenntnisses, zu beschreiben. Sicherlich läßt sich das, was wir unter ‚traditioneller Politik' verstehen, mit Stichworten wie dynastische Strategien, königliche Rechte, monarchische Autorität, ständische Privilegien, verstehen. Zwischen den vermeintlichen Rechten und ihrer tatsächlichen Chance zur Durchsetzung konnte freilich eine Kluft bestehen. Kompromisse und Konsense waren zu suchen, ob nun offen oder verdeckt. „Öffentlichkeiten der frühen Neuzeit" konnten dafür ein Forum bieten.[21] Der Räte, Agenten und Netzwerke

---

[19] *J. P. Cooper*, Differences between English and Continental Government in the Early Seventeenth Century, in: ders., Land, Men and Beliefs. London 1983, 97–114, hier 97.
[20] *Norman Jones*, The Birth of Elizabethan England. Oxford 1993, 35.
[21] *Esther-Beate Körber*, Öffentlichkeiten der frühen Neuzeit. Teilnehmer, Formen, Institutionen und Entscheidungen öffentlicher Kommunikation im Herzogtum Preußen von 1525–1618. Berlin 1998.

bediente sich Herzog Albrecht in Preußen ebenso wie König Philipp II. von Spanien im Reich. Und schließlich gab es die Ratgeber und Spezialisten, die Gesichtspunkte der Diskussionen und Debatten einzelner Disziplinen, wie der Theologie oder der Rechtswissenschaft, in die Entscheidungsfindung einbrachten. Insofern läßt sich die Diskussion um Adiaphora auch als politische Strategie verstehen, so sehr es um religiöse Fragen geht. Wir befinden uns mitten in der oben bereits analysierten Verzahnung von Religion und Politik.

Gerade für den Problemkomplex der Verzahnung von Religion und Politik im Zeitalter der Reformation ist die gemeinsame europäische Geschichte mit Händen zu greifen. Schrieben doch die Reformatoren nicht zuletzt in einer in ganz Europa rezipierten Sprache, dem Lateinischen, und wurden ihre Schriften in Zustimmung und Ablehnung in ganz Europa rezipiert. Historiker wie Andrew Pettegree, die zu Deutschland, England und Frankreich geforscht und veröffentlich haben, haben diese Ambivalenz des europäischen Kontextes und des lokalen oder regionalen ‚Spielfeldes' immer wieder nachhaltig betont.[22] Die bedeutende Rolle von Migranten, Flüchtlingen, Besuchern und Reisenden, aus England und Frankreich in das Reich, aus den südlichen in die nördlichen Niederlande, von Büchern und ihren Lesern, all das unterstreicht die Rolle von solchen Gruppierungen von Gläubigen, wissenschaftlichen Zirkeln, familiären Verbindungen, Gruppenkulturen, die sich nur mit Vorbehalt schwerpunktmäßig einem bestimmten regionalen oder gar ‚nationalen' Kontext zurechnen lassen. Patrick Collinson gewann auf diese Weise einen neuen Zugriff auf den ‚Puritanismus' des späteren 16. Jahrhunderts, indem er die Geschichte einer Glaubensbewegung erzählte, deren Protagonisten wenigstens ebenso an den verfolgten Glaubensbrüdern in den Niederlanden und Frankreich, und später der Pfalz und in Böhmen, gelegen war wie an den Nachbarn im eigenen Dorf, der Stadt oder dem Königreich.

Die Beiträge dieses Bandes spiegeln diese Ambivalenz. Zum einen lassen sie deutlich werden, wie überragend die besondere Rolle und das spezifische Gewicht der Monarchie in ihrer Gesellschaft für die Geschichte der Reformation jeweils war. Fragen wir, was mit ‚Politik' jeweils gemeint sein mochte, dann entschied das Gewicht der Monarchie in ganz grundlegender Weise darüber, in welchen Formen Entscheidungen gesucht und gefunden wurden. Jeder Blick auf die spätmittelalterliche Geschichte des Verhältnisses von Krone und Gesellschaft, beispielsweise in England und im Reich, zeigt dann sofort, daß die europäischen Gemeinwesen unter sehr unterschiedlichen Voraussetzungen mit der Reformation konfrontiert wurden.[23] Um Mißver-

---

[22] Siehe jetzt *Andrew Pettegree* (Ed.), The Reformation World. London 2000; *ders.*, Reformation and the Culture of Persuasion. Cambridge 2005.
[23] Vgl. beispielsweise *Ernst Schubert*, Königsabsetzung im deutschen Mittelalter. Göttingen 2005; *Christine Carpenter*, Resisting and Deposing Kings in England in the Thir-

ständnissen vorzubeugen – es geht hier nicht um ein ‚Mehr' oder ‚Weniger' an Politik, ein ‚Mehr' oder ‚Weniger' an Gehorsam oder ständischer Mitsprache, sondern um Gestaltwandel spätmittelalterlicher Konstellationen unter dem Druck der reformatorischen Entwicklung.

Die Beiträge von Martin Ingram und Ralph Houlbrooke unterstreichen die ungeheure Rolle der Krone in England. Die divergierenden Pläne englischer Reformer blieben weitgehend oder völlig abhängig von dem Spielraum, der ihnen durch die jeweilige monarchische Spitze eröffnet wurde. Felicity Heals Geschichte der Reformation auf den britischen Inseln hat diese Perspektive jüngst bestätigt. Und die Sorge des Regenten Northumberland über die Religion Maria Tudors, der Halbschwester Eduards, erwies sich denn auch als mehr als berechtigt. Die Rückkehr Englands in den Schoß der römischen Kirche unter Maria läßt sich bis heute als Beweis dieses ungeheuren Gewichtes der Krone verstehen. Die erzwungene Konversion des Regenten Northumberland, der den protestantischen Glauben gegen Maria durchsetzen wollte, zum Katholizismus „symbolizes more dramatically than that of any other indvidual during the English Reformation evangelical faith's entanglement with the serpentin coils of traditional political considerations" (Houlbrooke) – Maria besaß als Tochter Heinrichs den relativ besten Anspruch auf den Thron und setzte als Königin den Katholizismus wieder durch.[24] Dagegen erhob sich kaum Widerstand. Die Zahl der Märtyrer und Exulanten (rund 1100 in einer Bevölkerung von rund 3,5 Millionen) blieb gering. Erst seit den 1560er und 1570er Jahren gewannen die reformierten Gruppierungen innerhalb der englischen Kirche zunehmend ein Eigengewicht, welches Elisabeth nach 1588 noch bändigen, aber nicht mehr vollends kontrollieren konnte. Nicht zuletzt die Weigerung beinahe aller katholischen Bischöfe der Regierungszeit Marias, Elisabeths neue Wendung nachzuvollziehen, hatte die neue Königin gezwungen, in einem von ihr wohl selbst nicht gewünschtem Maße auf Reformer aus dem Exil zur Besetzung der Bischofsämter zurückzugreifen. Damit aber schuf sie in einer noch weithin unreformierten Kirche die Grundlage für eine große Gruppe nachhaltig nach weiterer Reform verlangender Geistlicher. Ralph Houlbrooke faßt in seinem Beitrag denn auch zusammen: „England escaped a religious civil war in the sixteenth century above all because the centre held. The legitimacy of the monarch was hardly ever seriously challenged." Martin Ingram stimmt zu: „What provided the dynamics of change was politics."

Von besonderem Interesse muß in diesem Zusammenhang Ingrams Erläuterung sein, daß die Frömmigkeitsformen der Laien für politisch inspirierte Neuerungen des Ritus von oben sehr anfällig blieben und daß das

---

teenth, Fourteenth and Fifteenth Centuries, in: Robert von Friedeburg (Ed.), Murder and Monarchy. Regicide in European History, 1300–1800. Houndmills 2004, 99–121.
[24] *Felicity Heal*, Reformation in Britain and Ireland. Oxford 2003.

protestantische Erziehungsprogramm der Regierungszeiten Elisabeths und Jakobs erfolgreich blieb. Er führt eine ganze Reihe von wichtigen Rahmenbedingungen für diese Erfolge an, etwa die Kritik an Geistlichen und an Klöstern, welche die Akzeptanz der Heinrichschen Reformen in England erklärt. Er führt jedoch auch das irische Gegenbeispiel an, wo es der Krone gelang, ihre religiöse Politik durchzusetzen.[25] Wir kennen vergleichbare Prozesse auch im Reich. Nachdem die seit 1556/59 lutherische Kurpfalz unter Kurfürst Friedrich III. (1559–1573) 1563 zur reformierten Konfession übergegangen war, suchte Friedrichs Sohn Ludwig VI. (1576–1583) wieder zum Luthertum zurückzukehren. Nach dessen Tod steuerte jedoch Pfalzgraf Johann Kasimir während seiner Regentschaft für den noch unmündigen Friedrich IV. (1583–1592) wieder in die andere Richtung und führte den Calvinismus erneut ein. Breite Teile der Bevölkerung baten 1576 ebenso um die Bewahrung des Calvinismus wie 1583 um die Bewahrung des Luthertums. „Es reichte in diesem Falle also ein Zeitraum von sieben Jahren aus, um eine Bevölkerung nicht nur von ihrer bisher gepflegten Glaubensübung abzuwenden, sondern sie so stark an eine neueingeführte Konfessionsform zu gewöhnen, daß sie dieselbe beizubehalten wünschte und sich der Rückkehr zu der vorausgegangen Konfessionsform widersetzte. Entscheidend scheint beidemal die Vertreibung der Pfarrer […] gewesen zu sein".[26] Inwieweit dann freilich diese Wechsel als Ausdruck ‚traditioneller Politik' verstanden werden können, ist eine andere Frage.

Mark Greengrass führt mit Frankreich den Fall einer Gesellschaft vor, die sich ohne die Krone nicht mehr zu organisieren im Stande war, in der die Krone von den Kräften der religiösen Mobilisierung jedoch überrannt wurde. Die französische Monarchie hatte nach dem Tode Karls des Kühnen und der Teilung des Herzogtums Burgund, und damit des Endes der burgundischen Valois als potentieller Alliierter aller Gegner der Könige von England vergleichsweise leichteres Spiel. Von der Zange zwischen England und Burgund befreit, wurden die Valois die wichtigsten Herausforderer der Habsburger in Spanien, den Niederlanden und im Reich. Die Konkordate der französischen Krone mit der Kurie sicherten der Krone entscheidenden Einfluß auf die Kirche in Frankreich. Aber eine ganze Abfolge minderjähriger Könige samt Regentschaften erschwerten es der Krone, die protestantische und katholische Massenmobilisierung der 1560er bis 1580er Jahre zu steuern. Man mag die Versuche der französischen Krone, durch die gezielte Ermordung der Häupter der Hugenotten 1572 und der katholischen Liga 1588

---

[25] Siehe jetzt *Steven G. Ellis*, Building the Nation: Patriotism and National Identity in Early Modern Ireland, in: Robert von Friedeburg (Hrsg.), Patria und Patrioten vor dem Patriotismus. Pflichten, Rechte, Glauben und die Rekonfigurierung europäischer Gemeinwesen im 17. Jahrhundert. (Wolfenbütteler Arbeiten zur Barockforschung, 41.) Wiesbaden 2005, 169–192.
[26] *Ernst Walter Zeeden*, Die Entstehung der Konfessionen. München 1965, 96.

Herr der Lage zu werden, mehr oder minder als traditionelle Politik bezeichnen. Die Ermordung der französischen Könige Heinrich III. 1589 und Heinrich IV. 1610 wurden jedoch sicherlich durch Attentäter mit Visionen ausgeübt.[27] Die Auffindung der römischen Katakomben im Jahre 1578 stimulierte neue Formen der Beschreibung des Lebens der Heiligen und Märtyrer, bestückt mit Bildern und Drucken, und löste auch unter den katholischen Gläubigen einen neuen Enthusiasmus für die frühen christlichen Märtyrer und den Märtyrertod aus. Reinhart Koselleck hat an anderer Stelle resümierend auf die Verknüpfung klassischer Topoi mit religiösen Pflichten im Begriff der Liebe zum Vaterland hingewiesen. Die „antiken Heroengeschichten", in denen „Dolche in den Körper des Tyrannen gejagt wurden"[28], standen neben der Erinnerung an die Märtyrer des Alten Testamentes. Der Psalter ist voll von Anweisungen und Berichten über die Kriege Gottes, und der Attentäter Heinrichs III. hörte möglicherweise am Ostersonntag eine Predigt über die Glückseligkeit derer, die durch einen mutigen Schlag das Vaterland retten.[29] Die mittelalterliche Verknüpfung zwischen den Pflichten der Gläubigen gegenüber dem himmlischen Vaterland und dem Königreich, in dem sie lebten, wurde in den Glaubenskonflikten der Reformation vielfach beschworen. Einerseits haben wir es damit sicherlich mit einem Beispiel der Verzahnung von Religion und Politik zu tun, aber andererseits zeigt sich hier doch auch der Gestaltwandel der mittelalterlichen Form dieser Verzahnung.

Die bereits von den Zeitgenossen wahrgenommene außerordentliche Gewalttätigkeit der Konflikte unter den französischen Untertanen wurde in protestantischen Flugschriften der Zeit nicht zuletzt mit Bezug auf den Topos der *multitudo bestialis* kolportiert – die katholischen Täter wurden als Bestien mit Tierköpfen dargestellt. Die Pazifikationen der Jahre 1563, 1568, 1570, 1576, 1577 und 1598 suchten ihr Heil in der Vermeidung jeder weiteren Diskussion oder Analyse der diversen Gewaltakte. Die Protestanten fürchteten noch in den 1620er Jahren, Opfer einer allgemeinen Auslöschung zu werden. Lieder, Predigten, Visionen und neu formulierte Vorbilder der Märtyrer beeinflußten die Gläubigen in nach wie vor schwer rekonstruierbarer Weise. Auch Magdeburger Flugschriften aus der Zeit des Interims bezogen sich auf Armageddon, auch sie riefen vereinzelt die Bürger Magdeburgs auf,

---

[27] Siehe neben dem hier gedruckten Beitrag von Mark Greengrass auch *ders.*, Regicide, Martyrs and Monarchical Authority in France in the Wars of Religion, in: von Friedeburg (Ed.), Murder and Monarchy (wie Anm. 23), 176–192; *Lucien Bely*, Murder and Monarchy in France, in: ebd. 195–211.
[28] *Reinhard Koselleck*, Patriotismus. Gründe und Grenzen eines neuzeitlichen Begriffs, in: von Friedeburg (Hrsg.), Patria und Patrioten (wie Anm. 25), 535–552, Zitat 543 und 546f.
[29] *Greengrass*, Regicide (wie Anm. 27), 183. Zahllose Beispiele, darunter Psalm 68, 1; 2, 1–9; bes. 137, 9.

für den Herren zu streiten. Aber im wesentlichen blieben die Kampfhandlungen im Schmalkaldischen Krieg, im Zuge der Belagerung Magdeburgs und im Fürstenaufstand von 1552 Kampfhandlungen von geworbenen Söldnerverbänden, die in erster Linie, wenn auch keineswegs ausschließlich, auf den bewaffneten Gegner zielten. Handgreiflichkeiten hatte es im Verlauf der städtischen Reformationen im Reich gegeben, aber sie standen in keinem Vergleich zu den völlig außer Kontrolle geratenen Bürgerkriegen Frankreichs.

Die Unterschiede zur Lage im Reich liegen auf der Hand. Die Überformung der durch die Reformation entstandenen Konfliktlage durch rechtsförmige Verfahren, durch Anstände, Ausgleiche, Verträge, und die auf diese Verfahren einwirkenden Diskussionen der Juristen und Theologen, scheinen von einer anderen Welt. Ihnen gelten die Beiträge von Luise Schorn-Schütte und Robert von Friedeburg. Handstreiche, wie etwa die Rückführung des Herzogs von Württemberg durch Philipp von Hessen, die Übertragung der sächsischen Kur und ernestinischen Länder an den Albertiner Moritz oder der Markgrafenkrieg, ja selbst der große Bauernkrieg, blieben entweder auf bestimmte Regionen beschränkte Ereignisse oder wurden selbst wieder durch rechtliche Verfahren gebändigt. Die Feststellung des Augsburger Religionsabschiedes, man habe erfolglos nach einer religiösen Einigung gesucht und suche nun zunächst, den Landfrieden zu bewahren, und die sich daran anschließenden Bestimmungen, spiegeln beispielhaft die Fähigkeit der Reichsstände, trotz der religiösen Konflikte zu einem Ausgleich zu gelangen. Hier fanden „akademische Gelehrsamkeit und politisches Kalkül"[30] zur Entwicklung von Konzeptionen zueinander, die helfen sollten, dies möglich zu machen.

Indem sie beide Gesichtspunkte gemeinsam berücksichtigen, die übergreifenden Fragestellungen (I) und die spezifischen Entwicklungen vor Ort (II), tragen die Beiträge dazu bei, den Blick für die europäischen Entwicklungen zu öffnen, ohne die Spezifika einzelner Gemeinwesen aus dem Auge zu verlieren. So sehr dies eine längst formulierte Forderung ist, so sehr bleibt dies doch auch eine Aufgabe der künftigen Forschung.

---

[30] *Axel Gotthard*, Der Augsburger Religionsfrieden Münster 2005, 171.

Eigenlogik oder Verzahnung?

Religion und Politik im lutherischen Protestantismus des Alten Reiches (16. Jahrhundert)

Von

Luise Schorn-Schütte

I.

Daß es im 16. Jahrhundert eine enge Verzahnung zwischen Religion und Politik gegeben hat, ist unbestritten. Trotz entgegengesetzter Absicht führte Luthers sola-Theologie zu einer neuerlichen Einbindung des Geistlichen in das Weltliche und gerade deshalb zu einer Intensivierung der Verzahnung beider Welten. Über die Charakterisierung dieser Verbindung allerdings gab es bereits unter den Zeitgenossen unterschiedliche Auffassungen, die sich mit der Zuspitzung der politischen Konflikte zwischen Kaiser und protestierenden Reichsständen bis zum Schmalkaldischen Krieg und den Auseinandersetzungen um das kaiserliche Religionsgesetz 1548 (*Interim*) noch verstärkten. Gelehrte Theologen und Juristen dienten den politischen Entscheidungsträgern als Berater, angesichts der Verbindung von Reichspolitik und reformatorischem Umbruch wuchs den protestantischen Theologen eine gewichtige politische Rolle zu, gegen die sich Luther zwar noch wehrte, die Mehrheit der zweiten und dritten Generation der Reformatoren aber nicht mehr.[1]

Die Debatte um den Charakter der Reichsverfassung, die Kontroversen um das Recht der Gegen- oder Notwehr, schließlich die Diskussionen um die Funktion der Drei-Stände-Lehre, die durch die lutherischen Theologen wie-

---

[1] Grundlegend zu Luthers Position und zu den Diskussionen u. a. zwischen Theologen und Juristen bis 1545 ist *Eike Wolgast*, Die Wittenberger Theologie und die Politik der evangelischen Stände. Studien zu Luthers Gutachten in politischen Fragen. Gütersloh 1977. Die Forschung hat sich in den letzten Jahren verstärkt der Rolle der zweiten und dritten Generation der Reformatoren zugewandt, siehe dazu u. a. *Luise Schorn-Schütte*, Politische Kommunikation in der Frühen Neuzeit. Obrigkeitskritik im Alten Reich, in: Geschichte und Gesellschaft 32, 2006, 273–314; *dies.*, Obrigkeitskritik und Widerstandsrecht. Die politica christiana als Legitimitätsgrundlage, in: dies. (Hrsg.), Aspekte der politischen Kommunikation im Europa des 16. und 17. Jahrhunderts. Politische Theologie – Res Publica-Verständnis – konsensgestützte Herrschaft. München 2004, 195–232; *Günter Wartenberg/Irene Dingel* (Hrsg.), Georg Maior (1502–1574). Ein Theologe der Wittenberger Reformation. Leipzig 2005.

der belebt worden war, sind gewichtige Aspekte dieser zeitgenössischen Reflexion über das Verhältnis von Religion und Politik. Von den Theologen, die als Politikberater herangezogen wurden, erwartete man prinzipielle Aussagen zum Verhältnis von Kirche und weltlicher Obrigkeit. Wiederholt formulierten sie derartiges in enger Abstimmung mit den gelehrten Juristen, die in Anknüpfung an die römisch-rechtlichen Traditionen argumentierten.[2] Trotz dieser offenkundigen Gemeinsamkeiten hat die Forschung seit Generationen daran festgehalten, daß es eine Gleichrangigkeit zwischen gelehrten Theologen und Juristen nicht gegeben habe, die protestantischen Theologen sich den Vorgaben der Rechtsgelehrten untergeordnet hätten. Sehr zutreffend ist jüngst darauf hingewiesen worden, daß sich diese Sichtweise seit der Charakterisierung des nachreformatorischen Luthertums als „Altprotestantismus" durch Ernst Troeltsch erneut verfestigt hat.[3]

Derartige Interpretationen halten Nachprüfungen nicht stand. Vielmehr erscheint die These tragfähig, wonach gelehrte Theologen und Juristen gemeinsam Grundlinien einer protestantischen politischen Ethik diskutiert und erprobt haben.[4] Daß die Frage nach den Grenzen zwischen Kirche und Welt eine gewichtige Rolle gespielt hat, ist offenkundig, ohne daß damit Einhelligkeit in der Auffassung bei beiden Gelehrtengruppen hätte bestehen müssen. Gerade der Konflikt über die Ordnung der Herrschaft ermöglicht es dabei dem Historiker, die unterschiedlichen Argumente nachzuvollziehen.

Anhand einiger zentraler Konfliktfelder soll dies im folgenden geschehen (II): die gegensätzlichen oder auch parallelen Meinungen zum Charakter der Reichsverfassung, die Legitimität der Not- bzw. Gegenwehr und die Akzeptanz der Dreiständelehre sind als „politische Sprache" der Zeitgenossen identifizierbar, deren verbindendes Thema war die Frage nach dem Verhältnis von weltlicher und geistlicher Ordnung (1). Da es sich in diesem Sinne um „politische Kommunikation" unter gelehrten Eliten handel-

---

[2] Dazu *Schorn-Schütte*, Kommunikation (wie Anm. 1), mit ausführlichen Nachweisen. Zentral zur Gemeinsamkeit der Kommunikation zwischen Juristen und Theologen *Merio Scattola*, Das Naturrecht vor dem Naturrecht. Zur Geschichte des ius naturae im 16. Jahrhundert. Tübingen 1999.

[3] Der nordamerikanische Rechtshistoriker *John Witte*, Emory University, hat sich mit dem Themenkomplex in letzter Zeit anregend auseinandergesetzt, siehe ders., Law and Protestantism. The Legal Teaching of the Lutheran Reformation. Cambridge 2002, 23–33. Zur Bedeutung der These Troeltschs für die Forschung zur Geschichte der Frühen Neuzeit bereits *Luise Schorn-Schütte*, Ernst Troeltschs Soziallehren und die gegenwärtige Frühneuzeitforschung. Zur Diskussion um die Bedeutung von Luthertum und Calvinismus für die Entstehung der modernen Welt, in: Friedrich Wilhelm Graf/Trutz Rendtorff (Hrsg.), Ernst Troeltschs Soziallehren. Studien zu ihrer Interpretation. Gütersloh 1993, 133–151.

[4] Diese These wird gestützt durch *Witte*, Law (wie Anm. 3), 5–23 u. ö.

te[5], ist es notwendig, deren sozialen und Bildungsort zu identifizieren (2). In einem abschließenden Teil (III) wird die Eingangsfrage nach Eigenlogik oder Verzahnung wiederaufgenommen werden.

II.

Mit der Etablierung der reformatorischen Bewegung als „Institution Kirche" entstanden Fragen nach dem Verhältnis zwischen Politischem und Religiösem, von deren nahtloser Integration Luther zunächst noch ausgegangen war. Aber die Konfrontation auf dem zweiten Speyrer Reichstag (1529) zwischen protestierenden Ständen einerseits, altgläubigen Ständen und dem Kaiser andererseits (Speyrer Protestation, 19. April 1529) belegt die politische Sprengkraft des Einsatzes traditionaler Rechte (hier des Minderheitenschutzes vor Rechtsbindungen durch Mehrheitsentscheidungen des Reichstages) in Verbindung mit religiöser Argumentation.[6] Denn deren Folge war, daß die Kompetenz des Reiches, in Glaubensfragen zu entscheiden, infrage gestellt wurde. Damit standen die Reichsreform und die Frage nach Legitimität und Umfang eines Widerstandsrechtes der Reichsstände gegen einen Kaiser zur Debatte, der in Glaubensfragen Zwang anzuwenden versuchte.

1. Für die Zeitgenossen stellte sich damit nicht, wie dies in der Forschung des 19./20. Jahrhunderts betont wurde, das Problem des individuellen Gewissensentscheids. Vielmehr stand unter den neuen Vorzeichen der reformatorischen Theologie die alte Frage des Kräfteverhältnisses zwischen Kaiser und Reichsständen auf dem Prüfstand. Aus dem Blickwinkel einiger „protestierender" Reichsstände löste sich der Kaiser aus der auf Wechselseitigkeit angelegten Lehnsbeziehung, die er in Gestalt der Wahlkapitulation anerkannt hatte, dann, wenn er das traditionale Recht des Minderheitenschutzes verletzte. In dieser Situation waren die Reichsstände als Lehnsleute an ihren Treueeid nicht mehr gebunden, der Kaiser verlor seine Eigenschaft als Obrigkeit, die Gehorsamspflicht endete.[7]

---

[5] Zum Konzept der „political languages" siehe *Luise Schorn-Schütte*, Einleitung, in: dies. (Hrsg.), Aspekte (wie Anm. 1), 1–12. Eine Auseinandersetzung mit dem angelsächsischen Konzept bei *Olaf Asbach*, Von der Geschichte politischer Ideen zur „History of Political Discourse"? Skinner, Pocock und die „Cambridge School", in: Zeitschrift für Politikwissenschaft 12, 2002, 637–667.

[6] Zur Bedeutung der Diskussionen auf dem Speyrer Reichstag jetzt umfassend *Armin Kohnle*, Reichstag und Reformation. Gütersloh 2002, bes. 363–375.

[7] Siehe zum Ganzen *Wolgast*, Theologie (wie Anm. 1), bes. 125–146, sowie *Diethelm Böttcher*, Ungehorsam oder Widerstand? Zum Fortleben des mittelalterlichen Widerstandsrechtes in der Reformationszeit (1529/30). Berlin 1991, 21–39, und *Robert von Friedeburg*, Widerstandsrecht und Konfessionskonflikt. Notwehr und Gemeiner Mann im deutsch-britischen Vergleich 1530–1669. Berlin 1999, 51–70, sowie zuletzt auch *Schorn-Schütte*, Obrigkeitskritik und Widerstandsrecht (wie Anm. 1), 206–225.

Diese der römischrechtlichen Tradition entstammende Argumentation der Juristen wurde zu Beginn der dreißiger Jahre des 16. Jahrhunderts mit den theologischen Ansätzen der Wittenberger Geistlichkeit verbunden, denn angesichts der reichspolitisch verhärteten Fronten sahen sich die protestantischen Theologen und Juristen gezwungen, sich „in einer bis dahin nicht gekannten umfassenden, detaillierten und zugleich grundsätzlichen Weise zum Verfassungsrecht des Reiches zu äußern".[8] Dies aber geschah in den Bahnen der spätmittelalterlichen politisch-theologischen Kommunikation. Nicht die neuen theologischen Wahrheitsansprüche führten zu gänzlich neuen politischen Diskussionen über die Legitimität von Herrschaft und Widerstand; vielmehr ging es allen Beteiligten darum, die Dynamik der bis dahin nicht gekannten religionspolitischen Konflikte zu bewältigen.[9] Dabei arbeiteten juristische und theologische Politikberater eng zusammen, der Rückgriff auf die jeweiligen Traditionsbestände wurde wechselseitig kommuniziert. In den dichten Debatten, die im Zusammenhang mit der Gründung des Schmalkaldischen Bundes seit 1530 geführt wurden, stand deshalb der beiderseitig definierte Begriff von weltlicher Obrigkeit, die Bestimmung der Aufgaben des Herrscheramtes, die Frage nach der jeweiligen Legitimation eines Widerstandsrechtes und schließlich die inhaltliche und formale Interpretation der Reichsverfassung zwischen Theologen und Juristen zur Diskussion.[10] Seit der Jahrhundertmitte intensivierten sich die Debatten um die Rolle des geistlichen Amtes und um die Legitimität des Teilhabeanspruches, der nicht zuletzt mit der Dreiständelehre verbunden war.

---

[8] *Eberhard Isenmann*, Widerstandsrecht und Verfassung in Spätmittelalter und Früher Neuzeit, in: Helmut Neuhaus/Barbara Stollberg-Rilinger (Hrsg.), Menschen und Strukturen in der Geschichte Alteuropas. Festschrift für Johannes Kunisch. Berlin 2000, 37-69, hier 50.

[9] So auch die Argumentation am Beispiel des schwäbischen Bundes bei *Horst Carl*, Landfriedenseinungen und Ungehorsam – der Schwäbische Bund in der Geschichte des vorreformatorischen Widerstandes im Reich, in: Robert von Friedeburg (Hrsg.), Widerstandsrecht im Europa der Neuzeit. Erträge und Perspektiven der Forschung im deutsch-britischen Vergleich. Berlin 2001, 85-112, hier 91.

[10] Siehe auch *Isenmann*, Widerstandsrecht (wie Anm. 8,) der 52f. sowohl die Kooperation der Theologen und Juristen als auch die Breite der Kommunikation über legitime Obrigkeit hervorhebt. Die Debatten, die sich zwischen 1530 und 1555 im Alten Reich stetig intensivierten, sind in der einschlägigen Forschung noch nicht zusammenhängend bearbeitet worden. So fehlen sie in den gewichtigen Werken von *Quentin Skinner*, The Foundations of Modern Political Thought. 2 Vols. Cambridge 1975, und *Friedrich Hermann Schubert*, Die deutschen Reichstage in der Staatslehre der Frühen Neuzeit. München 1966. Hinweise dagegen bei *v. Friedeburg*, Widerstandsrecht (wie Anm. 7). Die Untersuchung von *Witte*, Law (wie Anm. 3), bezieht sich ausdrücklich auf die Kooperation der Theologen und Juristen, wobei die Konzentration auf das Eherecht wichtig ist, denn damit wird das Obrigkeitsverständnis thematisiert. Andere Aspekte wie v. a. die große Bedeutung der wiederbelebten Dreiständelehre werden zwar für einzelne Autoren benannt, nicht aber in der ganzen Breite ihrer Rezeption durch Theologen und Juristen erkannt.

a) Zum Kreis der Politikberater aus der ersten Generation der Reformatoren gehörten die gelehrten Theologen bzw. Juristen *Justus Menius* (1499–1558)[11] und *Basilius Monner* (um 1500–1566)[12]. Beide waren durch die bewußte Erfahrung der Reformation und ihrer Resonanz sowie durch die Konflikte um deren Legitimität, etwa im Zusammenhang mit der Auseinandersetzung um die Einführung des kaiserlichen Religionsgesetzes (Interim) 1548, geprägt. Menius, seit 1529 Superintendent in Eisenach, hatte in unmittelbarem Kontakt mit Luther und Melanchthon den Gang der reformatorischen Bewegung in den Territorien maßgeblich geprägt. Seine „Oeconomia" ist das erste protestantische Hausbuch, eine Anleitung zur vorbildlichen Eheführung und Leitung des ganzen Hauses.[13] Die Schrift des Menius war eingebunden in eine breite Debatte um die Grundlagen eines Gegenwehr-, Notwehr- oder Widerstandsrechtes, die im Umkreis der Schmalkaldischen Bündnispartner schon seit den späten zwanziger und frühen dreißiger Jahren des 16. Jahrhunderts durch hessische, sächsische und einige reichsstädtische gelehrte Juristen geführt worden war und sich angesichts der militärischen Zuspitzung auch unter den juristisch geschulten Politikberatern intensivierte. Ein stark rezipierter Text aus letzterem Umfeld war das kurz zuvor (1546) anonym publizierte Gutachten[14] des Juristen Basilius Monner, der zum Zeitpunkt der Veröffentlichung als Prinzenerzieher und politischer Berater am Hof des sächsischen Kurfürsten Johann Friedrich tätig war.[15]

---

[11] *Friedrich Wilhelm Bautz/Traugott Bautz* (Hrsg.), Biographisch-bibliographisches Kirchenlexikon. Bd. 5. Herzberg 1993, 1263–1266.
[12] Zur Biographie siehe Allgemeine deutsche Biographie. Bd. 22. Leipzig 1885, 171.
[13] *Justus Menius*, An die hochgeborne Fürstin [...] Oeconomia christiana/ das ist/ von Christlicher haushaltung [...]. Wittenberg 1529 [Verzeichnis der im deutschen Sprachbereich erschienenen Drucke des 16. Jahrhunderts (künftig: VD 16): M 4542; Exemplar der Herzog-August-Bibliothek Wolfenbüttel (künftig: HAB): Li 55309]. Zur Gattung der Hausväterliteratur vgl. *Julius Hoffmann*, Die ‚Hausväterliteratur' und die ‚Predigten über den christlichen Hausstand'. Weinheim/Berlin 1959. Eine Untersuchung, die den neueren Forschungsstand integrierte, fehlt.
[14] Rechtliches Bedenken von der Defension und Gegenwehr, ob es nemblich von göttlichem, weltlichem und natürlichem Rechten zugelassen sey, wider die Tyranney, und unrechten Gewalt der Obrigkeit sich zu widersetzen, und Gewalt mit Gewalt zu vertreiben. O. O. 1546 [VD 16: 14:004896X; HAB: A: 48.3 Pol (5)].
[15] Zum Kontext vgl. *Luise Schorn-Schütte*, Politikberatung im 16. Jahrhundert. Zur Bedeutung von theologischer und juristischer Bildung für die Prozesse politischer Entscheidungsfindung im Protestantismus, in: Armin Kohnle/Frank Engehausen (Hrsg.), Zwischen Wissenschaft und Politik. Studien zur deutschen Universitätsgeschichte. Festschrift für Eike Wolgast zum 65. Geburtstag. Stuttgart 2001, 49–66. Zudem *Robert Kolb*, The Legal Case for Martyrdom. Basilius Monner on Johann Friedrich the Elder and the Schmalcaldic War, in: Irene Dingel/Volker Leppin/Christoph Strohm (Hrsg.), Reformation und Recht. Festschrift für Gottfried Seebaß zum 65. Geburtstag. Gütersloh 2002, 145–160; *Scattola*, Naturrecht (wie Anm. 2), 59–61; *Gabriele Haug-Moritz*, „Ob wir uns auch mit Gott / Recht und gutem Gewissen / wehren mögen / und Gewalt mit Gewalt vertreiben?" Zur Widerstandsdiskussion des Schmalkaldischen Krieges 1546/47, in:

Obgleich sich beide Texte in ihrer Argumentation unterschieden, da beide Autoren an verschiedenen Traditionsbeständen ansetzten, ergänzten sich juristische und theologische Denkweise doch. Für die folgenden Jahre blieb eine wechselseitige Kommunikation über den Obrigkeitsbegriff beherrschend.

Die Fronten verliefen durchaus quer durch das lutherische Lager. Während Menius und Monner den monarchisch zentrierten Herrschaftsanspruch des Kaisers kritisierten, verteidigten ihn andere lutherische Juristen, wie beispielsweise der Nürnberger Stadtschreiber Lazarus Spengler (1479-1534).[16] Beiden Positionen lag ein je eigenes Verständnis der Reichsverfassung zugrunde. Luthers Position dazu ist gut erforscht[17], sie war aber keineswegs unangefochten. Innerhalb der Gruppe der Wittenberger Reformatoren gab es ebenso wie unter den lutherischen Juristen jener Jahrzehnte durchaus voneinander abweichende Positionen.

Als einer der ersten *Theologen* hat der Wittenberger Stadtpfarrer Johannes Bugenhagen (1485-1558) in zwei Gutachten für den sächsischen Kurfürsten (1523 und 1529) seine eigenständige Position entwickelt, an die u. a. Menius anknüpfen konnte. Bugenhagen argumentierte mit einer schon in der spätmittelalterlichen Tradition gewichtigen Stelle des Alten Testaments, dem ersten Buch Samuel.[18] Selbstverständlich ist auch für ihn im Sinne des Paulusbriefes an die Gemeinde in Rom (Röm. 13,1) alle Obrigkeit von Gott eingesetzt. Aber diese Obrigkeit hat einen bestimmten Auftrag: Sie soll die Guten schützen und die Bösen strafen.[19] Sobald sie diese Aufgabe nicht oder

---

Luise Schorn-Schütte (Hrsg.), Das Interim im europäischen Kontext (1548-1550). Herrschaftskrise und Glaubenskonflikt. Gütersloh 2005, 486-509.

[16] Zu Spengler vgl. *Bernd Hamm*, Die reformatorische Krise der sozialen Werte – drei Lösungsperspektiven zwischen Wahrheitseifer und Toleranz in den Jahren 1525 bis 1530, in: Thomas A. Brady (Hrsg.), Die deutsche Reformation zwischen Spätmittelalter und Früher Neuzeit. München 2001, 91-122.

[17] Siehe *Wolfgang Günther*, Luthers Vorstellung von der Reichsverfassung. Münster 1976; *Hans-Joachim Gänssler*, Evangelium und weltliches Schwert. Hintergrund, Entstehungsgeschichte und Anlaß von Luthers Scheidung zweier Reiche oder Regimente. Wiesbaden 1983.

[18] In dem Gutachten für Kurfürst Johann bezieht sich Bugenhagen 1529 auf 1. Sam. 15,23: Gewalt, die sich gegen Gott und Gottes Wort richtet, ist verworfen. Der Einsatz des Samuelbuches für die Charakterisierung eines gerechten Königs hat bereits im Mittelalter Tradition, an sie konnte gerade in der Situation der dreißiger Jahre des 16. Jahrhunderts im Reich angeknüpft werden, denn mit diesem Verweis konnte die Frage nach dem Recht der Zentrierung von Herrschaft beim Kaiser erörtert werden. Zum Ganzen siehe *Annette Weber-Möckl*, „Das Recht des Königs, der über euch herrschen soll". Studien zu 1. Sam. 8, 11ff. in der Literatur der Frühen Neuzeit. Berlin 1986, 94-96 u. ö.

[19] *Johannes Bugenhagen*, Gutachten 1529, abgedruckt in: Heinz Scheible (Hrsg.), Das Widerstandsrecht als Problem der deutschen Protestanten. Gütersloh 1968, 26: „Darumb sol er [der Kaiser] sich erkenen für eynen keyser, nicht eynen moerder, [...] eynen herrn und vater und nicht eyneen tyrannen."

nicht mehr erfüllt, ist die Grenze für die Gehorsamspflicht ihr gegenüber erreicht. Als Beleg dafür verwies der Wittenberger Stadtpfarrer auf die alttestamentliche Figur des König Saul, der als von Gott erwählter Herrscher über besondere Gaben, aber auch besondere Pflichten gegenüber seinem Volk verfügte. In dem Augenblick, in dem er diese Aufgaben vernachlässigt, wird der König zu einer gottlosen Obrigkeit, „er verliert seine Legitimation, er hört auf, eine *obrigkeitliche* Gewalt zu sein".[20] Anders als zu diesem Zeitpunkt Luther und auch noch Melanchthon[21] eröffnete Bugenhagen damit bereits am Ende der zwanziger Jahre des 16. Jahrhunderts eine theologische Rechtfertigung in der zeitgenössischen Widerstandsdebatte. Und diese verband er mit der reichsrechtlichen Argumentation zumindest eines Teils der zeitgenössischen gelehrten Juristen. Indem er in seinem Gutachten von 1529 „Unterherrn" von „Oberherrn" unterschied und beiden aufgrund ihrer jeweiligen Schutzpflichten obrigkeitlichen Charakter zumaß[22], hatte er sich der Deutungstradition einer großen Gruppe der Reichsjuristen angeschlossen, die die Reichsverfassung durch die Existenz zweier Obrigkeiten: Kaiser einerseits, Reichstände andererseits, gekennzeichnet sah.[23] Die damit verbundenen Konsequenzen für die Debatte um das Recht der „Gegenwehr" gegenüber dem Kaiser[24] anerkannte Bugenhagen als Ergänzung seiner eigenständigen theologischen Interpretation. Für ihn waren beide Perspektiven nahtlos miteinander zu verbinden, was sich in den Debatten der nachfolgenden Jahre unter den beteiligten Gelehrten und Politikern nur allmählich durchzusetzen begann. Inhaltlich handelte es sich um zwei parallel verlaufende Deutungsmuster, die sich in der Kernaussage aufeinander zubewegten, sich nicht ausschlossen.[25]

---

[20] *Böttcher*, Ungehorsam (wie Anm. 7), 23. In seinem Gutachten von 1529 zitiert Bugenhagen: „Weil du nu des hern wort verworffen hast, hat er dich auch verworffen, das du nicht könig seyest." Abdruck bei *Scheible* (Hrsg.), Widerstandsrecht (wie Anm. 19), 27.
[21] Zu Melanchthons Haltung und deren Differenzierung siehe *Eike Wolgast*, Melanchthon als politischer Berater, in: Walter Sparn u. a. (Hrsg.), Melanchthon. Erlangen 1998, 179–208, dort 191–198 zur Einräumung eines Widerstandsrechtes gegenüber dem Kaiser seit 1535 auch durch Melanchthon.
[22] Gutachten gedruckt in: *Scheible* (Hrsg.), Widerstandsrecht (wie Anm. 19), 28. Entsprechend bewertet auch *Böttcher*, Ungehorsam (wie Anm. 7), 23–25. Er verweist zu Recht auf eine vergleichbare Argumentation durch Bugenhagen bereits in seinem Gutachten von 1523 (für Kurfürst Friedrich von Sachsen) abgedruckt bei *Scheible* (Hrsg.), Widerstandsrecht (wie Anm. 19), 18.
[23] Dazu *Wolgast*, Melanchthon (wie Anm. 21), 188–203; jüngst weiter differenzierend *Isenmann*, Widerstandsrecht (wie Anm. 8), 50–61.
[24] Zum Begriff und seiner Bedeutung für die zeitgenössische politische Kommunikation siehe *Gabriele Haug-Moritz*, Widerstand als „Gegenwehr". Die schmalkaldische Konzeption der „Gegenwehr" und der „gegenwehrliche" Krieg des Jahres 1542, in: *v. Friedeburg* (Hrsg.), Widerstandsrecht (wie Anm. 9), 141–161.
[25] Siehe entsprechend *Merio Scattola*, Widerstandsrecht und Naturrecht im Umkreis von Philipp Melanchthon, in: Schorn-Schütte (Hrsg.), Interim (wie Anm. 15), 459–487. Er verweist dort auf die Doppelung der Argumentationslinien: Selbstverteidigung ist legiti-

b) An Bugenhagens Position hat Menius in seiner bereits erwähnten, viel gelesenen Schrift von 1547 anknüpfen können. Bugenhagens Schriften waren ihm bekannt, beide hatten zusammen in Wittenberg studiert, Menius gehörte zum engsten Kreis um die Wittenberger Reformatoren. Es kann als sicher gelten, daß mit der Stimme des Menius auch die Position Melanchthons artikuliert wurde.[26] Denn seit der akuten Gefahr des militärischen Vorgehens des Kaisers gegen die schmalkaldischen Bündner hatte sich Melanchthons Haltung zur Begrenzung obrigkeitlicher Gewalt im Reich sichtbar verändert.[27] Als Aufgabe weltlicher Obrigkeit definierte er nunmehr den Schutz beider Gesetzestafeln (*custodia utriusque tabulae*)[28], eine Verletzung dieser Pflicht begründete ein Widerstandsrecht selbst dann, wenn es, wie im Gutachten von 1536 formuliert[29], um den *magistratus superior* geht, der Konzilsbeschlüsse umsetzt. Anders als noch 1530 berief sich Melanchthon bei dieser Argumentation ausdrücklich auf das Naturrecht, das Widerstandsrecht wurde als dessen Teil charakterisiert.[30] Zudem sicherte er seine Argumentation

miert durch das römische Recht (juristische Linie), sie ist zudem gerechtfertigt durch das theologisch-philosophische Konstrukt des Naturrechts. Das nahm auch Melanchthon auf und entfaltete es weiter. Drittens schließlich wird beides verbunden mit dem spätmittelalterlichen Recht der Gegenwehr (wiederum juristische Argumentation). Die bei *Skinner*, Foundations (wie Anm. 10), Vol. 2, 117f., 127–134, 204–208 u. ö. getroffene Unterscheidung eines konstitutionellen von einem privatrechtlichen Argumentationsmuster im Kontext der Widerstandsdebatte im Alten Reich erscheint unter diesen Voraussetzungen als nicht existent, zudem werden Begriffe des Konstitutionalismus des 19. Jahrhunderts verwandt, ein Verfahren, das Skinners eigenem methodischem Konzept widerspricht. Zur Kritik an Skinner siehe auch *v. Friedeburg*, Widerstandsrecht (wie Anm. 7), 56 mit Anm. 20.
[26] Siehe dazu *Luther D. Peterson*, J. Menius, Ph. Melanchthon and the 1547th Treatise „Von der Notwehr Unterricht", in: Archiv für Reformationsgeschichte 81, 1990, 138–157. Die Schrift des Menius beinhaltet zwei parallele Argumentationsstränge: die Hausstandsethik und die Notwehrargumentation. Sie wurden bei ihm nicht verschmolzen, was gegen *v. Friedeburg*, Widerstandsrecht (wie Anm. 7), 62, festgehalten werden muß. Siehe dazu auch die Bewertung durch *Scattola*, Widerstandsrecht (wie Anm. 25), 470. Zur Schrift des Menius als Teil der Kommunikation über Theologie und Politik siehe ebenso *Günter Wartenberg*, Theologischer Ratschlag in Zeiten politischen Umbruchs. Die Wittenberger Theologen und ihre Landesherrn, in: Anselm Doering-Manteuffel/Kurt Nowak (Hrsg.), Religionspolitik in Deutschland von der frühen Neuzeit bis zur Gegenwart. Martin Greschat zum 65. Geburtstag. Stuttgart 1999, 29–50, hier 42f.
[27] Dazu *Wolgast*, Melanchthon (wie Anm. 21), 190–206, sowie *ders.*, Theologie (wie Anm. 1), 224–230.
[28] *C. G. Bretschneider/H. E. Bindseill* (Hrsg.), Corpus Reformatorum. Philippi Melanchthonis opera quae supersunt omnia. 28 Bde. Halle 1834–1860 (künftig: CR), Bd. 21, 553.
[29] CR Bd. 3, 126ff., das Gutachten in Auszügen auch bei *Scheible* (Hrsg.), Widerstandsrecht (wie Anm. 19), 89ff. Unterzeichnet wurde das von Melanchthon formulierte Kollektivgutachten von Luther, Jonas, Bugenhagen, Amsdorf und Cruciger. Ausführlich dazu *Wolgast*, Theologie (wie Anm. 1), 225f.
[30] *Scattola*, Naturrecht (wie Anm. 2), 50–55, verweist auf den vormodernen Charakter dieses Naturrechtsverständnisses. Zu diesem gehört die Einpflanzung eines Rechts auf Selbstverteidigung des menschlichen Wesens gegen die Obrigkeit, ebd. 56.

mit Belegen aus dem Alten Testament ab. Eike Wolgast hat zu Recht darauf hingewiesen, daß mit dieser Position der Charakter der Reichsverfassung als Aristokratie, innerhalb derer mehrere Obrigkeiten neben- und miteinander existieren könnten, anerkannt wurde. Dies kam der Sicht der zeitgenössischen hessischen und kursächsischen Juristen nahe und entsprach der Bewertung durch Bugenhagen. Damit endete die abwartende Haltung der Wittenberger Theologen der ersten Generation. Alle Unterzeichner der Kollektivgutachten bekräftigten seitdem, daß in Notwehrlagen weltliche Obrigkeiten Rechte und Pflichten wahrnehmen sollten, über deren Beachtung Theologen *und* Juristen zu wachen haben.[31]

In der Ausarbeitung des Menius wurde diese Position der Wittenberger Theologen breit rezipiert. Menius erweiterte sie noch um den gewichtigen Aspekt der Parallelität von weltlicher Obrigkeit und *Elternamt*. Aus den daher rührenden patriarchalischen Fürsorgepflichten leitete er die Schutzaufgabe christlicher Obrigkeit her. Sobald sie gegen das „göttliche Gesetz" handelt, verstößt sie, weil beide als identisch betrachtet wurden, gegen das „natürliche Gesetz", mißachtet also selbst das erste Gebot. Die Untertanen sind dann geradezu verpflichtet, die natürliche Ordnung durch Ungehorsam gegenüber einer solchen Obrigkeit wiederherzustellen.[32] Über die Parallelisierung von Obrigkeit und Elternamt formulierte Menius das natürliche Recht der Kurfürsten, sich gegen die *atrox iniuria* des Kaisers zu wehren. Kurfürsten und Kaiser wurden als zweierlei Arten der Obrigkeit charakterisiert, die einander im Rahmen der Reichsverfassung über- und untergeordnet waren. Wie Bugenhagen und Melanchthon betonte auch Menius, daß die aristokratische Herrschaftsform der Reichsverfassung sich durch die Zuordnung von *magistratus inferior* und *superior* bezeichnen lasse.[33]

c) In der praktisch-politischen Auseinandersetzung um den Charakter der Reichsverfassung, die seit den dreißiger Jahren des 16. Jahrhunderts immer dichter wurde, gab es sehr verwandte Positionen zwischen Juristen und Theologen. Bei der Beantwortung der für die Zeitgenossen nicht weniger gewichtigen Frage nach den Ordnungsprinzipien von Herrschaft aber gingen beide Gruppen unterschiedliche Wege. Entscheidend dafür war ganz offensichtlich die unterschiedliche Struktur der protestantisch-theologischen und der juristischen Wissensbestände.[34] Zwar gingen beide Gruppen von der Existenz

---

[31] *Wolgast*, Melanchthon (wie Anm. 21), 226. Daß damit allerdings ein theologiefreier Raum für die Politiker geschaffen wurde, bleibt eine These, der die hier vorgelegten Ausführungen widersprechen.
[32] *Justus Menius*, Von der Notwehr Unterricht / nützlich zu lesen. Wittenberg 1547, C IIIr, C IVr [HAB 312.46 Theol (1); VD 16: M 4592]. Als biblischer Beleg dienen Menius ebenso wie Melanchthon und Bugenhagen: Apg. 5, 29.
[33] *Menius*, Notwehr (wie Anm. 32), a IV r+v.
[34] Entsprechend die Argumentation bei *Scattola*, Naturrecht (wie Anm. 2), 59f. mit Anm. 133.

eines Naturrechts aus; im juristischen Verständnis gab es deshalb ein natürliches Recht der Selbstverteidigung, was aus römisch-rechtlicher Tradition hergeleitet wurde. Demgegenüber gingen die Theologen von der natürlichen als göttlichen Ordnung, der Schöpfungsordnung, aus, innerhalb derer ein Notwehrrecht begründet ist. Zwar gab es einige wenige Teilnehmer dieser zeitgenössischen Kommunikation insbesondere unter den Theologen, die beide Legitimitätsstränge zusammenzuführen versuchten. Zu ihnen gehörte der Vertraute Melanchthons und Wittenberger Theologieprofessor Georg Maior (1502-1574). Auch er berief sich nie auf das römische Recht oder die Digesten, aber er kannte ein natürlich begründetes Selbstverteidigungsrecht, das er auch als Theologe aus der „Idee der allgemeinen Ordnung" herleitete.[35]

Die große Mehrzahl aber folgte den gruppenspezifischen Argumentationen der jeweiligen Wissensgebiete. Nur selten nahmen die Juristen das theologische Verständnis des Naturrechts zur Kenntnis. Offensichtlich wurden die wechselseitigen Wahrnehmungen erst dichter angesichts des sichtlichen Bedeutungszuwachses der von den Theologen sehr ernst genommenen Dreiständelehre, und das war erst in der zweiten Hälfte des 16. Jahrhunderts der Fall.

Beispielhaft für die Argumentation der Juristen ist die Begründung des Basilius Monner. Seine Schrift von 1546[36] ist in eben dem Kontext entstanden, der für Bugenhagen und Menius skizziert wurde. Monner argumentierte auf der Linie der kursächsischen Rechtsgutachten, die bereits in den dreißiger Jahren ein Notwehrrecht gegenüber dem kaiserlichen Oberherrn aus den wechselseitigen Bindungen des Lehnsrechts in Verbindung mit Argumenten des kanonischen und römischen Rechts begründet hatten.[37] Wie der spätmittelalterliche Rechtsgelehrte Bartolus setzte auch Monner die Schutzpflicht des Vaters gegenüber seinem Sohn mit derjenigen des Lehnsherrn gegenüber dem Lehnsuntertan gleich. Damit verband er römischrechtliche mit reichsrechtlichen Argumenten. Der Lehnsherr/Vater, der seine Pflicht als

---

[35] Zur Biographie vgl. *Timothy Wengert*, G. Major (1502-74). Defender of Wittenberg's Faith and Melanchthonian Exeget, in: Heinz Scheible (Hrsg.), Melanchthon in seinen Schülern. Wiesbaden 1997, 129-156. Seine Position formulierte Major in einer zunächst anonym erschienenen Schrift von 1546 (VD 16: M 2035). Zu deren Interpretation siehe *Scattola*, Naturrecht (wie Anm. 2), 62-66, sowie *Schorn-Schütte*, Obrigkeitskritik (wie Anm. 1), 210f., und *dies.*, Kommunikation über Herrschaft. Obrigkeitskritik im 16. Jahrhundert, in: Lutz Raphael/Heinz-Elmar Tenorth (Hrsg.), Ideen als gesellschaftliche Gestaltungskraft der Neuzeit. Beiträge für eine erneuerte Geistesgeschichte. Stuttgart 2006, 71-108.

[36] *Monner*, Bedencken (wie Anm. 14).

[37] Die Texte bei *Scheible* (Hrsg.), Widerstandsrecht (wie Anm. 19), 63-66. Zum Ganzen siehe *Böttcher*, Ungehorsam (wie Anm. 7), 136-146, sowie *Wolgast*, Theologie (wie Anm. 1), 165-168.

Obrigkeit nicht erfüllte, nämlich Bosheit und Sünde öffentlich zu strafen und die gehorsamen Lehnsleute/Kinder zu schützen und zu schirmen, verwirkte sein obrigkeitliches Amt. Gegenüber einer Obrigkeit aber, die keine mehr ist, konnte es keine Gehorsamspflicht geben.[38]

Gleichberechtigt neben dieser Rechtsfigur stand das natürliche Recht jedes Menschen auf Notwehr gegenüber Mördern oder Räubern, die fremdes Gut oder Eigentum antasteten.[39] Da die Normierungen des römischen Rechts ebenso wie die Reichsordnungen niemanden von diesen Grundsätzen ausnahmen, galt jener Rechtssatz auch für das Verhältnis zwischen Obrigkeit und Untertan. Und das hieß: wenn die Obrigkeit selbst diese natürlichen Rechte der Untertanen mißachtete, war sie wie eine Privatperson zu betrachten, gegen die der bedrohte Untertan im Rechtssinn keinen Widerstand leistete, sondern seine Angehörigen und sein Eigentum gegen unrechtmäßige Angriffe *verteidigte*.[40]

In der aktuellen Konfliktlage des Reiches in den vierziger Jahren des 16. Jahrhunderts bündelte Monner mit dieser Beweisführung die verschiedenen Begründungen für die Legitimität des Widerstandes, die die zeitgenössischen Debatten beherrschten. Indem er einerseits den aristokratischen Charakter der Reichsverfassung betonte, nahm er das institutionelle Argument von der Gleichrangigkeit der niederen und der höheren Obrigkeiten auf. Andererseits fand dieses Recht seine Grundlage im Naturrecht der Notwehr. Zum dritten schließlich beruhte es auf der Verpflichtung der christlichen Amtsinhaber, ihr Amt nicht zu mißbrauchen.[41]

Dieses aristokratische Verständnis der Reichsverfassung war, wie erwähnt, sicherer Bestandteil der Argumentation zahlreicher weiterer Juristen, die als Berater städtischer und landesherrlicher Obrigkeiten nach dem Augsburger Reichstag von 1530 mit Gutachten und Stellungnahmen an die Öffentlich-

---

[38] *Monner*, Bedencken (wie Anm. 14), 15. Monner publizierte unter den Pseudonymen Regius Selinus und Christoph Cunradt. 1554 wurde er zum ersten juristischen Professor an die neu gegründete Universität Jena berufen. Es ist bemerkenswert, daß Monner wie Bugenhagen auf verschiedenen Argumentationslinien (lehns- und römischrechtliche hier, alttestamentliche dort) zu inhaltlich gleichen Ergebnissen kamen. Damit wird die These von der Parallelität der Argumentationen innerhalb unterschiedlicher Wissensbestände bestätigt.
[39] *Monner*, Bedencken (wie Anm. 14), 17.
[40] Ebd.; siehe das Zitat bei *Scattola*, Naturrecht (wie Anm. 2), 60 mit Anm. 135.
[41] Sehr präzise hat *Kolb*, Case (wie Anm. 15), 151, diese Sachlage charakterisiert: „These arguments [individuelles natürliches Recht der Notwehr, Recht zur Abwehr von Amtsmißbrauch, Pflicht, der höheren Obrigkeit zu widerstehen, sofern sie die Grenzen des Amtes überschreitet – d. Vf.in] had been in the process of development within Hessian and Saxonian circles since 1529 and Monner did no more than to apply them with special reference to the legal tradition."

keit getreten waren.[42] Meinungsführer dieser Gruppe waren (neben den kursächsischen) die hessischen Juristen, die als Berater des Landgrafen Philipp die Reichsverfassung als reichsrechtlich verankerten Vertrag zwischen Kaiser und Reichsständen charakterisierten. Sollte der Kaiser seine eidliche Verpflichtung verletzen, die Stände bei ihrem alten Recht zu belassen, waren sowohl das Vertragsverhältnis als auch der Gehorsamseid der Stände mit allen Konsequenzen gegenstandslos.

Während sich die sächsischen Juristen strikt auf die juristischen Argumente stützten, versuchten die hessischen und einige städtische Rechtsgelehrte theologische und juristische Argumentationsmuster zusammenzuführen. So betonten die Hessen, daß das Gehorsamsgebot des Apostels Paulus im Römerbrief nur in seinem historischen Zusammenhang verständlich sei, eine wörtliche Übertragung des Bibeltextes auf die aktuelle Situation nicht zulässig sei.[43] Vor allem aber interpretierte der Münsteraner Syndikus Johannes Wick in einem Gutachten von 1531 das Gehorsamsgebot des Römerbriefs in enger Verbindung mit dem Paulusbrief an die Gemeinde in Korinth (2. Kor. 10): die Obrigkeit hat die Aufgabe zu bessern und zu schützen, wer durch Widerstand gegen eine in diesem Sinne pflichtvergessene Obrigkeit Besserung erreicht, der hat das Recht auf seiner Seite. In der Verknüpfung beider Texte bezog sich der westfälische Jurist auf die Auslegungen, die zuerst durch Johannes Bugenhagen am Ende der zwanziger Jahre vorgelegt worden waren.[44]

Diese vorerst noch spärlichen Versuche, theologische und juristische Argumentationslinien zusammenzuführen, intensivierten sich in der Krisensituation von 1547, Breitenwirkung erreichten sie in der Interimskrise von 1548 bis 1550. Gerade weil die theologischen und juristischen Wissensbestände parallel vorhanden waren, ist die Frage nach einer wechselseitigen Rezeption falsch gestellt. Von einer strikten Trennung gelehrter juristischer und theologischer Bildung, Argumentation und politischer Absicht sollte für die Jahrzehnte zwischen 1530 und 1550 nicht länger gesprochen werden. Statt dessen ist von einer gemeinsamen „politischen Sprache" auszugehen, die praktische Wirkungen erzielte. Merio Scattola hat dies im Blick auf die Wissenstraditionen zusammengefaßt: „Die Idee der gerechten Gegenwehr wur-

---

[42] Grundlegende Darstellung dazu weiterhin *Wolgast*, Theologie (wie Anm. 1), 163–175. Ferner *Isenmann*, Widerstandsrecht (wie Anm. 8), 57–62, der sich in seiner sonst anregenden Interpretation leider nicht auf Wolgast bezieht.

[43] *Isenmann*, Widerstandsrecht (wie Anm. 8); *Wolgast*, Theologie (wie Anm. 1), 169f.

[44] D. Johann Wicks zu Bremen Bedencken, ob man dem Käyser widerstreben möge? De Anno 1531, in: Johann Christian Lünig, Europäische Staats-Consilia ... Leipzig 1715, Gutachten Nr. XIII, 45–52. Vgl. *Isenmann*, Widerstandsrecht (wie Anm. 8), 56. Den Nachweis verdanke ich Patrizio Foresta, Mitarbeiter im von mir geleiteten Teilprojekt E3 des KFK/SFB „Wissenskultur und gesellschaftlicher Wandel" an der Universität Frankfurt am Main.

de aus dem römischen Völkerrecht entliehen; die Idee der göttlichen Ordnung, die freilich von dem Apostel Paulus stammt, geht auf das Naturrecht stoischer Prägung zurück, das in die mittelalterliche Philosophie und Theologie eingegliedert und darin ausgebaut wurde. Insofern sind die Argumente zur Rechtfertigung des Widerstandes kein Sonderprodukt einer speziellen, individuellen Entwicklung, sondern Teil eines gemeinsamen Gedankenguts." Die parallelen Deutungsstrategien konnten von Theologen und Juristen in Anspruch genommen werden, weil „sie tief greifenden Strukturen des juristischen, politischen und theologischen Denkens entsprachen".[45]

d) In dieses Ergebnis muß die zeitgenössische Debatte um die *Träger* legitimer Notwehr, Selbstverteidigung oder Gegenwehr eingepaßt werden, die seit den vierziger Jahren des 16. Jahrhunderts als Kontroverse um den Geltungsbereich der Dreiständelehre geführt wurde. Die Forschung hat sich diesem Thema selten gewidmet[46], vor allem ist kaum etwas bekannt über die Verzahnung von theologischen und juristischen Wissensbeständen. Daß es sie gegeben hat, wurde bislang lediglich etwas lakonisch konstatiert.[47] Unter den Wittenberger Theologen begegnet die Lehre von der Ordnung der drei Stände erstmals in der Mitte der zwanziger Jahre bei Johannes Bugenhagen, sie gewann an Bedeutung im Hausbuch Menius' von 1528, sie erhielt weiteres Gewicht in Melanchthons Schriften seit 1535, sie wurde eingesetzt in (auch gedruckten) Predigten und der wachsenden Hausväterliteratur im Vorfeld des Schmalkaldischen Krieges, begegnete als Argumentation in den ganz konkreten Konflikten um die Einführung des Interims und prägte deshalb auch die „Magdeburger Confessio", schließlich erhielt sie weiteres Gewicht in den seit den sechziger Jahren vielfältig ausgetragenen Konflikten um die Rolle der (auch sozial) neuen Gruppe der protestantischen Geistlichkeit.

In ihren frühen Schriften haben Menius und Bugenhagen ein Muster formuliert, an das in den folgenden Jahren immer wieder angeknüpft werden konnte.[48] Aufgrund des Rechtes, sich einer Obrigkeit zu widersetzen, die ihre Amtspflicht verletzt, stehen sich in Bugenhagens Verständnis weltliche und geistliche Amtsträger gleichberechtigt gegenüber. In Anknüpfung an die aristotelischen Kategorien formulierte auch Menius 1528 in seiner „Oecono-

---

[45] *Scattola*, Widerstandsrecht (wie Anm. 25), 480.
[46] Siehe mit Nachweis der Literatur zuletzt *Schorn-Schütte*, Kommunikation (wie Anm. 1).
[47] *Martin Heckel*, Staat und Kirche nach den Lehren der evangelischen Juristen Deutschlands in der ersten Hälfte des 17. Jahrhunderts. München 1968, 140: „Als die Dreiständelehre von den lutherischen Theologen entwickelt war, ist sie Schritt für Schritt in die juristische Literatur eingedrungen." Heckel stellt dann allerdings ohne Nachweis fest, daß eine Annäherung zwischen Juristen und Theologen erst seit dem Beginn des 17. Jahrhunderts stattgefunden habe; dem widersprechen die hier skizzierten Befunde.
[48] Zum Folgenden siehe mit allen Nachweisen *Schorn-Schütte*, Politikberatung (wie Anm. 15).

mia" jene Doppelung der Schöpfungsordnung, wonach einem leiblich-weltlichen Teil ein geistlicher Teil gegenübersteht. Ersterer besteht aus der *oeconomia* und der *politia*, letzterer tritt als *ecclesia* den beiden weltlichen Ordnungen gegenüber. Die Doppelung der Schöpfungsordnung wird zur Ordnung der drei Stände. Für beide ist die Grundlage aller legitimen Herrschaft der Dekalog, konkret das vierte Gebot; das gilt für alle drei Stände (oder Ordnungen: der Sprachgebrauch ist zunächst nicht eindeutig). Deshalb auch sind alle drei Stände aufgerufen, den Mißbrauch, die Amtsverfehlung zu ahnden. Notwehr oder Widerstand sind keine Individualrechte. Ihre Ausübung ist immer nur möglich für legitime Amtsinhaber, für das Haupt jedes der drei Stände. Mit dieser „Amtsbindung" erfüllte die Dreiständelehre eine strukturierende, das Notwehrrecht in die ständische Ordnung einbindende Funktion. Nicht eine aufrührerische Masse stand zu befürchten, wie es die Gegner des Notwehrrechtes einwandten und wie es als Vorwurf insbesondere von seiten der Altgläubigen formuliert wurde. Statt dessen handelte eine klar begrenzte, ständisch gebundene Gruppe. Dies unterstrich Melanchthon mit seinem Votum von 1535 als er betonte, daß es nicht die Masse sei, die hier angesprochen werde, sondern die „reliquia politia, cui Deum gladius dedit".[49]

Diese ständisch ordnende Rolle erklärt, warum die Dreiständelehre in den folgenden Jahrzehnten eine so dominierende Funktion erhielt.[50] Weil mit dem Anspruch der protestantischen Geistlichkeit, ein Wächteramt gegenüber den beiden anderen Ständen zu üben, die Grenzen zwischen den Ständen/Ämtern zur Disposition gestellt waren, eröffnete sich ein Konfliktpotential, auf das die gelehrten Juristen ebenso wie die weltlichen Obrigkeiten zu reagieren gezwungen waren. Das Problem war stets heikel, denn mit der Beschreibung der Aufgabe des *status politicus* als Schutz und Strafamt, als Wächter über beide Tafeln des Dekalogs, war schon in der ersten Generation der Reformatoren die Grenze undeutlich geblieben.[51] Dies aber nicht in der Absicht, die Position des *pius magistratus* zu stärken, sondern mit dem Ziel, die weltliche Obrigkeit auf ihre Schutzaufgabe für die noch gefährdete Kirche zu verpflichten. In dem Augenblick, in dem die Existenz der protestantischen Kirche im Kern nicht mehr gefährdet war, führte diese Schutzzuweisung zur Stärkung des *status politicus*, womit das Gleichgewichtsmodell der Dreiständeordnung nachhaltig gefährdet schien.

In der zeitgenössischen politischen Kommunikation herrschte breiter Konsens über die herrschaftsbegrenzende Funktion dieses Modells. An den Debatten darüber beteiligten sich einerseits die Theologen, andererseits vornehmlich städtische Amtsträger und gelehrte Juristen. Das Beispiel der

---

[49] *Philipp Melanchthon*, Loci Communes. Wittenberg 1535, zitiert nach *Scattola*, Widerstandsrecht (wie Anm. 25), 476 mit Anm. 48.
[50] Siehe in anderer Interpretation *v. Friedeburg*, Widerstandsrecht (wie Anm. 7), 51-70.
[51] *Melanchthon*, Loci (wie Anm. 49). Dazu auch *Peterson*, Menius (wie Anm. 26), 141f.

Bürgerhauptleute der Stadt Braunschweig ist bekannt[52], es läßt sich ergänzen um den Verweis auf die Diskussionen in der politisch sehr selbständigen Stadt Bremen. Im Rahmen verschiedener Konflikte um die Grenzen zwischen geistlichem und weltlichem Amt griffen mehrere juristisch gebildete Bürgermeister in den 60er Jahren des 16. Jahrhunderts auf die Dreiständelehre zurück. „Es ist richtig", so argumentierte Bürgermeister Dietrich von Büren Anfang 1562 gegen seinen innerstädtischen Gegner, den Bürgermeister Johann Esig, „die Obrigkeit ist Hüterin auch der ersten Gesetzestafel. Aber ihre Macht erstreckt sich keineswegs über die äußere Diszplin hinaus. Das Urteil aber über die Lehre steht jedenfalls der ganzen Kirche zu." Und in anderem Zusammenhang wiederholte er: „Vnd offwoll J:W:E: alse de Ouericheit Custodes primae tabulae und syn, so höred doch dat ordell van der lehre der ganzen Kercken tho deren de Ouericheit men ein deill ys."[53] Es ist nicht verwunderlich, daß die Lehre in den tagespolitischen Auseinandersetzungen mit Bezug auf bestimmte Interessen eingesetzt wurde, das galt für Juristen und Theologen. Aber das Ordnungsmodell war außerordentlich präsent, es war Teil der politischen Sprache. Und in Gestalt protestantischer, von Juristen verfaßter Regentenspiegel war es zugleich Norm der juristischen Herrschaftslehre, wie es das Beispiel des Johannes Ferrarius belegt.[54]

2. Aufgrund ihrer gemeinsamen Funktion als Berater in politischen Entscheidungsphasen haben Juristen und protestantische Theologen seit dem ersten Drittel des 16. Jahrhunderts in engem Austausch über die politisch-theologischen Prinzipien der Strukturierung von Herrschaft gestanden. Diese beschränkte sich nicht, so konnte gezeigt werden, auf den Austausch unter den jeweiligen Gelehrten zumeist der Universitäten, sondern schloß den beratenden oder konflikthaften Kontakt in den Auseinandersetzungen vor Ort (u. a. im Umkreis der Durchsetzung des Interims) ein. Schon vor der Reformation hatte es zumal in den Städten lebhaften geistigen Austausch zwischen humanistisch gebildeten Laien und Klerikern gegeben, und die Träger der reformatorischen Bewegung in den Städten waren bekanntermaßen gelehrte Juristen, juristisch gebildete Amtsträger in landesherrlichen oder städtischen Diensten und ehemalige, theologisch gebildete Kleriker. Die ge-

---

[52] Siehe ausführlich *Luise Schorn-Schütte*, Evangelische Geistlichkeit in der Frühneuzeit. Deren Anteil an der Entfaltung frühmoderner Staatlichkeit und Gesellschaft. Gütersloh 1996, 416–421.
[53] Zitat nach *Chang Soo Park*, Die Dreiständelehre als politische Sprache in der zweiten Hälfte des 16. Jahrhunderts am Beispiel des T. Heshusius (1527–1588), in: Bremisches Jahrbuch 83, 2004, 50–69, hier 60f.
[54] Siehe dazu ausführlich *Luise Schorn-Schütte*, „Den eygen nutz hindan setzen und der Gemeyn wolfart suchen." Überlegungen zum Wandel politischer Normen im 16./17. Jahrhundert, in: Neuhaus/Stollberg-Rilinger (Hrsg.), Menschen (wie Anm. 8), 167–184, bes. 172–176; zudem *Witte*, Law (wie Anm. 3), 140–153.

meinsame gelehrte Bildung ebenso wie die häufig reiche praktische politische Erfahrung vor Ort erwiesen sich trotz aller Umbrüche zumindest für die erste Generation derjenigen, die die reformatorische Bewegung trugen, als kontinuitätsstiftend.

Die Autoren der hier untersuchten Texte (Gutachten, Predigten, Regentenspiegel, Hausväterliteratur), die in den beschriebenen Debatten eine Rolle gespielt haben, gehörten für den Zeitraum zwischen 1500 und 1600 fünf Generationen an.[55] Dementsprechend unterschiedlich verliefen die Lebenswege und Kommunikationsweisen der Gruppen. Die erste und zweite Generation setzte sich aus Juristen und Theologen gleichermaßen zusammen, letztere waren mehrheitlich bis zum Ende der zwanziger Jahre des 16. Jahrhunderts katholische Kleriker gewesen. Mehrere von ihnen hatten während der gleichen Zeitspanne an der gleichen Universität studiert, fast alle hatten in den zwanziger bis dreißiger Jahren des Jahrhunderts ihr Studium (sei es in der theologischen, sei es in der juristischen Fakultät) in Wittenberg absolviert und dort in direktem Kontakt mit dem Kreis der Reformatoren um Luther, Melanchthon, Jonas, Bugenhagen und Major gestanden. Wie viele aus der ersten Generation der Reformatoren stammten auch diese Autoren aus städtischen Ratsfamilien, waren also Angehörige der stadtbürgerlichen Führungsgruppen jener Zeit. Häufig wurden sie über ihre Ehefrauen eingebunden in das mit den beiden ersten Generationen entstehende neue Netz protestantischer stadtbürgerlicher Entscheidungsträger, die nicht zuletzt als juristisch oder theologisch geschulte Berater von Stadträten und/oder Landesherrn amtierten.

Dieses Netz entfaltete und verdichtete sich in den beiden folgenden Generationen sichtlich.[56] Das zeigt sich z. B. deutlich an der Differenzierung der bevorzugten Studienorte. Während auch die zweite Generation mehrheitlich einmal im Laufe des Studiums in Wittenberg anzutreffen war, traten für die dritte und vierte Generation, diejenigen also, die geboren wurde, als sich die Reformation bereits etabliert hatte, Tübingen und Leipzig hinzu. Für die fünfte Generation schließlich wurden vermehrt die Universitäten bedeutsam, die für das heimische Territorium als Ausbildungsstätten dienten. Hier griff die gezielte Förderung des eigenen Nachwuchses mit Hilfe landes-

---

[55] Für die Sammlung der hier nur zu einem kleinen Teil ausgewerteten 200 Basistexte, wurden schematische „Generationen" angesetzt, denen die Einzelfälle zugeordnet wurden. I: vor 1500: 3; II: 1500–1524: 9; III: 1525–1549: 17; IV: 1550–1574: 14; V: 1575–1599: 10. Biographische Details entstammen zumeist den vorhandenen Lexika; sie sind Bestandteil einer umfassenderen Datensammlung, die am Lehrstuhl Neuere allgemeine Geschichte unter besonderer Berücksichtigung der Frühen Neuzeit der Johann Wolfgang Goethe-Universität Frankfurt am Main geführt wird. Sie ist Ergebnis verschiedener Projektforschungen, die u. a. durch die DFG, die VW-Stiftung und die Thyssenstiftung gefördert wurden.
[56] Hier die Generationen II und III/IV.

herrlicher Stipendienanstalten. Selbst wenn von einer Regionalisierung der Kommunikationswege und sozialen Beziehungen für die hier betrachtete Gruppe durchaus nicht gesprochen werden kann, ist doch nun die Herausbildung von verschiedenen, einander nicht immer tangierenden Kommunikationsnetzen zu beobachten, die sich aber erst gegen Ende des 16. Jahrhunderts allmählich auf die Gruppe der gelehrten Theologen konzentrierten. Die biographischen Daten legen die Erklärung nahe, daß für die dritte und vierte Generation die im Zuge einer gemeinsamen Amtstätigkeit verdichteten Kommunikationswege stärkere Bedeutung erhielten.[57]

Auch für diese Generationen galt, daß die Einbindung in das Kommunikationsnetz protestantischer Entscheidungsträger und gelehrter Politikberater häufig über die Eheschließung geschah. Nachdrücklich ist hervorzuheben, daß sich die sozialen, beruflichen und politischen Kommunikationskreise nicht auf die Geistlichkeit reduzierten. Selbst wenn in der vierten und fünften Generation die Verfasser der untersuchten Texte mehrheitlich Theologen waren, so blieben sie über Elternhaus, Ehepartner und Berufe der Kinder bzw. Schwiegerkinder in der überwiegenden Zahl der Fälle in die Gruppe der stadtbürgerlichen Entscheidungsträger und/oder in diejenige des sogenannten „Territorialbürgertums" eingebunden, eine Gruppe also, die in Diensten des Landesherrn als häufig juristisch gebildete Fachleute politische Entscheidungen vorbereiteten und umsetzten, ohne daß damit deren distanzlose Nähe zu den Herrschaftsträgern vorgegeben gewesen wäre.[58] Diese soziale Nähe der theologisch und/oder juristisch gebildeten Autoren erklärt ihre große Vertrautheit mit den zeitgenössischen politischen Konflikten ebenso wie mit den juristisch-theologischen Debatten um die Legitimation von Herrschaft – auch und gerade im Kleinen.

Angesichts dieser Tatbestände kann es gerade nicht als Aufgabe der gelehrten Juristen und Theologen angesehen werden, „die sozialen und ideologischen Positionen derart umzudefinieren, daß sie der modernen Staatenbildung nicht im Wege standen".[59] Diese Beschreibung der Aufgabe frühneuzeitlicher „Intellektueller" verkennt die Eigenständigkeit der theologischen

---

[57] Die chronologische Aufschlüsselung der Amtsorte ist z. B. für J. Bugenhagen und J. Menius aufschlußreich: zeitgleich mit Bugenhagen war Caspar Cruciger Professor in Wittenberg, Bugenhagen, Freder, Menius und Mörlin hatten zur gleichen Zeit in Wittenberg studiert, Mörlin und Bugenhagen waren zeitgleich Pfarrer an Wittenberger Kirchen gewesen. Als Jurist gehörte B. Monner zu dieser vernetzten Gruppe hinzu. Der Blick auf die Autoren von Interimsschriften bestätigt diese Vernetzung, sie wird durch weitere Namen ergänzt (u. a. Medler und Beyer).
[58] Für die Gruppe der Hofprediger ausführlich *Luise Schorn-Schütte*, Prediger an protestantischen Höfen der Frühneuzeit, in: Herman Diederiks/Heinz Schilling (Hrsg.), Bürgerliche Eliten in den Niederlanden und in Nordwestdeutschland. Köln/Wien 1985, 275-336.
[59] So die Charakterisierung bei *Jutta Held*, Intellektuelle in der Frühen Neuzeit, in: dies. (Hrsg.), Intellektuelle in der Frühen Neuzeit. München 2002, 8-15, 11. Diese Beschrei-

und juristisch geschulten Gruppen, die sich in deren sehr autonomem Umgang mit traditionalen Deutungsmustern zeigte. Die Neuordnung von politisch-theologischen Debatten und Interpretationsmustern beruhte gerade nicht auf deren „Funktionalisierung" für jene frühneuzeitliche „Staatlichkeit", deren Existenz mehr denn je fragwürdig geworden ist.[60] Vielmehr gelang es den hier charakterisierten Gruppen, die parallel vorhandenen Wissensbestände in den politisch aufgeladenen Debatten der Mitte des 16. Jahrhunderts zu aktivieren und einander anzunähern. Diese allerdings betonten die Dimension von Herrschaftsbegrenzung, nicht von Herrschaftszentrierung.

III.

Religion und Politik waren, so läßt sich der Durchgang für das 16. Jahrhundert zusammenfassen, in der Wahrnehmung der juristisch und theologisch geschulten Amtsträger so eng ineinander verwoben, daß eine strikte Trennung in der jeweiligen Amtsführung nie zur Debatte stand. Das aber schloß die Anerkennung der Verschiedenartigkeit der inneren Logik und der Traditionen beider Wissensbestände nicht aus. Drei Aspekte diese Befundes sollen festgehalten werden.

1. Die zeitgenössischen Debatten, die um Reichsverfassung, Notwehrrecht/Naturrecht und die Dreiständelehre geführt wurden, waren politisch und theologisch hochbrisant, die Kompetenz der beteiligten Sachverständigen war groß, der Austausch der Argumente zwischen gelehrten Juristen und Theologen eng. Auch für die Zeitgenossen aber war sichtbar, daß trotz gemeinsamer Fragestellungen die unterschiedliche Struktur der theologischen und juristischen Wissensbestände und der damit verzahnten Wissenstraditionen zu verschiedenen Antworten führen musste. Es war die Leistung der beteiligten Juristen und Theologen, die verschiedenen Aspekte zusammengeführt und in ihrer Paßfähigkeit artikuliert zu haben. Die damit verbundenen, zeitweilig sehr kontrovers geführten Debatten sind ein Muster-

---

bung entspricht den hier skizzierten Befunden nicht, die Bedeutung von Traditionserneuerung wird in der dort dokumentierten Debatte vollständig unterbewertet.

[60] Siehe dazu *Schorn-Schütte*, Obrigkeitskritik (wie Anm. 1). Jüngst sehr anregend *Markus Meumann/Ralf Pröve*, Die Faszination des Staates und die historische Praxis. Zur Beschreibung von Herrschaftsbeziehungen jenseits teleologischer und dualistischer Begriffsbildungen, in: dies. (Hrsg.), Herrschaft in der Frühen Neuzeit. Umrisse eines dynamisch-kommunikativen Prozesses. Münster 2004, 11-49; *Dagmar Freist*, Staatsbildung, lokale Herrschaftsprozesse und kultureller Wandel in der Frühen Neuzeit, in: dies/Ronald G. Asch (Hrsg.), Staatsbildung als kultureller Prozess. Strukturwandel und Legitimation von Herrschaft in der Frühen Neuzeit. Köln/Weimar/Wien 2005, 1-47, nimmt leider trotz vergleichbarer Fragestellungen weder auf Schorn-Schütte noch auf Meumann/Pröve Bezug.

beispiel dafür, was „politische Kommunikation" bedeutet. Von beiden Seiten wurden traditionsgeladene Begriffe zur Charakterisierung von Problemen politischer Ordnungsleistung eingesetzt, ohne daß damit zunächst auch Vergleichbares gemeint war. Dadurch, daß die Tragfähigkeit der traditionalen Inhalte auch für eine aktuell veränderte Situation in Gestalt des Austausches zwischen Juristen und Theologen geprüft wurde, entstand die Chance, den schon immer bekannten Begriff in einer für alle Beteiligten anerkannten Bedeutung zu verwenden. Damit wurde er Teil der aktuell akzentuierten „political language".

2. Schon diese Charakterisierung zeigt, daß die an der Kommunikation Beteiligten gleichberechtigte Partner waren. Die immer wieder betonte Unterordnung der Theologen unter die Juristen traf für die hier untersuchte Zeitspanne nicht zu. Bestätigt wird diese Gleichrangigkeit zudem durch den sozial- und bildungsgeschichtlichen Befund: Theologen und Juristen verfügten über gemeinsame Bildungsinstitutionen, über gemeinsame personale Netzwerke und damit seit den 60er Jahren des 16. Jahrhunderts über ein gemeinsames, protestantisch geprägtes Selbstverständnis als gelehrte Amtsträger. Dieses umfaßte eine durchaus skeptische Distanz zur weltlichen Obrigkeit.

3. Die gemeinsame politische Sprache, die sich seit den Debatten der dreißiger Jahre unter den juristisch und theologisch geschulten Politikberatern herausgebildet hatte, enthielt allerdings Konfliktpotential. Dieses zeigte sich darin, daß die im Kern als herrschaftsbegrenzend anerkannte Dreiständelehre in der aktuellen Debatte des ausgehenden 16. Jahrhunderts die Gegensätze zwischen den Ordnungen/Ständen zuspitzte. Das geistliche Wächteramt kollidierte nunmehr mit dem Auftrag des *status politicus*, Wächter beider Tafeln des Dekalogs zu sein. Diese Kontroversen sind hinlänglich bekannt, aber es waren Konflikte zwischen gleichberechtigten Amtsträgern um die Grenzen des jeweiligen Aufgabenbereichs, nicht die Debatten um die Dominanz des *status politicus*. Die Zeitgenossen selbst haben zumindest hier sehr viel differenzierter argumentiert, als es die historische Forschung angenommen hat.

„Officium in rempublicam"

Fürstliche Herrschaft und Territorialstaat in politischen und rechtlichen Reflexionen und Projektionen im Jahrhundert der Reformation

Von

Robert von Friedeburg

Nicht allein im Jahr der 450. Wiederkehr des Augsburger Religionsfriedens bleibt das Verhältnis von Reformation und Territorialstaat ein zentrales Anliegen der Reformationsgeschichte. Jüngere Überblicksdarstellungen halten an der zentralen Rolle des Zusammenhangs von Territorienbildung und Reformation entweder fest oder setzen den Bestand solcher Territorien als fürstlicher Herrschaftsbereiche am Vorabend der Reformation sogar voraus.[1] Jeder Vergleich einer Reformationsgeschichte des Reiches mit Dar-

---

[1] Beispielsweise ist bei *Olaf Moerke*, Die Reformation. Voraussetzungen und Durchsetzung. München 2005, 107, die Rede von der „objektiven Bedeutung des politischen Prozesses der Territorialisierung des Reiches". *Ulinka Rublack*, Reformation in Europe. Cambridge 2005, 6, formuliert: „The Empire [...] consisted of territories governed by a prince or by a bishop". *Axel Gotthard*, Das Alte Reich 1495–1806. Darmstadt 2003, spricht 51 vom *ius reformandi* als dem „Recht der Obrigkeit auf die Festsetzung und Veränderung der Religionsverhältnisse in ihrem Territorium", ohne daß der Begriff in der an dieser Stelle vom Autor behandelten Quelle, dem Augsburger Religionsfrieden, verwendet wird oder vom Autor selbst behandelt worden wäre. Er findet sich noch nicht einmal im Register. Ders., Der Augsburger Religionsfrieden. Münster 2004, verlegt S. 82f., 283f. die „ ‚frühmoderne' Territorialisierung" vor allem in die zweite Hälfte des 16. Jahrhunderts, geht jedoch auf die rechts- und verfassungsgeschichtlichen Fragen der Entwicklung des *ius territorialis* nicht ein. Vielmehr argumentiert er ebd. 284: „Der Religionsfrieden dokumentiert, wie sehr die Herrschaftsausübung für Politiker des 16. Jahrhunderts bereits territorialisiert war. In seiner Kombination von Ius reformandi und Ius emigrandi spricht der Religionsfrieden den Reichsständen Herrschaft über Territorien, nicht über Gewissen zu: über bestimmte Räume, nicht über Personenverbände". Das ist eine erstaunliche Feststellung, bedenkt man die Aussagen der Quelle und den Stand der Forschung. Zur Quelle: Im Augsburger Religionsfrieden ist nur, beispielsweise in Paragraph 15, von „Fuerstenthumen, Landen und Herrschaften" die Rede. Paragraph 16 findet zu einer Aufzählung von „Haab, Guetern, liegend, fahrend, Landen, Leuthen, Herrschafften, Obrigkeiten, Herrlichkeiten und Gerechtigkeiten, Renthen, Zinsen, Zehenden", welche die Realität fürstlicher Herrschaft, nämlich die Summe unterschiedlicher Rechte, abbildete, wie jüngst noch einmal *Ernst Schubert*, Fürstliche Herrschaft und Territorium im späten Mittelalter. München 1996, 1–6, feststellt: „fürstliche Herrschaft ist die Wahrnehmung einzelner Herrschaftsrechte". Die Bestimmungen des Religionsfriedens waren innerhalb der fürstlichen Herrschaftsbereiche also nicht in einem geschlossenen Raum, sondern zunächst in den mehr oder minder geschlossenen Ämtern, gegen-

stellungen zu Frankreich oder England stößt unmittelbar auf die zentrale Rolle der Krone in England (siehe die Beiträge von Martin Ingram und Ralph Houlbrooke in diesem Band) oder die verheerenden Folgen des Verlustes der Fähigkeit der Krone zur Steuerung der Geschehnisse in Frankreich (siehe Mark Greengrass). Wie sehr auch immer sich die jüngere Kulturgeschichte der Reformation von der Geschichte politischer Ereignisse und verfassungsrechtlicher Strukturen entfernt haben mag[2], sie operiert dennoch weiterhin mit Annahmen, die fundamental durch die Entstehung fürstlicher Anstalts- und Flächenstaaten im Reich geprägt sind.

Unstrittig reflektierte in der zweiten Hälfte des 17. Jahrhunderts Samuel Pufendorf diese Entwicklung, wenn er das Reich als „Monstrum" bezeichnete. Wir wissen jedoch, daß selbst nach dem Dreißigjährigen Krieg nur mit Vorbehalt von geschlossenen Territorialstaaten gesprochen werden kann.[3] Enklaven und Exklaven blieben allenthalben die Regel. Die Rechtsverhältnisse zwischen Landständen und Fürsten blieben nicht nur umstritten, die vermeintlichen Untertanen der Fürsten brachten ihren Herren noch bis weit ins 18. Jahrhundert schwere verfassungsrechtliche Niederlagen bei. Der Mecklenburger Herzog verlor im Ausgleich von 1755 die von ihm angestrebte Machtposition im Territorium; die Trierer Ritter erkämpften sich

---

über den direkten Untertanen und gegenüber den Lehnsvasallen durchzusetzen. Die Einführung der Reformation erfolgte jedoch ganz überwiegend nicht allein in den Reichsstädten, sondern auch durch die Reichsstände, gerade in Einklang und Absprache mit den Ständen. Dabei soll gar nicht bestritten werden, daß die reichsständische Herrschaft über Ämter und Vasallen sich in der Folge vor das Problem gestellt sah, bei Streitigkeiten mit Nachbarn in Religionsfragen Abgrenzungskriterien zu entwickeln, die sich dann, wenigstens seit der Wende zum 17. Jahrhundert, als *ius territorialis* und *ius reformandi* im als geschlossenen Rechtsbezirk gedachten Territorium darstellten, nur war davon wenigstens in der Quelle des Augsburger Reichsabschieds vom September 1555, des Religionsfriedens, noch keine Rede. Die besonderen Probleme bei dynastischen Aufteilungen der Rechte einer fürstlichen Familie oder der dynastischen Neu-Zusammenfassung verschiedener Herrschaften sind dabei noch nicht einmal benannt. Es bleibt auch unklar, wen er unter „Politiker" subsumiert. Für Berater in Sachen *prudentia civilis* wie Lazarus Schwendi bestand das Reich noch 1570 nicht aus Territorien, die Begrifflichkeit des *ius territorialis* entwickelte sich vermutlich erst (siehe unten) im Verlauf der 1580er Jahre, und die Politica des ersten Drittels des 17. Jahrhunderts, die in der Tat häufig – nicht immer – den Territorialstaat kannte, fußte ihrerseits auf Entwicklungen der Jurisprudenz, die heute in den 1590er Jahren bis in die Zeit nach der Wende zum 17. Jahrhundert verortet werden. Es macht sich bemerkbar, daß Gotthard die einschlägige Arbeit von *Bernd Christian Schneider*, Ius reformandi. Die Entwicklung eines Staatskirchenrechts von den Anfängen bis zum Ende des Alten Reiches. Tübingen 2001, nicht mehr verwerten konnte (siehe *Gotthard*, Augsburger Religionsfrieden, 8 Anm. 25).

[2] Vgl. beispielsweise *Bernhard Jussen/Craig Koslofsky* (Hrsg.), Kulturelle Reformation. Göttingen 1999.

[3] *Georg Schmidt*, Der Westfälische Frieden – eine neue Ordnung für das Alte Reich?, in: Reinhard Mußgnug (Hrsg.), Wendemarken in der deutschen Verfassungsgeschichte. Berlin 1993, 45–72; *Karl Otmar von Aretin*, Das Alte Reich 1648–1806. 4 Bde. Stuttgart 1993-2000, Bd 1.

noch 1729 die Reichsunmittelbarkeit.[4] Angesichts der inzwischen teils pejorativen Bewertung des Verhältnisses von Obrigkeit und Reformation, aber auch der breiten vergleichenden Anlage des vorliegenden Bandes, will der folgende Beitrag sich vom Allgemeinen zum Besonderen vorarbeiten. Dazu wird im folgenden zunächst an einige Meilensteine der historiographischen Behandlung des Problems erinnert (I). Es folgt ein Abschnitt zur Begrifflichkeit, Bedeutung und zeitlichen Einordnung der Reflexion und Projektion einer territorialen Herrschaftsordnung im Reich und zum Problem des Verhältnisses dieser Entstehung zum *ius reformandi* (II), um danach einen Blick auf die Terminologie zur Beschreibung der Herrschaftsordnung zu werfen, nämlich in einem bedeutenden Rechtslexikon der 1540er Jahre und bei Philipp Melanchthon (III). Der Beitrag schließt mit vergleichenden Überlegungen (IV, V).

I.

In der Geschichte der Reformation im Reich dominierte lange Zeit eine Sicht, nach der die Reformation dem sterbenden spätmittelalterlichen Reich den letzten Todesstoß versetzt habe, um dem fürstlichen Territorialstaat zum Durchbruch zu verhelfen. Bereits 1892 formulierte Karl Wilhelm Nitzsch, „die Geschichte der Reformation ist zugleich die einer Neubildung von Staaten [...]. Die politischen Faktoren, welche sich bisher feindlich gegenüberstanden, vereinigten sich jetzt zur Erreichung derjenigen Ziele, aus denen der moderne Staat sich gebildet hat [...]. Die Reformation hat trotz des Zwiespalts, den sie hervorrief, für das nationale Leben, welches so tief zerklüftet war, [...] eine entschieden heilende Wirkung gehabt."[5] Nitzsch vertrat damit zum Ende des 19. Jahrhunderts eine auf den nationalen Machtstaat konzentrierte Perspektive, die beispielsweise für Ranke bedeutungslos gewesen war.[6] Diese Perspektive wurde durch die Schulpolitik des preußischen

---

[4] *Hermann Weber*, Frankreich, Kurtrier, der Rhein und das Reich 1623–1635. Bonn 1969, 12. Zur spektakulären Vertreibung einzelner Fürsten in den genannten Beispielen siehe *Robert von Friedeburg*, Natural Jurisprudence, Argument from History and Constitutional Struggle in the Early Enlightenment: Gottlieb Samuel Treuer's 1719 Anti-absolutist Polemic, in: Timothy J. Hochstrasser/Peter Schröder (Eds.), Early Modern Natural Law Theories. Dordrecht etc. 2003, 141–167; *Aloys Winterling*, Der Hof des Kurfürsten von Köln 1688–1794. Bonn 1986; *Sigrid Jahns*, ‚Mecklenburgisches Wesen' oder absolutistisches Regiment? Mecklenburgischer Ständekonflikt und neue kaiserliche Reichspolitik 1658–1755, in: Paul-Joachim Heinig (Hrsg.), Reich, Regionen und Europa in Mittelalter und Neuzeit. Berlin 2000, 323–351.
[5] *Karl Wilhelm Nitzsch*, Geschichte des deutschen Volkes bis zum Augsburger Religionsfrieden. 2. Aufl. Leipzig 1892, 429.
[6] Zur gegenwärtigen Rankeforschung vgl. *Jörg Baberowksi*, Der Sinn der Geschichte. Geschichtstheorien von Hegel bis Foucault. München 2005.

Kultusministeriums unterstützt, das für die Schulbücher des preußischen Königreiches Karten zeichnen ließ, die den Eindruck der Zersplitterung des Alten Reiches hervorrufen sollten.[7] Walther Sohm, der Sohn des Kirchenhistorikers, sah in der Reformation sogar die Grundlegung für „ein Staatsgefühl und ein Staatsgefüge" gelegt, die „im Zeitalter der Aufklärung stark genug war[en], den Gedanken des Christlichen zu entbehren". Zur Erklärung dieser Bewertungen sind eine ganze Reihe von wissenschaftlichen Rahmenbedingungen heranzuziehen.[8] Die Geschichte des Territorialstaates als Teil der Verklärung des nationalen Machtstaates in der Historiographie des letzten Drittels des 19. Jahrhunderts ist nur eine dieser Rahmenbedingungen.

Wir müssen uns die historiographischen Weichenstellungen der letzten achtzig Jahre nicht zuletzt deswegen vor Augen führen, weil die positive Wertung des Machtstaates im späten 19. Jahrhundert keineswegs eine Herabstufung aller Bürger zu Untertanen, sondern vielmehr die Durchsetzung einer im Kern als „bürgerlich" verstandenen Rechts- und Lebensordnung unter dem Dach der Monarchie und gegen den Adel favorisierte. Der – fürstliche – Machtstaat wurde als Garant der Einheit, nicht als Unterdrücker von Freiheit, gleich gar nicht bürgerlicher oder bäuerlicher Freiheit, gefeiert. Reinhold Koser beispielsweise beschrieb die Durchsetzung der „Absoluten Monarchie" nicht zuletzt als Konsequenz ihrer Unterstützung durch Bürger und Bauern im Kampf gegen den das Land beherrschenden Adel.[9] Es ist bezeichnend, daß die deutschen Rechtshistoriker der germanistischen Schule, allen voran Otto von Gierke, die sich um die staatsrechtliche Bedeutung des Genossenschaftsprinzips als Teil der politischen Traditionen der deutschen Nation bemühten, keineswegs die Rolle der Monarchie zurückzudrängen, sondern vielmehr die Beteiligung der Bürger und Bauern im monarchischen Staat zu legitimieren suchten.[10] Zwar war und blieb „die ältere deutsche

---

[7] Vgl. *Thomas Würtenberger*, Staatsverfassung an der Wende vom 18. zum 19. Jahrhundert, in: Mußgnug (Hrsg.), Wendemarken (wie Anm. 3), 85–121, und *Schmidt*, Der Westfälische Frieden (wie Anm. 3), sowie die Diskussionsbeiträge in diesem Band.

[8] *Walter Sohm*, Territorium und Reformation in der hessischen Geschichte 1526–1555. Marburg 1915. Vgl. zu dessen Vater Rudolph Sohm und der von ihm vertretenen These, die wahre Natur der Kirche sei mit einer formellen rechtlichen Ordnung unvereinbar, *Wilfried Härle*, Kirche, Religion und Recht in reformatorischer Sicht, in: Irene Dingel u. a. (Hrsg.), Reformation und Recht. Festgabe für Gottfried Seebaß zum 65. Geburtstag. Gütersloh 2002, 270–287, hier 270–272. Die Bewertung der Leistungen des – vermeintlich – säkularen Fürstenstaates sind nicht zuletzt auch vor diesem Hintergrund zu verstehen.

[9] *Reinhold Koser*, Die Epoche der absoluten Monarchie, in: Historische Zeitschrift 61, 1889, 246–287.

[10] *Otto von Gierke*, Deutsches Genossenschaftsrecht. 4 Bde. Berlin 1868–1913. Zur doppelten Frontstellung von Gierke siehe *Otto G. Oexle*, Otto von Gierkes Rechtsgeschichte der deutschen Genossenschaft, in: Notker Hammerstein (Hrsg.), Deutsche Geschichtswissenschaft um 1900. Stuttgart 1988, 193–219, hier 199–202. Zur zeitgenössischen Diskussion um den Ort der Souveränitätsrechte im Kaiserreich *Christoph*

Städtegeschichte [...] die Geschichte des bürgerlichen Emanzipationskampfes gegen den das Land bestimmenden Feudalismus"[11], aber eben gegen den „Feudalismus" als Prinzip adligen Übermutes und der Zersplitterung nationaler Einheit, nicht gegenüber der Monarchie als Garant eben dieser Einheit im zu gründenden Nationalstaat.

Dem standen in der Rechtsgeschichte Überlegungen zur Bedeutung der Rezeption des Römischen Rechts für die Entstehung des Staatsrechts zur Seite. Die dominierende Figur war hier sicherlich Paul Laband, der in seiner Rektoratsrede von 1880 auf die Bedeutung der Rezeption des römischen Rechts für die Entstehung des Staatsrechts hinwies und dafür Peter von Andlaus „Libellus de Cesarea monarchia" von 1460 anführte. Laband führte aus, daß im allgemeinen die Rezeption des Römischen Rechts allein im Hinblick auf das Privatrecht angenommen und untersucht würde, während „dagegen alles, was das öffentliche Recht betreffe, von der Rezeption ausgeschlossen sei".[12] Laband konzedierte umstandslos, „die Verfassungszustände des Deutschen Reiches waren zu allen Zeiten von denen des Römischen Kaiserreiches so unendlich verschieden, die Grundlagen der Staatsgewalt, die Aufgaben und Einrichtungen des Staates, die Gliederung seiner Organe, die Formen seiner Willensakte so vollkommen abweichend, daß man kaum verstehen kann, wie in irgendeiner Epoche auf diesen historisch gegebenen deutschen Staat die im Römischen Recht in Geltung gewesenen Vorschriften für anwendbar erklärt werden konnten. Die Forschungen über die Rezeption des römischen Rechts beschäftigen sich daher auch vorzugsweise mit dem Eindringen des Privatrechts in Deutschland [...]." Er wandte dann jedoch ein, „[...] man verschließt sich im Allgemeinen wohl nicht der Ansicht, daß die politischen Verhältnisse eine der Hauptursachen [der Rezeption, R. v. F.] waren. Zu einer vollen Würdigung dieses Zusammenhangs ist man aber noch nicht gelangt und die eigenthümliche Wechselwirkung zwischen der Umgestaltung des gesamten deutschen Staatsrechts und der wachsenden

---

Schönberger, Das Parlament im Anstaltsstaat. Zur Theorie parlamentarischer Repräsentation in der Staatsrechtslehre des Kaiserreiches (1871-1918). Frankfurt 1997, 338-367 zur „Genossenschaftslehre" bei Otto von Gierke und Hugo Preuß.
[11] *Paul Sander*, Feudalstaat und bürgerliche Verfassung. Berlin 1906, 4; *Luise Schorn-Schütte*, Stadt und Staat. Zum Zusammenhang von Gegenwartsverständnis und historischer Erkenntnis in der Stadtgeschichtsschreibung der Jahrhundertwende, in: Die Alte Stadt. Zeitschrift für Stadtsoziologie und Denkmalpflege 10, 1983, 228-266.
[12] Vgl. *Joseph Huerbin*, Der Libellus de Cesarea monarchia von Hermann Peter aus Andlau, in: Zeitschrift der Savigny Stiftung für Rechtsgeschichte, Germanistische Abteilung 12, 1891, 34-102; *Paul Laband*, Rede über die Bedeutung der Rezeption des Römischen Rechts für das deutsche Staatsrecht (anlässlich des Rektoratswechsels an der Kaiser-Wilhelms-Universität Strassburg am 1. Mai 1880), in: ders., Dissertationen, Abhandlungen und Beiträge (1858-1917). Leipzig 1983, 540-573, 544f. Der Text jetzt besser zugänglich und kommentiert in *Peter von Andlau*, Kaiser und Reich. Libellus de Cesarea Monarchia. Hrsg. durch Rainer A. Müller. Frankfurt am Main 1998.

Herrschaft des römischen Rechts gehört noch zu den am wenigsten aufgeklärten Punkten der Rezeptionsgeschichte."[13]

Sowohl jene Sichtweise, die die territoriale Monarchie als Schutz der Bürger oder als einheitsstiftende Kraft verstand, als auch die erwähnten Annahmen über die historische Entstehung des Staatsrechts, wurden mittlerweile gründlich revidiert. Die Rechtsgeschichte handhabt nicht allein die Begriffe „Staat" und „Staatsrecht" vorsichtiger. Sie verlagerte die Entwicklung eines öffentlichen Staatsrechts völlig aus dem 15. und 16. Jahrhundert in das 17. Jahrhundert. Die Entstehung eines öffentlichen Rechts von Reich und Territorien, oder selbst die Wurzeln dieser Disziplinen, werden nun gerade in der beginnenden Emanzipation *vom* Römischen Recht gesucht, nicht in seiner Rezeption.[14] Die Entstehung eines öffentlichen Rechts im Reich, und damit auch einer begrifflichen Erschließung und Definition des Territorialstaats als Herrschaftsgebilde sui generis, sei erst seit dem Ende des 16. Jahrhunderts im Zuge der zunehmenden Ausdifferenzierung eines dann als *jus publicum* bezeichneten Gegenstandes von der Zivilistik in Gang gekommen. Die faktische Verdichtung gesetzgeberischer Maßnahmen auf territorialer Ebene durch Policeyordnungen, territoriale Gerichtspraxis usf. sei der expliziten Reflexion vorausgegangen.[15] Hinzu kommt, daß die Forschung zur Geschichte des römischen Rechtes inzwischen die Grundlagen seiner Erforschung aus dem 19. Jahrhundert, Mommsens römisches Staatsrecht, zunehmend kritisch bewertet, obgleich Mommsens Werk Ausgangspunkt der historischen Forschung bleibt.[16]

Die Deutung der Reformation als Durchbruch bürgerlicher Emanzipationsziele gegen den Adel und den ultramontanen Katholizismus und die Deutung Luthers in diesem Zusammenhang[17] sind durch die deutsche Ka-

---

[13] *Laband*, Rede (wie Anm. 12), 545f.

[14] Vgl. bereits *Rudolf Hoke*, Die Emanzipation der deutschen Staatsrechtswissenschaft von der Zivilistik im 17. Jahrhundert, in: Der Staat 15, 1976, 211–230.

[15] Ebd.; *Michael Stolleis*, Geschichte des öffentlichen Rechts in Deutschland. Bd. 1: Reichspublizistik und Policeywissenschaft 1600–1800. München 1988, 58–70, 334f.

[16] *Wilfried Nippel*, Geschichte und System in Mommens „Staatsrecht", in: Hans Markus von Känel/Maria R.-Alföldi/Ulrike Peter/Holger Komnick (Hrsg), Geldgeschichte vs. Numismatik. Kolloqium aus Anlass des 100. Todestages von Theodor Mommsen. Berlin 2004, 215–228.

[17] *Leopold von Ranke*, Deutsche Geschichte im Zeitalter der Reformation. Hrsg. v. Paul Joachimsen. München 1925/26; *Ernst Troeltsch*, Luther, der Protestantismus und die moderne Welt, in: ders., Aufsätze zur Geistesgeschichte und Religionssoziologie. (Gesammelte Schriften, Bd. 4.) Tübingen 1925, 202–254. Vgl. zur Inanspruchnahme Luthers durch die deutsche Nationalbewegung *Werner Conze*, Zum Verhältnis des Luthertums zu den mitteleuropäischen Nationalbewegungen im 19. Jahrhundert, in: Bernd Moeller (Hrsg.), Luther in der Neuzeit. Gütersloh 1983, 178–193, hier 181f.; *Luise Schorn-Schütte*, Ernst Troeltschs Sozialllehren und die gegenwärtige Frühneuzeitforschung. Zur Diskussion um Luthertum und Calvinismus für die Entstehung der modernen Welt, in: Friedrich-Wilhelm Graf/Trutz Rendtorff (Hrsg.), Ernst Troeltsch Sozialllehren. Studien zu ihrer Interpretation. Gütersloh 1991, 133–151. Zur Kritik an der Troeltsch'schen Sicht

tastrophe der Jahre 1933-1945 schließlich zwar revidiert worden, jedoch in eigentümlicher Perspektive. Nun geriet der Fürstenstaat zunehmend zum Signum eines im Verhängnis endenden und zu perhorreszierenden deutschen Sonderweges. Aus der Unterstützung des Fürstenstaates durch die politische Theorie des 17. und 18. Jahrhunderts, auf die die Forschung des 19. und frühen 20. Jahrhunderts ganz zu Recht hingewiesen hatte, wurde nun eine Ideologie verinnerlichter Freiheit, die die deutsche Mentalität vermeintlich nachhaltig prägte, und die den Anspruch auf Mitsprache in öffentlichen Angelegenheiten für Bauern und Bürger aufgab.[18] Bauern und Bürger blieben die Helden der Darstellung, jedoch nun in ihrem Widerstand gegen diesen Fürstenstaat, einem Widerstand, der unter anderem in Alltag und Organisationsformen von Land- und Stadtgemeinde aufzusuchen sei.[19]

---

und besonders an der daran anschließenden der lutherischen Orthodoxie vgl. den Forschungsüberblick bei *Wolfgang Sommer*, Gottesfurcht und Fürstenherrschaft. Studien zum Obrigkeitsverständnis Johann Arndts und lutherischer Hofprediger zur Zeit der altprotestantischen Orthodoxie. Göttingen 1988, 16f. Zur Forschung nach 1945, insbesondere zum Widerstandsproblem *Eivind Bergrav*, Wenn der Kutscher trunken ist. Luther über die Pflicht zum Ungehorsam gegenüber der Obrigkeit (1941), wiederabgedr. in: Arthur Kaufmann (Hrsg.), Widerstandsrecht. Darmstadt 1972, 135-150; *Hans Emil Weber*, Von den Kirchenrechtstheorien im Alten Luthertum (1946), in: ders., Gesammelte Aufsätze. Hrsg. v. Ulrich Seeger. München 1965, 224-243; *Johannes Heckel*, Widerstand gegen die Obrigkeit? Pflicht und Recht zum Widerstand bei Martin Luther (1954), wiederabgedr. in: ders., Das blinde, undeutliche Wort „Kirche". Gesammelte Aufsätze. Hrsg. v. Siegfried Grundmann. Köln 1964, 288-306; *ders.*, Lex charitatis. Eine juristische Untersuchung über das Recht in der Theologie Martin Luthers. München 1953; *Martin Honekker*, Cura Religionis Magistratus Christiani. Studien zum Kirchenrecht des 17. Jahrhunderts insbesondere bei Johann Gerhard. München 1968; *Martin Heckel*, Art. „Rechtstheologie Luthers", in: Evangelisches Staatslexikon. Stuttgart 1966, Sp. 2051-2083; *Martin Brecht*, Art. „Luther I", in: Theologische Realenzyklopädie. Bd. 21. Berlin/New York 1991, 514-530; *Karl Heinz zur Mühlen*, Art. „Luther II", in: ebd. 531-567; *Martin Brecht*, Die Rezeption von Luthers Freiheitsverständnis in der frühen Neuzeit, in: Lutherjahrbuch 62, 1992, 121-151, hier 125; *Walter Sparn*, Art. „Lutherische Orthodoxie", in: Evangelisches Kirchenlexikon. Bd. 3. Göttingen 1992, Sp. 1954-1958; *Dietrich Braun*, Luther über die Grenzen des Staates, in: Archiv für Reformationsgeschichte 78, 1987, 61-80; *Jörg Baur*, Lutherisches Christentum im konfessionellen Zeitalter – ein Vorschlag zur Orientierung und Verständigung, in: Dieter Breuer (Hrsg.), Religion und Religiosität im Zeitalter des Barock. Wiesbaden 1995, 43-62; *Robert Stupperich*, Melanchthon und die Täufer, in: Kerygma und Dogma 3, 1957, 150-169; *Wilhelm Maurer*, Luther und die Schwärmer, in: ders., Kirche und Geschichte 1: Luther und das evangelische Bekenntnis. Hrsg. v. Ernst-Wilhelm Kohls u. Gerhard Müller. Göttingen 1970, 103-133; *James M. Stayer*, Luther und die Schwärmer, in: Norbert Fischer/Marion Kobalt-Groch (Hrsg.), Außenseiter zwischen Mittelalter und Neuzeit. Festschrift für Hans Jürgen Goertz. Leiden 1990, 269-288.

[18] Vgl. besonders *Leonard Krieger*, The German Idea of Freedom. History of a Political Tradition. PhD Thesis Yale 1957, unter der Anleitung von Hajo Holborn.

[19] Siehe vor allem die Begriffsbildung „Kommunalismus" durch *Peter Blickle*, Kommunalismus und Republikanismus in Oberdeutschland, in: Helmut G. Koenigsberger (Hrsg.), Republiken und Republikanismus im Europa der frühen Neuzeit. München

Es versteht sich, daß die Reformationsgeschichtsschreibung seit den 1920er Jahren nicht eine, sondern gleich eine ganze Reihe von Entwicklungen durchlaufen hat, auf die hier im einzelnen gar nicht eingegangen werden kann.[20] Die Niederlage Deutschlands im Ersten Weltkrieg, die damit zusammenhängende scharfe Konturierung der Verteidigung der politischen, aber auch moralischen Legitimität des deutschen Staates gegen die Kriegsschuldthese der Ententemächte einerseits, die bereits seit den 1930er Jahren einsetzende kritische Neubewertung des deutschen frühmodernen Fürstenstaates andererseits, schließlich die Annäherung evangelischer und katholischer Kirchengeschichtsschreibung durch gemeinsame Tagungen, nicht zuletzt im Rahmen der Erforschung der Konfessionalisierung im Reich, haben das Gesicht der Reformationsgeschichtsschreibung tiefgreifend verändert. Ohne auch nur entfernt die verschiedenen Gesichtspunkte dieser Veränderung umfassend benennen zu wollen, galt dabei doch ein größeres Augenmerk der Reformation in der Stadt und durch die Stadt, auf dem Lande und unter Bürgern und Bauern, während die Reformation in den Territorialstaaten nicht zuletzt unter dem Gesichtspunkt struktureller Konflikte und mehr oder minder erfolgreicher oder gescheiterter Staatsbildungsprojekte verfolgt wurde.[21] Die Neubewertung des Alten Reiches seit den 1970er Jahren hat ihren Anteil dazu beigetragen, den Territorialstaat der Reformation in seiner Bedeutung zu relativieren.[22] Die Sozialgeschichtsschreibung der Reformation galt ihrerseits in erster Linie städtischen, aber auch ländlichen Gruppierungen, die Haupt- und Staatsereignisse der fürstlichen Politik traten demgegenüber in den Hintergrund. Als Teil dieser Veränderungen gewann die Geschichte der Mentalitäten und der sie formenden und auf sie reagie-

---

1988. 57–75; *ders.*, Kommunalismus, Parlamentarismus, Republikanismus, in: Historische Zeitschrift 242, 1986, 529–556.

[20] Vgl. beispielsweise *Geoffrey Dickens/Arthur G. Dickens/John Tonkin*, The Reformation in Historical Thought. Oxford 1985.

[21] *Bernd Hamm*, Reformation ‚von unten' und Reformation ‚von oben': Zum Problem reformhistorischer Klassifizierungen, in: Hans R. Guggisberg (Ed.), Reformation in Germany and Europe: Interpretations and Issues. Gütersloh 1993, 256–279; *Volker Press*, Calvinismus und Territorialstaat. Regierung und Zentralbehörden der Kurpfalz 1559–1619. Stuttgart 1970.

[22] *v. Aretin*, Das Alte Reich (wie Anm. 3), Bd. 1–4; *Volker Press*, Kriege und Krisen: Deutschland 1600–1715. München 1991; *Peter Moraw*, Von offener Verfassung zu gestalteter Verdichtung. Das Reich im späten Mittelalter 1250–1490. Berlin 1985; *Horst Rabe*, Der Augsburger Religionsfriede und das Reichskammergericht 1555–1600, in: ders./Hansgeorg Molitor/Hans-Christoph Rublack (Hrsg.), Festgabe für Ernst Walter Zeeden. Münster 1976, 260–280; *Paul-Joachim Heinig*, Die Vollendung der mittelalterlichen Reichsverfassung, in: Mußgnug (Hrsg.), Wendemarken (wie Anm. 3), 7–31; *Schmidt*, Der Westfälische Frieden (wie Anm. 3); *ders.*, Der Wormser Reichstag von 1495 und die Staatlichkeit im hessischen Raum, in: Hessisches Jahrbuch für Landesgeschichte 46, 1996, 115–136; *ders.*, Der Dreißigjährige Krieg. München 1995, 94–98.

renden Flugblattpublizistik größeres Gewicht.[23] Nicht zuletzt die Zunahme forschungsintensiver Monographien und die produktive Auffächerung der Forschung haben in den letzten Jahren zur Formulierung höchst widersprüchlicher Ansätze und Thesen geführt.[24]

Es steht außer Frage, daß diese Entwicklungen in ihrer Gesamtheit unsere Kenntnis der Geschichte der Reformation im Reich wesentlich erweitert haben. Weniger deutlich zeichnen sich vor diesem Hintergrund freilich die Konturen der Reformation im Reich gegenüber den Reformationen in anderen Ländern ab. In einer Hinsicht ist sich die Forschung sicherlich einig – von einem deutschen Sonderweg, gleich gar von einer Entwicklung staatsfrommer Gesinnung von Luther bis in die nationalistische Katastrophe des Dritten Reiches kann nicht mehr gesprochen werden.[25]

Nicht zuletzt die parallele Ausdifferenzierung und Spezialisierung der historischen Forschung in den Nachbarländern hat die Konturierung einer zuverlässigen europäischen Geschichte ungleich schwieriger gemacht, als das noch vor drei Jahrzehnten der Fall war. Wo noch in den 1970er Jahren Geoff Dickens die Geschichte der Reformation in Europa aus einer Hand kenntnisreich und mit scharfer Diktion beschreiben konnte, haben viele seiner vergleichenden Bewertungen Widerspruch erregt. Vor diesem komplexen forschungsgeschichtlichen Hintergrund eignet sich das Verhältnis von Politik und Theologie in besonderer Weise als Leitfrage vergleichender Beiträge zur Reformation in England, Deutschland und Frankreich. Im Vergleich ragen neben der Vielzahl der Universitäten, der großen Anzahl unabhängiger und wohlhabender Städte und den vielen Druckerpressen im Reich sicherlich auch die besondere Natur der landesherrlichen Obrigkeit und ihre Stärkung durch die Reformation hervor. Trotz der unstrittig belasteten Forschungsgeschichte gerade dieses Problemkomplexes wird es im folgenden um die Frage der Stärkung der landesherrlichen Obrigkeit durch die Reformation gehen; damit kann der Frage nach der Traditionalität der durch die Reformation hervorgerufenen Veränderungen in der politischen Ordnung nachgegangen werden. Dazu ist jedoch in erster Linie zu prüfen, wann eigentlich fürstliche Herrschaft nicht allein als Herrschaft über auf ihrem

---

[23] *Robert W. Scribner*, For the Sake of the Simple Folk. Popular Propaganda for the German Reformation. Oxford 1994.
[24] Nur ein Beispiel für solche gegensätzlichen Auffassungen sind die beiden Arbeiten von *Susan Karant-Nunn*, The Reformation of Ritual. An Interpretation of Early Modern Germany. London 1997, einerseits, und *Thomas Fuchs*, Protestantische Heiligenmemoria im 16. Jahrhundert, in: Historische Zeitschrift 267, 1998, 587–614, andererseits.
[25] *Heinz Schilling*, Wider den Mythos vom Sonderweg – Die Bedingungen des deutschen Weges in die Neuzeit, in: Heinig (Hrsg.), Reich, Regionen und Europa (wie Anm. 4), 699–714. Schon vorher *Luise Schorn-Schütte*, Obrigkeitskritik im Luthertum? Anlässe und Rechtfertigungsmuster im ausgehenden 16. und im 17. Jahrhundert, in: Michael Erbe (Hrsg.), Querdenken. Festschrift für Hans R. Guggisberg. Mannheim 1995, 253–270.

Kammergut siedelnde bäuerliche Untertanen oder Lehnsnehmer verstanden wurde, sondern als Herrschaft über alle Einwohner eines flächenmäßig begriffenen Rechtsbezirks, des Territorialstaats. Daran folgt die Frage, in welchem Zusammenhang diese Veränderung mit der Reformation und besonders dem *ius reformandi* stand.

II.

Die Lektüre der Beiträge von Martin Ingram und Ralph Houlbrooke macht die überragende Rolle der englischen Krone und zentraler Personen in unmittelbarer Umgebung des Herrschers deutlich. Unabhängig von der kontroversen Bewertung der Stärke der katholischen Kirche in England am Vorabend der englischen Reformation kann an der entscheidenden Rolle der Krone und ihrer Berater in den Regierungszeiten Heinrichs, seines Sohnes und der beiden Töchter Maria und Elisabeth wenig Zweifel bestehen. Natürlich hat sich auch die deutsche Forschung der Motive der politisch Handelnden, seien es Kaiser Karl V. oder sein Bruder Ferdinand, seien es einzelne Fürsten, seien es Berater einzelner Bünde, angenommen.[26] Hervorzuheben ist jedoch, daß – im Unterschied zu anderen Gemeinwesen in Europa – solche Motive in die Bewertung der Lage im Reich insgesamt eingebettet blieben. Es gab kein einzelnes, alle anderen überragendes Gravitationszentrum politischer Entscheidungen. Die Abwendung Karls V. vom Ketzerrecht nach 1530 galt beispielsweise allein für das Reich, nicht für seine Besitzungen in den Niederlanden.[27] Karl reagierte hier realistisch auf die Lage im Reich, in der ihm eine kompromißlose Verfolgung der Anhänger Luthers nicht gangbar schien. Damit reagierte er auch auf die Realitäten kaiserlicher und fürstlicher Macht im Reich. Diese wandelten sich freilich ihrerseits. Nicht allein ausschlaggebend, aber sehr wohl entscheidend für diese Veränderungen war dabei ein bemerkenswerter Wandel von Begriffen und Theorien. Vor diesem Hintergrund gewinnen die Formeln, die im Verlauf der Ereignisse gefunden wurden, um Einigungen zu erreichen, einen hohen eigenen Stellenwert. Natur und Umfang der fürstlichen Herrschaftsbereiche wurden auch durch solche Begriffe ‚begriffen' und verändert.

---

[26] Vgl. beispielsweise *Armin Kohnle*, Reichstag und Reformation. Kaiserliche und ständische Religionspolitik von den Anfängen der Causa Lutheri bis zum Nürnberger Religionsfrieden. Gütersloh 2001; *Gabriele Haug-Moritz*, Der Schmalkaldische Bund (1530–1541/42). Eine Studie zu den genossenschaftlichen Strukturelementen der politischen Ordnung des Heiligen Römischen Reiches Deutscher Nation. Leinfelden-Echerdingen 2002; *Thomas A. Brady*, Protestant Politics. Jacob Sturm (1489–1553) and the German Reformation. Atlantic Highlands, N. J. 1995.
[27] *Horst Rabe*, Abschied vom Ketzerrecht? Zur Religionspolitik Karls V., in: Dingel u. a. (Hrsg.), Reformation und Recht (wie Anm. 8), 40–57.

In der Bewertung Horst Rabes stehen im Hinblick auf die verfassungsrechtlichen Veränderungen im Reich als Antwort auf die Religionskonflikte die Veränderungen auf der Ebene des Reiches im Mittelpunkt, die Veränderungen in den Territorien an zweiter Stelle. Der „Verzicht auf die Durchsetzung der Allgemeingültigkeit des katholischen Kirchenwesens" und die Errichtung einer „Politischen Friedensordnung für die neu entstehenden Konfessionskirchen" mit dem Augsburger Religionsfrieden von 1555 untergruben die „universalistischen Bezüge des Kaisertums" – das Kaisertum geriet zum „Annex des Königtums".[28] Im Kern dieser Friedensordnung stand auch das *ius reformandi,* obgleich die Begrifflichkeit erst im weiteren Verlauf der zweiten Hälfte des 16. Jahrhunderts so entwickelt wurde. Es geriet, nicht zuletzt in der Deutung und Ausformulierung der die Streitfälle begleitenden und interpretierenden Juristen, bald zum „kostbarsten Stück der Landeshoheit".[29] Für die Reichsstände wurde dieses Recht ein besonders bedeutender Baustein für die Entwicklung geschlossener Territorien.[30] Insofern liegt in dieser Entwicklung der Reformation auch eine zentrale Wurzel der Territorialstaatsbildung, und zwar nicht nur der besonderen Rahmenbedingungen von Politik im Reich im Zeitalter der Reformation, sondern auch der Veränderung dieser Rahmenbedingungen.

Unstrittig blieben die Stände innerhalb der Territorien bedeutsam, sie konnten zudem auch in Zeiten der Krankheit oder Minderjährigkeit des Fürsten oder bei Zwistigkeiten innerhalb der fürstlichen Familie erheblichen Einfluß geltend machen.[31] Zu Recht hat die Forschung bei der Bewertung des Verhältnisses von Ständen und Fürsten darauf hingewiesen, daß bestimmte Grundkonstellationen, wie sie sich innerhalb einzelner Gebiete bis zum Ende der Reformation ausgebildet hatten, so die Präsenz und Stärke des Adels unter den Ständen eines Territoriums, entscheidenden Anteil am Gewicht von Fürst und Ständen besaßen.[32] Ebenso zu Recht ist auf die verwaltungs-, behörden- und finanzgeschichtlichen Tatbestände hingewiesen worden, die im Laufe des 16. Jahrhunderts den fürstlichen Zentralverwaltungen zugute kamen. Viele dieser Entwicklungen gingen bis ins 15. Jahrhundert und damit in die Zeit vor der Reformation zurück. Bei der Entstehung

---

[28] *Horst Rabe,* Reich und Glaubensspaltung. Deutschland 1500–1600. München 1986, 432.
[29] *Horst Rabe,* Deutsche Geschichte 1500–1600. München 1991, 644.
[30] *Martin Heckel,* Deutschland im konfessionellen Zeitalter. 2. Aufl. Göttingen 2001.
[31] Zu den Ständen siehe *Cordula Nolte,* Der kranke Fürst. Vergleichende Beobachtungen zu Dynastie- und Herrschaftskrisen um 1500, ausgehend von den Landgrafen von Hessen, in: Zeitschrift für Historische Forschung 27, 2000, 1–36, hier 17–19. Im Überblick jetzt *Kersten Krüger,* Die landständische Verfassung. München 2003, 12f.
[32] *Volker Press,* Formen des Ständewesens in den deutschen Territorien des 16. und 17. Jahrhunderts, in: Peter Baumgart (Hrsg.), Ständetum und Staatsbildung in Brandenburg-Preußen. Berlin 1983, 280–318.

territorialstaatlicher Herrschaft ging es jedoch nicht alleine um die Vollendung ohnehin angelegter Strukturen. Sie ist vielmehr zu sehen vor dem Hintergrund der spätmittelalterlichen Natur der Herrschaftsbeziehungen im Reich. Noch um 1500 war der präzise Umfang reichsfürstlicher Herrschaft in der Regel keineswegs eindeutig umrissen.[33]

Für die Zeit um 1500, ja selbst 1555, blieben insbesondere Begriff und Gegenstand des „Territoriums" oder „Territorialstaates" problematisch. Zwar deutete der spätmittelalterliche Plural von den „deutschen Landen" die Vielfalt dessen an, was gemeint war. In einer der wenigen Aufzählungen konkreter einzelner deutscher Länder in einer Urkunde von 1422 finden sich jedoch mit „Schwaben, Beyern, Franken, am Reyn, in Elsass, in der Wederawe, in Hessen, Dorjngen, Sachsen, Westfalen, Bravant, Holland, Seeland Gulch, Gelre" keineswegs fürstliche Jurisdiktionen, Herrschaftsbereiche oder der fürstlichen Herrschaft unterworfene Personenverbände, sondern, mit den Worten Ernst Schuberts, „Stammesgebiete" und „traditionsreiche Marken". Die Zeitgenossen nahmen, jedenfalls im Hinblick auf die strukturelle Zusammensetzung des Reiches in unterschiedliche Einheiten, „die fürstliche Herrschaft nicht wahr"[34], sie verstanden das Reich gerade nicht als eine Ansammlung von Territorialstaaten oder fürstlichen Hoheitsgebieten.

Inwieweit die Reformation dies änderte, und in welchem Sinne, bleibt die Frage. Zwar gilt nach wie vor, daß die Reformation nicht nur zu Konflikten zwischen Kaiser und evangelischen Reichsständen, sondern auch zwischen

---

[33] Vgl. *Peter Moraw*, Zu Stand und Perspektiven der Ständeforschung im spätmittelalterlichen Reich, in: ders., Über König und Reich. Aufsätze zur deutschen Verfassungsgeschichte des späten Mittelalters. Hrsg. v. Rainer Christoph Schwinges. Sigmaringen 1995, 243-275; *Horst Carl*, Landfriedensordnung und Ungehorsam – der Schwäbische Bund in der Geschichte des vorreformatorischen Widerstandsrechts im Reich, in: Robert von Friedeburg (Hrsg.), Widerstandsrecht im Europa der frühen Neuzeit. Ergebnisse und Perspektiven der Forschung im deutsch-britischen Vergleich. (Zeitschrift für Historische Forschung, Beih. 26). Berlin 2002, 85-112; *Gabriele Haug-Moritz*, Widerstand als „Gegenwehr". Die schmalkaldische Konzeption der „Gegenwehr" und der „gegenwehrliche Krieg" des Jahres 1542, in: ebd. 141-161; *Hillay Zmora*, State and Nobility in Early Modern Germany. The Knightly Feud in Franconia, 1440-1567. Cambridge 1997; zu Hessen vgl. *Schmidt*, Wormser Reichstag (wie Anm. 22), 115-136.

[34] *Schubert*, Herrschaft und Territorium (wie Anm. 1), 1. Vgl. jetzt auch *Christian Hesse*, Amtsträger der Fürsten im spätmittelalterlichen Reich. Göttingen 2005, 192, der feststellt: „Walter Schlesinger hat vor mehr als dreissig Jahren bereits betont, daß das Land nicht in Ämter eingeteilt war, sondern sich aus ihnen zusammengesetzt hat. Der unterschiedliche Entwicklungsstand der Ämterorganisation innerhalb der hier untersuchten Territorien und noch mehr die mit der Verwaltung der Finanzen betrauten Funktionen und Amtsträger bestätigen seine Aussage ausdrücklich." In der Tat hatte sich die Struktur der Ämter als lokaler Verwaltungsdistrikte bis zum Ende des 15. Jahrhunderts vielfach gefestigt, aber eben nicht die der Fürstentümer, die in der Verwaltungspraxis eine wechselnde Vielfalt verschiedener Ämter und anderer lokaler Strukturen darstellten, keinesfalls selbst geschlossene Verwaltungsdistrikte, auch wenn sie, insofern sie als Lehen betrachtet wurden, als Einheit behandelt wurden.

den Reichsständen und Personengruppen führte, über die von diesen Reichsständen Herrschaft beansprucht wurde. Obwohl beim Reichskammergericht Prozesse gegen reformierende Obrigkeiten bereits in den ersten Jahrzehnten der Reformation anhängig wurden, kam es jedoch erst seit der zweiten Hälfte des 16. Jahrhunderts zur Ausbildung der Terminologie, in deren Rahmen mit Begriffen wie „Landeshoheit" und „superioritas territorialis" etwas genuin Neues gekennzeichnet wurde, nämlich ein umfassendes Hoheitsrecht in weltlichen und Kirchensachen. Laut der rechtsgeschichtlichen Forschung kam diese Entwicklung erst mit der Ausdifferenzierung eines öffentlichen Rechtes des Reiches seit dem späten 16. Jahrhundert[35] in Gang, besonders mit Andreas Knichens „De iure territorii".[36] Die historische Forschung deutet dies als Folge und Konsequenz der durch die Juristen von Kaiser, Reichsständen und nachgeordneten Ständen immer schärfer gefaßten Rechtsprobleme, die die Anwendung des *ius reformandi* auf nachgeordnete Gruppen und Korporationen mit sich brachten. Mußten sich diese den Landesherren fügen, weil sie sich in deren Territorium oder unter deren Jurisdiktion befanden? Und was genau umfaßte die Jurisdiktion oder das Territorium eines Fürsten?

Andreas Knichen führte deswegen einen Durchbruch herbei, weil er gerade nicht mehr von einzelnen Jurisdiktionen ausging, sondern von der „umfassenden Beschreibung der landesherrlichen Territorialgewalt", einer Hoheitsgewalt (*superioritas*), die alle Rechte im Territorium (*ius territorii*) potentiell umfaßte. Nun wurde ein geographischer Raum – das Territorium – zum Rechtsbezirk, innerhalb dessen der Landesherr das Hoheitsrecht über alle dort lebenden Personengruppen besaß.[37] Aus dem Besitz spezifischer, in manchen Fällen greifender, in manchen aber auch nicht greifender Jurisdiktionen, wurde die Obrigkeit über alle Untertanen innerhalb des territorialen Rechtsbezirks, auch die Stände. „Untertan ist nicht nur der auf dem Kammergut siedelnde Hintersasse des Fürsten, sondern ohne Rücksicht auf einen besonderen Rechtsstatus jeder, der sich in den Grenzen des Territoriums niedergelassen hat".[38]

Weder der Passauer Vertrag von 1552 noch der Augsburger Religionsfrieden kannten solche Territorien, sondern nur „Churfürsten, Fürsten und Stände des Heiligen Reichs".[39] Die Formel von ‚Kurfürsten, Fürsten und

---

[35] *Hoke*, Emanzipation (wie Anm. 14).
[36] Frankfurt 1600. Dazu *Dietmar Willoweit*, Rechtsgrundlagen der Territorialgewalt. Köln 1975, 121.
[37] *Willoweit*, Rechtsgrundlagen (wie Anm. 36), 123.
[38] Ebd. 125.
[39] Der Augsburger Reichsabschied vom 25. September 1555, in: *Arno Buschmann*, Kaiser und Reich. Verfassungsgeschichte des Heiligen Römischen Reiches Deutscher Nation vom Beginn des 12. Jahrhunderts bis zum Jahre 1806 in Dokumenten. T. 1: Vom Wormser Konkordat 1122 bis zum Augsburger Reichsabschied von 1555. Baden-Baden 1994, 220, 222.

Ständen' fand sich beispielsweise bereits im Ewigen Landfrieden von 1495.[40] Die Formel vom *cuius regio, eius religio* ist dagegen überhaupt erst seit 1587 aus Prozessen belegt und erhielt ihren Eingang in die rechtstheoretische Reflexion erst um die Wende zum 17. Jahrhundert.[41] Obwohl also der dieser begrifflichen Entwicklung auch zugrunde liegende Konflikt, die Abgrenzung der Rechte von Kaiser, Reichsständen und Landständen vor allem mit Bezug auf Religionssachen, sich unmittelbar mit der Reformation selbst ergab und in ihrem Verlauf Verfahren am Reichskammergericht anhängig wurden, ließ schon die Formulierung der Zielvorgabe einer Territorialherrschaft Jahrzehnte auf sich warten, von ihrer regional unterschiedlichen Durchsetzung ganz zu schweigen.

Gehen wir in der Zeit noch etwas vor 1500 zurück und sehen, wie Herrschaft im Reich unter anderem beschrieben wurde. Der „Libellus de Cesarea monarchia" von Peter von Andlau informierte beispielsweise über die *translatio imperii* an den Kaiser und über die Kurfürsten und die Wahlmodalitäten. Er diskutierte, ob ein Nicht-Deutscher gewählt werden könne, ob der Papst einspringen könne, falls die Kurfürsten die Wahl versäumten, und unterstrich die Gottesunmittelbarkeit des gewählten Kaisers, vor allem im Verhältnis zum Papst. Auch die besondere Dignität des Kaisers im Vergleich zu anderen Königen kam zur Sprache. Demgegenüber zählte er zwar die Ränge des Adels im Reich auf, vom Herzog bis zum Baron.[42] Dabei wurden jedoch die Umrisse einer gestuften Hierarchie deutlich, weniger ein Dualismus aus Kaiser und Fürsten, Fürsten und Untertanen. Allen Gruppen, Fürsten wie Adel, sei das „officium in rempublicam in terris [....]" eigen.[43]

Andlau kam es vor allem darauf an, das stellte bereits Paul Laband zu Recht fest, die aus seiner und der Sicht vieler Zeitgenossen chaotischen Verhältnisse im Reich einer geordneten und durchsetzbaren Rechtsordnung zuzuführen.[44] Er befand sich damit, ungeachtet seiner pro-kaiserlichen Schwerpunktsetzung, im Einklang mit vielen anderen Vorschlägen zu einer Reform des Reiches.[45] Er unterstrich allerdings, die kaiserliche Autorität sei nie allein mit Waffen, sondern auch mit Gesetzen bewaffnet: „Imperatoriam majestatem non solum armis decoratam, sed eciam legibus oportet esse armatam, ut utrumque tempus et bellorum et pacis recte possit gubernari".[46] Ihm ging es schließlich ganz besonders um die Durchsetzung der Rechtsprechung durch gelehrte Juristen und um die soziale Aufwertung ihres Standes.

---

[40] Der Ewige Landfriede von 1495, in: *Lorenz Weinrich* (Hrsg.), Quellen zur Reichsreform im Spätmittelalter. Darmstadt 2001, 450f.
[41] *Schneider*, Ius reformandi (wie Anm. 1), 239-245.
[42] *Huerbin*, Andlau (wie Anm. 12), 163-197.
[43] Ebd. 197, mit Andlau, lib II, c 12.
[44] Andlau, lib II, c 16, in: *Huerbin*, Andlau (wie Anm. 12), 207-210.
[45] Vgl. jetzt *Weinrich* (Hrsg.), Quellen zur Reichsreform (wie Anm. 40).
[46] Andlau, lib II, c 16, in: *Huerbin*, Andlau (wie Anm. 12), 209.

Lassen wir die besonderen Wünsche Andlaus für den eigenen Berufsstand und die an Friedrich III. herangetragenen Ziele beiseite, so zeigt dieser kurze Ausblick, daß die Forderung nach einem gelehrten Gebrauch des römischen Rechts keiner bestimmten Sozialgruppe im Reich, etwa allein den Fürsten, zugute kommen mußte, sondern ganz unterschiedlichen politischen Schwerpunktsetzungen dienen konnte. Werke von Juristen, die einer größeren Bedeutung des römischen Rechts das Wort sprachen, blieben überdies auch nicht auf die lateinische Sprache beschränkt. Volkssprachlich verfaßte Handbücher, beispielsweise Johannes Oldendorps (1480–1567) Ratgeber „Wat byllick und recht ys" (1529) und „Van radtslage" (1530), standen den lateinischen Arbeiten zum Römischen Recht zur Seite. Die gelehrten Juristen wurden von allen Seiten zu Rate gezogen, um Argumente für den jeweils eigenen Rechtsstandpunkt zu finden. Sie kommentierten in diesem Zusammenhang auch eine Entwicklung, in der ganz unabhängig von der Wertschätzung des römischen Rechts bei der Rechtfertigung von Kampfhandlungen innerhalb des Reiches, insbesondere durch städtische Obrigkeiten und Fürsten, eine immer deutlichere und klarere Definition der Stellung von Obrigkeiten und Untertanen zueinander zum Tragen kam.

In der gesamten Debatte über ein mögliches Widerstandsrecht gegen den Kaiser spielten sehr früh die besonderen historischen Rechte der Fürsten in der Wahlmonarchie des Reiches einerseits, die Pflichten niederer Magistrate gegenüber ihren Untertanen andererseits eine zentrale Rolle. Für die geistlichen Berater der besonders betroffenen evangelischen Stände war, auch nachdem sie sich dazu durchgerungen hatten, eine Gegenwehr der evangelischen Obrigkeiten gegen den Kaiser im Falle eines rechtsbrecherischen Angriffs zu konzedieren, immer klar, daß damit nicht Übergriffe auf benachbarte Fürsten gemeint sein könnten. Selbst wo diese Argumentation nach unten durchbrochen wurde, wie durch den Rat der Stadt Magdeburg, wurde die Betonung der eigenen Position als Obrigkeit zu einer zentralen Argumentationsfigur des Widerstandsrechtes. Vermutlich auch ohne, aber sicherlich gerade auch nach den Erfahrungen von Bauernkrieg und Täuferreich ging es bei den Diskussionen um das Problem einer organisierten Gegenwehr gegen einen unrechtmäßigen Angriff des Kaisers in erster Linie um Magistrate. Die Diskussionen zum Widerstandsrecht prononcierten daher die immer wichtiger werdende Unterscheidung von Untertanen und Obrigkeiten.[47]

Es kann kein Zweifel daran bestehen, daß die Tendenzen zur Konsolidierung fürstlicher Herrschaftsgewalt in territorialstaatlicher Perspektive vor das 17. Jahrhundert zurückreichen und ihre Wurzeln besonders auch in der

---

[47] *Robert von Friedeburg*, Magdeburger Argumentationen zum Recht auf Widerstand gegen die Durchsetzung des Interim (1550–1551) und ihre Stellung in der Geschichte des Widerstandsrechts im Reich, 1523–1627, in: Luise Schorn-Schütte (Hrsg), Das Interim, Gütersloh 2005, 389–437; *ders.* (Hrsg.), Widerstandsrecht (wie Anm. 33).

Reformation lagen.⁴⁸ Das *ius reformandi* kann nach wie vor als eines der wichtigsten Instrumente der Territorialstaatsformung verstanden werden, insofern es die Spreu vom Weizen trennte, zwischen denjenigen Gruppen im Reich unterschied, die es für sich beanspruchen konnten, und denen, die das nicht konnten. Darüber sollte es zwischen Fürsten und nachgeordneten Rittern und Städten, über die sich Fürsten Obrigkeit zusprachen, zu Konflikten kommen. Zur Anwendung des *ius reformandi*, und damit auch für seine Funktion als Movens der „Verrechtlichung des Religionszwiespalts"⁴⁹, bedurfte es dann der Überführung der vielfach gestuften spätmittelalterlichen hierarchischen Personenverbände in geschlossene Territorien mit einer einheitlichen, über alle anderen Personen als Untertanen gebietenden Obrigkeit. Der neue Begriff des Territoriums als eines geschlossenen Rechtsbezirks, auf den oben eingegangen wurde, sprang hier ein.

Bereits in den Reformationsprozessen der 1530er Jahre spielte die Frage eine zentrale Rolle, ob klagende kirchliche Würdenträger, die der römisch-katholischen Kirche angehörten, tatsächlich der betroffenen reformatorischen Obrigkeit unterworfen waren oder nicht, wie beispielsweise im Falle der Klage der Abtei Kaufungen gegen den Landgrafen von Hessen. Untertanen, das stand für die Assessoren am Kammergericht jedenfalls fest, hatten dem Willen ihres Landesherren zu gehorchen.⁵⁰ Die Konsolidierung des eigenen Untertanenverbandes ließ sich also vorantreiben. Das *ius reformandi* wurde ein zentraler Hebel zur Konsolidierung der fürstlichen Herrschaftsrechte und zur Vereinheitlichung der Untertanenschaft eines geschlossenen Territoriums, weil es auf den neuen Status der Landstände als Untertanen besonderen Standes, aber doch gleichwohl Untertanen, abhob – auch wenn die Konflikte hierüber bis weit in das 17. und frühe 18. Jahrhundert hinein anhielten.⁵¹ Während die Konflikte um die Reformation der Kirche bis 1555 im wesentlichen zwischen Reichsständen und Kaiser stattfanden⁵², kam es im Verlauf der zweiten Hälfte des 16. Jahrhunderts zwischen konkurrierenden Obrigkeiten sowie zwischen Rittern, Grafen und Fürsten auch im Gefolge von reformierter Konfessionalisierung und der Konversion lutherischer Reichsstände zur römisch-katholischen Konfession zu Konflikten zwischen Ständen unterschiedlichen Ranges. Hier schälte sich im Verlauf der Vielzahl

---

⁴⁸ *Willoweit*, Rechtsgrundlagen (wie Anm. 36).
⁴⁹ *Martin Heckel*, Ius reformandi. Auf dem Wege zum ‚modernen' Staatskirchenrecht, in: Dingel u. a. (Hrsg.), Reformation und Recht (wie Anm. 8), 75-126, 80.
⁵⁰ *Gero Dolezalek*, Die juristische Argumentation der Assessoren am Reichskammergericht zu den Reformationsprozessen 1532-1538, in: Bernhard Diestelkamp (Hrsg.), Das Reichskammergericht in der deutschen Geschichte. Wien 1990, 25-58, 43.
⁵¹ *Raingard Esser*, Landstände und Landesherrschaft. Zwischen „Status provinciale" und „superioritas territorialis". Landständisches Selbstverständnis in deutschen Territorien des 17. Jahrhunderts, in: Zeitschrift für Neuere Rechtsgeschichte 23, 2001, 177-194.
⁵² Vgl. jetzt *Kohnle*, Reichstag und Reformation (wie Anm. 26).

unterschiedlicher Konflikte heraus, daß die Landeshoheit, die *superioritas territorialis*, das entscheidende Kriterium für die Zuweisung des *ius reformandi* sein sollte.[53] Die Stoßkraft der Verbindung von Landeshoheit und *ius reformandi* entwickelte sich also, folgt man den jüngeren einschlägigen Befunden, in erster Linie in der zweiten Hälfte des 16. Jahrhunderts und am Beginn des 17. Jahrhunderts.

In der Tat wissen wir für diesen Zeitraum von einer Vielzahl von Konflikten, die zu Prozessen vor dem Reichskammergericht und damit auch einer immer schärferen inhaltlichen Klärung der zugrundeliegenden Interpretationsfragen des Augsburger Religionsfriedens führten. Konflikte zwischen reichsständischen Obrigkeiten und anderen Ständen, im Zuge des Versuchs einer „Zweiten Reformation" bzw. reformierten Konfessionalisierung wie etwa der Grafen von Lippe mit lutherischen Städten, der Stadt Pforzheim mit dem Markgrafen Ernst Friedrich von Baden-Durlach, der lutherischen Stände in Brandenburg mit ihrem Kurfürsten sind Beispiele der inzwischen gut untersuchten Sprengkraft der Konfessionalisierung für die landständisch-reichsständischen Beziehungen.[54] Der wachsende Herrschaftsanspruch der Obrigkeiten und die Intensivierung der Normgebung gerade in Religionssachen mußte sich mit dem Widerstand der nachgeordneten Korporationen und Stände auseinandersetzen. Hier spielte das *ius reformandi* zusammen mit einer weiteren neuen Begrifflichkeit eine zentrale Rolle, nämlich der Begriffe zur Beschreibung landesfürstlicher Herrschaft über das Territorium als geschlossenem Rechtsbezirk. Formeln wie die vom *cuius regio, eius religio*, von den Brüdern Stephani um die Wende zum 17. Jahrhundert popularisiert[55], spiegeln die Hebelfunktion, die das *ius reformandi*

---

[53] *Schneider*, Ius reformandi (wie Anm. 1), 239–245.
[54] *Heinz Schilling*, Konfessionskonflikt und Staatsbildung. Eine Fallstudie über das Verhältnis von religiösem und sozialem Wandel in der Frühneuzeit am Beispiel der Grafschaft Lippe. Gütersloh 1981; *Volker Leppin*, Im Schatten des Augsburger Religionsfriedens. Die Begründung korporativen Widerstandsrechts in Religionsdingen bei den Juristen Peter Ebertz, in: Dingel u. a. (Hrsg.), Reformation und Recht (wie Anm. 8), 243–251; *Martin Heckel*, Reichsrecht und „Zweite Reformation". Theologisch-juristische Probleme der reformierten Konfessionalisierung, in: Heinz Schilling (Hrsg.), Die reformierte Konfessionalisierung in Deutschland – das Problem der Zweiten Reformation. Gütersloh 1986, 11–43.
[55] *Joachim Stephani*, Institutiones Iuris Canonici. Frankfurt 1604, 2. Auflage 1612, lib I, vii, De iure episcopali: „Ut et ideo hodie religionem regioni cohaerere dici potest, ut cuius sit regio hoc est ducatus, Principatus, territorium seu ius territorii eius etiam sit religio, hoc est ius episcopale seu iurisdictio spiritualis." Vgl. *Martin Heckel*, Staat und Kirche nach den Lehren der evangelischen Juristen Deutschlands in der ersten Hälfte des 17. Jahrhunderts. München 1968, 79–82, 227–235; *ders.*, Religionsbann und landesherrliches Kirchenregiment, in: Hans-Christoph Rublack (Hrsg.), Die lutherische Konfessionalisierung in Deutschland. Gütersloh 1992, 130–162; *Ernst Walter Zeeden*, Die Einwirkung der Reformation auf die Verfassung des Heiligen Römischen Reiches Deutscher Nation, in: Trierer theologische Zeitschrift 59, 1950, 207–226, 214.

zusammen mit der Idee eines Herrschaftsverbandes über alle Personen innerhalb eines solchen Gebietes besaß.

Die Umsetzung des *ius reformandi* durch die Reichsstände führte im Verlauf der gesamten zweiten Hälfte des 16. und bis in das 17. Jahrhundert hinein zu Auseinandersetzungen zwischen reichsständischen und besonders reichsfürstlichen Obrigkeiten einerseits und Städten und Ständen in den von ihnen beanspruchten Gebieten andererseits. In diesen Konflikten kam der Durchsetzung des *ius reformandi* unstrittig ganz entscheidende Bedeutung bei der Konsolidierung der verschiedenen Herrschaftsbeziehungen in geschlossene Herrschaftsräume zu, in denen alle dort Lebenden, trotz ihrer variierenden ständischen Qualität, in neuer Weise nur mehr der entstehenden Landesherrschaft unterworfen sein sollten. Diese Konflikte betrafen freilich keineswegs allein niederadlige Gruppierungen und Städte, sondern auch benachbarte Reichsritter und sogar Reichsgrafen, die, wie beispielsweise die Reichsritter der Wetterau und die Grafen von Waldeck, um ihre Unabhängigkeit gegenüber den Landgrafen von Hessen fürchten mußten.[56] Zur Lösung dieser Konflikte bedurfte es nicht allein deswegen auch neuer Terminologien, weil die zugrundeliegende Problemlage, die Glaubensspaltung und Konfessionalisierung, neu war, sondern auch, weil das spätmittelalterliche Reich mit seiner „offenen Verfassung", deutlich im Gegensatz zu England oder Frankreich, keine apriorische Handhabe zur Zuordnung der Souveränitätsrechte an eine einzelne Instanz kannte.[57]

In der Tat kann daher für das gesamte 16. Jahrhundert von der Prägung juristischer Begriffe und Formeln in strategischer Absicht gesprochen werden, die ein im Kern neues Verständnis von Landesherrschaft implizierten und dann auch durchsetzen helfen sollten. Bereits bei der Formulierung des *ius reformandi* haben insbesondere protestantische Juristen eine hervorragende Rolle gespielt. Und sie leisteten auch bei der Formulierung neuer Begriffe Schützenhilfe, die das vom *ius reformandi* eines Reichsstandes betroffene Gebiet definieren halfen. Dabei ging es um die schließlich auch vor den Reichsgerichten durchzusetzende These, daß bei Streitigkeiten zwischen Streitgegnern verschiedener ständischer Qualität um den Status des ständisch Niederen die Frage entscheidend war, ob er seinen Wohnsitz auf dem Gebiet des ständisch Höheren habe. Sei das der Fall, dann sei gegebenenfalls auch davon auszugehen, daß es sich um einen Untertan handelte, vorausge-

---

[56] *Gerhard Menk*, Recht und Raum in einem waldeckischen Reichskammergerichtsprozess, in: Geschichtsblätter für Waldeck 88, 2000, 12–47; *ders.*, Die Beziehungen zwischen Hessen und Waldeck von der Mitte des 16. Jahrhunderts bis zum Westfälischen Frieden. Territorialstaatliches Verhalten im Spannungsfeld von Lehnrecht und Superiorität, in: Geschichtsblätter für Waldeck 75, 1987, 45–206; *ders.*, Rechtliche und staatstheoretische Aspekte im waldeckischen Herrschaftskonflikt, in: Geschichtsblätter für Waldeck 72, 1984, 45–74.

[57] Vgl. *Moraw*, Zu Stand und Perspektiven der Ständeforschung (wie Anm. 33).

setzt, die betreffende Personengruppe könne nicht den expliziten Gegenbeweis führen. Die Frage der Einwohnerschaft in einem bestimmten abgeschlossen Bezirk wurde so ein bestimmender Grund, um in Streitfällen den Rechtsstatus einer Person zu bestimmen. Auch deshalb ergab sich für die Juristen der Reichsstände die Zielvorgabe, die Herrschaftsrechte ihrer Auftraggeber als Rechte über geschlossene Bezirke zu entwerfen – auch dort, wo sie das noch keineswegs waren. Innerhalb eines solchen Bezirkes wurde dann dessen Einwohnern der Nachweis aufgebürdet, von bestimmten Pflichten der Untertanen entbunden zu sein.[58]

Dabei wird in der Forschung inzwischen einerseits davon ausgegangen, daß alle entscheidenden Begrifflichkeiten und Formeln der neuen Territorialstaatlichkeit bis um 1600 entwickelt waren.[59] Andererseits werden die Ursprünge des *ius reformandi* weder in der spätmittelalterlichen, teils auch durch Konkordate abgesicherten Praxis landesfürstlicher Obrigkeit gesehen, sich der Kirche und ihrer Belange anzunehmen und Verbesserungen in einzelnen Punkten zu befördern – eben weil dies immer im Rahmen der einen Kirche geschah –, noch in lutherischen Elementen der theoretischen Reflexion auf die Rolle der weltlichen Obrigkeit, da die der weltlichen Gewalt zugeordnete Handhabung des *usus politicus legis* nicht in die Kirche selbst hineinreichte.[60] Entsprechend ist gerade in jüngerer Zeit auf den energischen Widerstand lutherischer Geistlicher gegen Versuche ihrer weltlichen Obrigkeit hingewiesen worden, in Sachen der Kirche einzugreifen.[61] Tatsächlich läßt sich das *ius reformandi* als reflektierte Theorie der Praxis rechtsförmiger Konflikte seit 1526 und noch während der zweiten Hälfte des 16. Jahrhunderts begreifen, in denen zunächst einmal an Hand von „Verfahrens- und Besitzstandsregeln" Fragen der rechtlichen Handlungsfähigkeit in Kirchensachen ausgefochten wurden. Dabei standen einerseits die verschiedenen Interessen der Religionsparteien an divergierenden Auslegungen des Augsburger Religionsfriedens im Mittelpunkt.[62] Innerhalb eines Gemeinwesens mußte aber andererseits die Stellung der Obrigkeit zur Debatte stehen.[63]

---

[58] *Willoweit*, Rechtsgrundlagen (wie Anm. 36). Siehe auch *ders.*, Der Usus Modernus oder die geschichtliche Begründung des Rechts. Zur rechtstheoretischen Begründung des Methodenwandels im späten 17. Jahrhundert, in: ders. (Hrsg.), Die Begründung des Rechts als theoretisches Problem. München 2000, 229–268.
[59] *Schneider*, Ius reformandi (wie Anm. 1), 273, 411.
[60] *Heckel*, Ius reformandi (wie Anm. 49), 87f.
[61] *Luise Schorn-Schütte*, Evangelische Geistlichkeit in der Frühneuzeit. Deren Anteil an der Entfaltung frühmoderner Staatlichkeit und Gesellschaft. Dargestellt am Beispiel des Fürstentums Braunschweig-Wolfenbüttel, der Landgrafschaft Hessen-Kassel und der Stadt Braunschweig (16.–18. Jahrhundert). Gütersloh 1996.
[62] *Heckel*, Ius reformandi (wie Anm. 49), 92, 93–97. Zu den Reformationsprozessen der 1530er Jahre siehe *Dolezalek*, Juristische Argumentation (wie Anm. 50).
[63] Allerdings zeigt *Schneider*, Ius Reformandi (wie Anm. 1), 146f., daß wenigstens die fürstliche Obrigkeit im reformatorischen Aufbruch nach innen in der Regel keineswegs

Die Entwicklung und der Gebrauch neuer Formeln, mittels derer die rechtliche Natur der Herrschaftsverhältnisse beschrieben wurde, führte sowohl in der strittigen Frage des Widerstandsrechts als auch in der strittigen Frage der Handlungsrechte der Obrigkeit in Kirchensachen zu Veränderungen dieser Herrschaftsverhältnisse selbst. Die produktive Neuformulierung und Neudefinition von Begriffen der weltlichen Herrschaftssphäre mit dem Ziel, diese im Sinne der streitenden Parteien neu zu deuten, muß daher nicht zuletzt im Jahrhundert der Reformation selbst und bei den Juristen gesucht werden.

III.

Wir sind über die tatsächliche Umsetzung der den Reichsständen im Kompromiß von 1526, im Passauer Vertrag und schließlich im Augsburger Religionsfrieden gewährten Rechte und ihre juristische Verteidigung und Deutung in der Auseinandersetzung mit anderskonfessionellen Ständen durch jüngere Studien gut informiert.[64] Wir wissen, daß der Herrschaftsbereich der Pfälzer Kurfürsten empfindlich schrumpfte, daß sich die bedeutenderen Adligen der Konsolidierung dieses Herrschaftsbereiches erfolgreich entzogen[65] und daß in den österreichischen Landen der Habsburger die lutherischen Stände bis in den Dreißigjährigen Krieg hinein ihre eigene Konfession behaupteten.

Die präzise Gestalt der juristischen und damit auch politischen Durchsetzung der Anerkennung territorialherrschaftlicher Gewalt, also der Umdeutung reichsständischer Herrschaftsrechte in geschlossene Rechtsbezirke, bleibt aber nach wie vor undeutlich, auch wenn wir an einzelnen Fällen bereits nachvollziehen können, wann und warum die Frage nach dem flächenmäßigen Charakter reichsständischer Herrschaft zum Tragen kam. An die Formulierung reichsständischer Herrschaft als einer über geschlossene Territorien und an ihre Qualität als *superioritas territorialis* wurde jedoch auch die Ausdehnung des *ius reformandi* im Streitfall geknüpft. Konzeptionelle Vorbilder für das neue geschlossene Territorium gehen jedoch wenigstens bis auf das Ende der *ersten* Hälfte des 16. Jahrhunderts zurück und liegen noch vor der Abfassung des Passauer Vertrages vor. Das gilt insbe-

---

auf eine umständliche rechtliche Argumentation angewiesen war. Wenn überhaupt auf rechtliche Legitimationen hingewiesen wurde, dann nur ausnahmsweise auf das Reichsrecht (um 1526, 1541 und nach 1555), aber auch auf biblische Gestalten und Fürsten wie Samuel, Josias oder auch David.
[64] Vgl. *Schneider*, Ius reformandi (wie Anm. 1), aber auch *Dolazek*, Juristische Argumentation (wie Anm. 50), und die dort aufgeführte Literatur; *Kohnle*, Reichstag (wie Anm. 26).
[65] *Press*, Calvinismus (wie Anm. 21).

sondere für die juristische Engführung des Begriffs *patria* durch protestantische Juristen.

Diese gleich weiter zu erläuternde Engführung wurde von der Forschung bei der Untersuchung konzeptioneller Entwürfe fürstlicher Herrschaft bisher nicht ins Auge gefaßt. Das liegt nicht zuletzt an der Arbeitsteilung der Forschung. Sie gliedert sich zum einen in die Geschichte der Kommentierung von Aristoteles' Politik und die Geschichte der politischen Philosophie im 16. und 17. Jahrhundert, vor allem im Hinblick auf die wachsende Bedeutung des Naturrechts. Die bis heute maßgeblichen Schneisen wurden durch Horst Dreitzel mit seiner Studie „Protestantischer Aristotelismus und absoluter Staat" über die „Politica des Henning Arnisaeus" geschlagen. Dreitzel kritisiert dort die problematische Schwerpunktsetzung der Geschichte der Politik auf Machiavelli, Bodin und Hobbes und konzentriert sich statt dessen auf die Geschichte der Kommentierung von Aristoteles in Helmstedt. Er skizziert auch, wie Melanchthon im Rahmen der Unterscheidung von Gesetz und Evangelium die Aristotelische Politik als Klassiker zur Organisation des weltlichen Gemeinwesens fruchtbar machte.[66] Seine Befunde sind von der Forschung zu Melanchthon im wesentlichen bestätigt worden. Sie hob nicht zuletzt auf die wachsende Bedeutung des Naturrechts bei Melanchthon ab. Dabei handelte es sich für Melanchthon um die durch Gott den Menschen eingegebenen *notitiae*. Umfang und Bedeutung des Naturrechts nahmen in Melanchthons Werk im Lauf der Jahre zu. Melanchthon schrieb eine wachsende Zahl normativer Vorgaben dem Naturrecht zu und stand damit in einer größeren Strömung, die dieses zu einer ethischen Grundlage des Rechts ausbaute. Das weltliche Gemeinwesen, von Melanchthon beispielsweise zunächst als Folge des Sündenfalls konzipiert, wurde schließlich selbst als Teil des Naturrechts verstanden. Die Selbstverteidigung in Notwehr wurde von Melanchthon ebenfalls als Naturrecht beschrieben, nachdem er sie als *defensio* von der allein den Magistraten zugesprochenen *vindicta* unterschieden hatte. Die Vaterlandsliebe wurde ebenfalls als eine solche *nota* verstanden, insofern sie helfen konnte, den schwachen und allen möglichen guten und unguten Einflüssen ausgesetzten Willen in Richtung der Verteidigung eines Gemeinwesens zu lenken, sofern Gottes Wort durch dieses Gemeinwesen verteidigt würde.[67]

---

[66] *Horst Dreitzel*, Protestantischer Aristotelismus und absoluter Staat. Die „Politica" des Henning Arnisaeus (ca. 1575-1636). Wiesbaden 1970.
[67] Vgl. zur weltlichen Herrschaftsordnung als Folge des Sündenfalls *Philipp Melanchthon,* Omnia Opera, in: Corpus Reformatorum (künftig: CR). Hrsg. v. Karl Bretschneider. Bd. 3. Halle 1836: CR 21 (Capita 1520), 23-28; *ders.*, CR 21 (Loci Communes 1521), 118; *ders.*, CR 21 (Themata de duplici iustitia regimineque corporali et spirituali), 227: „iustitia mundi non est vita sed mors et peccati poena". Zur Beschreibung der weltlichen Herrschaftsordnung als Teil des Naturrechts *ders.*, Commentarii ad Epistolam Pauli ad Romanos 1532; De dignitate legum 1538, De Magistratus Civilibus (alle CR 21); *ders.*,

Zum anderen liegen ältere und neuere Arbeiten zu einzelnen Juristen der ersten Hälfte des 16. Jahrhunderts vor. Während für Ulrich Zasius vor allem sein Einfluß auf die humanistische Verbesserung der lateinischen Textgrundlage und sein Bestehen auf der rechtlichen Einbindung der Magistrate hervorgehoben wurde, wurde für die lutherischen Juristen Eisermann und Oldendorp der Einfluß von Melanchthon beschrieben. Oldendorp suchte insbesondere, die Zehn Gebote als Grundlage des Naturrechts und dieses als allgemeine Grundlage des römischen Rechts zu beschreiben, um so zu einer systematischen und hierarchischen Beschreibung des Rechts zu gelangen, die auf einzelne positive Gesetze und deren Deutung anwendbar sein sollte.[68]

Die Tatsache, daß Melanchthon und die ihn rezipierenden Juristen die Rolle des christlichen Fürsten als Wächter der Gesetze unterstrichen, wird in Gestalt der Rechtsbindung der Magistrate und damit der Möglichkeit, Widerstand gegen Rechtsbrüche einzureichen, auch in der englischsprachigen Literatur zur Kenntnis genommen.[69]

Vor diesem Hintergrund ist zu sehen, wie Melanchthon und die protestantische Jurisprudenz zum einen das Verhältnis von Magistrat und Recht beurteilten, und wie zum anderen die Herrschaft der Magistrate beschrieben wurde. Vermeintliche Vorbilder aus dem römischen Recht dienten beispiels-

---

CR 21 (Loci Communes 1543), 701-723. Zur Beschreibung der Selbstverteidigung in Notwehr als Teil des Naturrechts ebd. 702-723. Zentral zu Melanchthons Rolle bei der Entwicklung des Naturrechts als ethischer Grundlage des Rechts vgl. *Werner Elert*, Societas bei Melanchthon, in: ders., Ein Lehrer der Kirche. Hrsg. v. Max-Keller Hüschemenger. Berlin 1967, 32-42; *Günter Frank*, The Reason of Acting: Melanchthon's Concept of Practical Philosophy and the Question of the Unity and Consistency of His Philosophy, in: Jill Kraye/Risto (Eds.), Moral Philosophy on the Threshold of Modernity. Springer 2005, 217-233; *Jill Kraye*, Stoicism in the Renaissance from Petrach to Lipsius, in: Grotiana NS. 22/23, 2001/02, 21-45; *Christoph Strohm*, Zugänge zum Naturrecht bei Melanchthon, in: Günter Frank (Hrsg.), Der Theologe Melanchthon. Stuttgart 2002, 339-356; *Robert von Friedeburg*, Widerstandsrecht und Konfessionskonflikt. Berlin 1999, 57f.; ders., The Office of the Patriot: The Problems of Passions and of Love of Fatherland in Protestant Thought, Melanchthon to Althusius, 1520s to 1620s, in: Studies in Medieval and Renaissance History 3, 2006, 241-274. Zur Naturrechtsdebatte bei Melanchthon zuletzt *Merio Scattola*, Das Naturrecht vor dem Naturrecht. Zur Geschichte des „ius naturae" im 16. Jahrhundert. Tübingen 1999.

[68] *Hans-Helmut Dietze*, Johannes Oldendorp als Rechtsphilosoph und Protestant. Königsberg 1933; *Albert Freybe*, Einleitung, in: Johannes Oldendorp, Was billig und Recht ist. Hamburg 1894, Ndr. Frankfurt am Main 1969; *Peter Macke*, Das Rechts- und Staatsdenken des Johannes Oldendorp. Köln 1966; *Brita Eckert*, Der Gedankte des Gemeinen Nutzens in der lutherischen Staatslehre des 16. und 17. Jahrhunderts. Diss. phil. Frankfurt am Main 1976; *Steven Rowan*, Ulrich Zasius. A Jurist in the German Renaissance, 1461-1535. Frankfurt am Main 1987. Die jüngste sehr weiterführende Darstellung gibt *John Witte*, Law and Protestantism. The Legal Teachings of the Lutheran Reformation. Cambridge 2002.

[69] Siehe beispielsweise *Witte*, Law (wie Anm. 68), 138.

weise Oldendorp dazu, die Herrschaftsbereiche der Fürsten als geschlossene Rechtsbezirke zu beschreiben. Dafür wurde der Begriff *patria* bedeutungsvoll. Die protestantische Jurisprudenz, etwa der Marburger Jurist Nicolas Vigelius, erweiterte die amorphe Vielfalt des Begriffs *patria*, der sich auf eine Fülle unterschiedlicher „Heimaten" des Bürgers – der Himmel für den Christen, eine Landschaft, Stadt, oder auch Land – um die Bedeutung „Territorium". Die Juristen orientierten sich dabei an den Rechten der *praesides provinciarum*, der Vorsteher der Provinzen im Römischen Reich, deren Machtfülle hinter derjenigen der Kaiser zurückstand, aber innerhalb ihres Machtbereiches verschiedene exekutive und jurisdiktionelle Rechte in charakteristischer Weise vereinte. Nachzuverfolgen ist diese Entwicklung in den einschlägigen juristischen Begriffslexika. Bereits das durch Johannes Spiegel, einen Schüler von Ulrich Zasius, 1549 herausgegebene „Lexicon Iuris Civilis", eines der wichtigsten Rechtshandbücher der Zeit, führte neben der väterlichen Gewalt (*patria potestas*) als weitere *significatio* von *patria* die *provincia* auf[70], in der alle zur *gubernatio* nötigen politischen Ordnungen (*ordinationes politiae*) unter einem Magistrat zusammengefaßt seien. Der ebenfalls einflußreiche Jurist Johannes Oldendorp führte in seiner allgemeinen Einführung in das Recht bei der Interpretation des Gehorsamsgebotes des Dekalogs gegenüber den Eltern mit Hinweis auf Pomponius[71] an, „quod Pomponius addens exempla Iuris Gentium naturali ratione constituti, hoc est, Iuris vere naturalis & Divini: Ut parentibus (inquit) & patriae pareamus. Complectitur enim in se patria, quicquid ad eam gubernandam est necessarium, id est, totam politiae ordinationem: scilicet magistratus, potestas, dominia, & cetera huiusmodi."[72]

Nicht allein den Eltern gegenüber, sondern auch dem im obigen Sinne als flächenmäßiger Herrschaftsdistrikt zu verstehenden Vaterland gegenüber gebe es laut Gottes Geboten die Pflicht zum Gehorsam. In seinem „Lexicon Iuris seu Epitome Definitionum, Ex Omnibus, qua Clarissimus Joannes Oldendorpius in lucem partim edidit" hatte Oldendorp die *civitas* dieses Vaterlandes bereits korporationsrechtlich als *universitas civium*, die notwendig eines Magistrats bedürfe, „qui administret Rem Publicam", definiert. Diese

---

[70] Lexicon Iuris Civilis, ex variis autorum commentariis. Leiden 1549, 426. Aufgenommen wurden hier die entsprechenden Passagen aus *Johannes Oldendorp*, Lexicon Iuris, Epitome definitionum [...]. Marburg 1546. Zu Spiegel und zur breiten Rezeption dieses Lexikons als Standardwerke siehe *Rowan*, Ulrich Zasius (wie Anm. 68), 222.

[71] Zur Rolle der Ansätze der justinianischen Rechtsbücher, besonders von Pomponius, zur späteren Umbewertung der lateinischen *Respublica* zur korporativen *Universitas* vgl. *Wolfgang Mager*, Art. „Republik", in: Geschichtliche Grundbegriffe. Ein Lexikon zur politisch-sozialen Sprache. Hrsg. v. Otto Brunner, Werner Conze u. Reinhart Koselleck. Bd. 5. Stuttgart 1984, 549–605, 559.

[72] *Johannes Oldendorp*, Leges Divinae Tabulae Decem Praeceptorum, in: Opera Partim Recens Edita. Vol. 1: Elementaria Introductio, ad Studium Iuris et aequitatis. Basel 1559, 9.

Ordnung ergab sich für Oldendorp aus der göttlichen Einsetzung der Obrigkeit und aus dem göttlichen Naturrecht.[73]

Die Auflage des „Lexicon Iuris Civilis" von 1577 übernahm den Passus zur *patria* und führte überdies den im selben Werk abgedruckten Kommentar Johannes Oldendorps in „Verba Legum XII Tabularem Scholia" an, wo in Titel II „De Magistratibus" Kapitel XV über die „Praecepta iuris de Magistratibus" eigens auf die *presides provinciarum* und ihre besondere Machtzusammenfassung unter Iustinian hingewiesen wird. Diese *presides* werden als Vorsteher der Provinzen bzw. *patriae* angesprochen. Darüber hinaus führte es eigens einen weiteren Abschnitt über die Pflicht der *caritas* für das Vaterland ein. Alle diese Hinweise wurden in der Ausgabe des Lecixon Iuridicum von 1612 übernommen.[74] Bis dahin war *patria* also als Begriff für eine Provinz unter der Kontrolle eines Vorstehers mit einer besonderen Herrschaftskonzentration, die aus derjenigen der *presides provinciarum* abgeleitet wurde, etabliert – ein für die Fürsten und ihr Interesse an der Konsolidierung ihrer Herrschaft innerhalb der Territorien sicherlich hilfreiches Konstrukt.

Es wäre jedoch verfehlt, aus dem Vorhergehenden zu folgern, diese Belege stützten die These von der Überhöhung der weltlichen Obrigkeit durch die protestantische Reformation zugunsten eines unbedingten Gehorsams der Untertanen. Hier seien eben die Entwicklungen in der Reformation angelegt, die am Beginn des 17. Jahrhunderts in die territorialabsolutistische Konzeption eines Henning Arnisaeus mündeten, nach der das korporative Gemeinwesen schlechthin als „ordo inter parentes et imperantes, dependens potissimum ab una summa potestate, quam nos Majestatem proprie dici" beschrieben wurde, als Herrschaftsordnung unter dem Fürsten.[75] Die protestantische Jurisprudenz im Reich vollzog nur die Entwicklung der Beschreibung des Gemeinwesens in ganz Europa mit, in der ein Staat als Herrschaftsordnung der Gesellschaft zunehmend als unabdingbar verstanden wurde. Diese Entwicklung war sogar durch Kommentatoren der Republik Florenz mitgetragen wurden. Es war schließlich Leonardo Bruni selbst, der berühmte Florentiner, der zu den ersten gehörte, welche das Gemeinwesen als *societas civilis* einerseits, als *res publica* andererseits beschrieben, und damit einen Platz schufen für die *res publica* als institutionalisierte Konfiguration der Herrschaftsordnung, welcher die Gesellschaft für ihr Funktionieren be-

---

[73] *Oldendorp*, Lexikon (wie Anm. 70), 66. Vgl. *Macke*, Oldendorp (wie Anm. 68), 29–57.
[74] *Nicolaus Vigelius*, Lexicon Iuridicum. Köln 1612, 2010f.; *Johannes Oldendorp*, In Verba Legum XII Tabularem Scholia, in: ders., Titulus II De Magistratibus, c. XV, 39, der ausführte, die Rechte der ‚presides provinciarum' seien als Teil der ‚translatio imperii' auch im gegenwärtigen Reich als ‚mandatis principum' vorhanden. Zu den Häuptern und Vorstehern der Provinzen siehe *Nicolaus Vigelius*, Methodus Iuris Civilis. Basel 1601, 32f.
[75] *Henning Arnisaeus*, De Re publica. Frankfurt 1615, 2, 1, 1, Nr. 12, zit. nach *Mager*, Art. „Republik" (wie Anm. 71), 568.

dürfe.[76] In der politischen Theorie wurde der Staat als Herrschaftsordnung längst schärfer gefaßt und von der Gesellschaft als solcher unterschieden. Im Reich blieb die *res publica* jedoch nicht allein an das göttliche und natürliche Recht gebunden, sie blieb auch auf das ihr eigene menschliche Recht verpflichtet; das galt auch für ihre Magistrate. Sie allein verwalteten die *res publica*, waren ihren Gesetzen aber ebenso wie die Bürger unterworfen. Daher beantwortet Oldendorp die Frage, ob die Magistrate den Gesetzen vorhergehen, mit der Antwort, daß die Magistrate „legum ministri sunt".[77] Daher diskutiert Oldendorp auch die Frage der Bestrafung staatlicher Rechtsbrüche in seinem *De iure et aequitate* und bejaht sie insgesamt. Beispiele beziehen sich auf Strafen des Reiches, repräsentiert durch den Kaiser, gegen einzelne Territorien.[78]

Richtungsweisend für diese Konzeption der eindringlichen Konturierung einer dann auch flächenmäßig definierten Herrschaftsordnung unter Magistraten, aber mit Verantwortlichkeit der Magistrate, waren bereits die Reflexionen von Philipp Melanchthon zu den Texten von Aristoteles. Melanchthons Aristoteles-Rezeption durchlief, zunächst unter dem Einfluß Luthers und der Auseinandersetzungen um die Frage eines „freien menschlichen Willens", dann unter dem Einfluß des Bauernkrieges, eine ganze Reihe von Wandlungen.[79] Dabei gerieten die gottgefällige Erhaltung des weltlichen Gemeinwesens und die damit verbundenen Tugenden, wie etwa die Vaterlandsliebe, in den Fokus seines Interesses.[80] Die jüngst erschienene Monographie von Wolfgang Matz bietet uns die Möglichkeit, die Hintergründe für den Ort, den Vaterlandsliebe schließlich bei Melanchthon einnehmen konnte, näher zu bestimmen. Matz rekonstruiert in seiner Arbeit mehrere Phasen der Auseinandersetzung Melanchthons mit dem Problem und der Stellung des Willens sowie der damit zusammenhängenden Rolle der Affekte. In den

---

[76] *Leonardo Bruni*, Aristotelis libri politicorum, in: ders., Aristotelis opera cum Averrois commentariis. Vol. 3: libri moralem totam philosophiam complectentes. Venedig 1562, 3, 2.

[77] *Olderndorp*, Lexicon Iuris (wie Anm. 70), 272; *Wolfgang Matz*, Der befreite Mensch. Die Willenslehre in der Theologie Philipp Melanchthons. Göttingen 2001, 79.

[78] Vgl. *Johannes Oldendorp*, De iure et aequitate, in: ders., Collatio iuris civilis et canonici, maximum afferens boni et aequi cogitationem. Lyon 1547, 136–141, 138: „In iis, quae faciendo committuntur contra Ius, si talia fuerit, quae ad solam Universitatis potestatis pertinent, ut statuere, Ius dicere, exactionem facere tunc delictum potest universitati [...] imputari".

[79] *Matz*, Der befreite Mensch (wie Anm. 77); *Nicole Kuropka*, Philipp Melanchthon. Wissenschaft und Gesellschaft. Ein Gelehrter im Dienst der Kirche (1526–1532). Tübingen 2002.

[80] Siehe insbesondere *Frank* (Hrsg.), Der Theologe Melanchthon (wie Anm. 67). Darin v. a. *Strohm*, Zugänge zum Naturrecht bei Melanchthon (wie Anm. 67), und *Henning Ziebritzki*, Tugend und Affekt. Ansatz, Aufriss und Problematik von Melanchthons Tugendethik, dargestellt anhand der Ethica doctrinae elementa von 1550, 357–374; *Matz*, Der befreite Mensch (wie Anm. 77).

„Loci communes" von 1521 blieb die Frage nach der Möglichkeit einer freien Wahl zwischen verschiedenen Handlungsalternativen für Melanchthon gegenüber der zentralen Rolle der Prädestination noch ganz im Hintergrund. In den „Theologicae Hypotyposes" von 1522 begann Melanchthon jedoch bereits, Möglichkeiten einer Wahl in bezug auf weltliche Dinge ins Auge zu fassen. Der *intellectus* könne hier eine Entscheidung treffen und diese dem Willen vorhalten. Dieser bleibe jedoch völlig unter dem Einfluss der *affectus carnales*.[81] Die Argumentationsführung im Hinblick auf das Problem der Willensfreiheit wurde so nicht kompromittiert.[82]

Nicht zuletzt unter dem Eindruck des Bauernaufstandes wurde beispielsweise in den „Scholia in Epistolam Pauli ad Colossenses" von 1527 die Unterscheidung von Gesetz und Evangelium weiter ausgeführt.[83] Das erlaubte auch die Unterscheidung zwischen der Erörterung der Fähigkeiten des Willens, geführt von der Vernunft, und der damit zusammenhängenden Rolle der Affekte, auf der einen Seite und der Frage der göttlichen Gnade und ihrer Erlangung auf der anderen.[84] Im Verlauf der 1530er Jahre wurde diese Differenzierung weiter entwickelt. Gemäß den „Fragmenta Locorum communium" von 1533 hatte der Sündenfall alle Affekte beeinträchtigt.[85] Aber im Blick auf äußere Werke (*opera externa*) blieb doch eine gewisse *libertas voluntatis*. Der Wille wurde seinerseits von den Affekten beeinflußt.[86] Die Unterscheidung zwischen der Erlangung der Gnade und der Übung (weltlicher) Gerechtigkeit gab den Leidenschaften also einen möglichen Ort gottgefälligen Wirkens, nämlich bei der Beeinflussung des Willens. Diese konnte so geschehen, damit er auch tatsächlich das wollte, was von der Vernunft als das Richtige erkannt worden war. Andere Forscher stützen Matz' Ergebnisse.[87] Melanchthon erklärte in seinen „Philosophia moralis epitome"[88], einzelne Affekte könnten sehr wohl einen wichtigen und gottgewollten Einfluß auf die Vernunft ausüben, indem tugendhaftes Verhalten durch sie stimuliert werde. Diese Affekte seien uns durch Gott eingepflanzt.

---

[81] *Melanchthon,* CR 21, 96; *Matz,* Der befreite Mensch (wie Anm. 77), 82.
[82] *Melanchthon,* CR 21, 71-97.
[83] Vgl. allgemein *Heinz Scheible,* Die Bedeutung der Unterscheidung von Gesetz und Evangelium für theologische Ethik und praktische Theologie am Beispiels Melanchthons, in: Wilhelm Gräb u. a. (Hrsg.), Christentum und Spätmoderne. Stuttgart 2000, 93-100.
[84] Melanchthons Werke in Auswahl. Hrsg. v. *Robert Stupperich.* Bd. 1-7. Gütersloh 1951-1980, Bd. 4, 225ff.
[85] *Melanchthon,* CR 21, 276-280; *Matz,* Der befreite Mensch (wie Anm. 77), 116f.
[86] *Melanchthon,* CR 21 (De peccato), 270ff.; *Matz,* Der befreite Mensch (wie Anm. 77), 136.
[87] *Kraye,* Stoicism (wie Anm. 67), 33f.
[88] *Melanchthon,* CR 16, 21-164, 51f.: „Alii [affectus] cum ratione consentiunt, ut amor coniugium, liberorum, benevolentia erga bene meritos, misericordia erga calamitoso, irasci his qui inferunt iniruriam. Hi affectus boni [...] erantque futuri in natura hominis, etiamsi non fuisset corrupta vitio originis. Et hi affectus sunt impetus ad virtutem".

Vor diesem Hintergrund konnte insbesondere die Vaterlandsliebe eine wichtige positive Rolle spielen. In einem Brief an Graf Schlick, der einer Edition von Tacitus' „Germania" von 1538 beigegeben worden war, führte Melanchthon im einzelnen aus, wie die Vaterlandsliebe sich auf das Handeln der Menschen positiv auswirken könne. Sie sei den Menschen von Gott in das Herz gepflanzt, um sie zur Verteidigung des Glaubens und der Gesetze des Vaterlandes anzuhalten.[89] Ebenso wie andere Affekte war die Vaterlandsliebe im Blick Melanchthons also imstande, den menschlichen Willen zu beeinflussen; sie konnte daher benutzt werden, um die Menschen im Hinblick auf die *justitia civilis* zu Taten anzuhalten, die Gott wohlgefällig waren.[90] Auf dieser Grundlage ermunterte Melanchthon in der eben erwähnten Vorrede zu Tacitus zur Lektüre von Geschichten über das Vaterland, die mit *ad virtutem exempla* unsere Vaterlandsliebe wecken und uns helfen, uns „servitutis impatiens, inimica crudelitati, libidinibus, tyrannidi" zu machen.[91] Besonders die Heranwachsenden sollten mit Hilfe solcher Texte angeleitet und erzogen werden. Im Rahmen der Unterscheidung von Gesetz und Evangelium, Gnade und Gerechtigkeit in weltlichen Angelegenheiten konnte die Vaterlandsliebe also sehr wohl eine wichtige Rolle spielen, um die Bürger zum Kampf mit dem Tyrannen zu motivieren. Wenigstens im frühen Calvinismus behauptete Melanchthon einen bedeutenden Platz, wie wir aus den Forschungen von Christoph Strohm inzwischen wissen.[92] Das gilt nicht nur für den Genfer Calvinismus, sondern auch für die deutsch-reformierte Richtung des Calvinismus, die durch den Philippismus beeinflußt blieb.[93]

---

[89] *Melanchthon,* CR 7, 565-567, No. 1708: „Divinitus omnium hominum pectoribus mirificus quidam patriae amor insitus est, credo, ut extimularetur ad defensionem illarum maximarum rerum, quas patria continet, religionis, legum disciplinae, imo vero ut admoneremur, etiam illam coelestem sedem, unde animorum origo est, amandam et appetendam esse. Nemo igitur tam ferreo est animo, quem non cupiditas aliqua teneat, cognoscendi antiquitatem patriae et quasi picturam veterum, sicut videre iuvat illa tecta, quae nascentes primum exceperunt." Im gleichen Jahr beendete Melanchthon seine „Philosophiae moralis epitome", in welcher die Integrierung der Philosophie in die neue Theologie weitestgehend vollendet war.
[90] *Karl-Heinz zur Mühlen,* Melanchthons Auffassung vom Affekt in den Loci Communes von 1521, in: Michael Beyer/Günther Wartenberg (Hrsg.), Humanismus und Wittenberger Reformation. Festgabe anläßlich des 500. Geburtstages des Praeceptor Germaniae Philipp Melanchthon am 16. Februar 1997. Leipzig 1996, 327-336.
[91] *Melanchthon,* CR 7, No. 1708, 565.
[92] *Christoph Strohm,* Melanchthon Rezeption im frühen Calvinismus, in: Johanna Loehr (Hrsg.), Dona Melanchthonia. Festgabe für Heinz Scheible zum 70. Geburtstag. Stuttgart 2001, 433-455.
[93] Vgl. *Horst Dreitzel,* Althusius in der Geschichte des Föderalismus, in: Emilio Bonfatti u. a. (Hrsg.), Politische Begriffe und historisches Umfeld in der Politica Methodice digesta des Johannes Althusius. Wiesbaden 2002, 49-112, hier 55-57 mit weiterführender Literatur zum Problem.

Zwar wird die Stoßrichtung von Melanchthons Beschäftigung mit Aristoteles und der Platz der Ethik in wichtigen Nuancen unterschiedlich beurteilt.[94] Seine Hinweise zum weltlichen Gemeinwesen selbst zielten jedoch in erster Linie auf die funktionale Rechtfertigung weltlichen Regiments als Friedenswahrung. Monarchie, Aristokratie und „Politie", die Herrschaft der Vielen, waren dabei kasuistisch zu beurteilende Formen des Regiments. Die fürstliche Herrschaft stand ebenso unter Gesetzen wie die stadtbürgerliche Herrschaft. Die „Loci communes" von 1521 enthielten im Abschnitt *de magistratibus* gerade rund 80 Zeilen zum Problem. Sie konzentrierten sich ganz auf Röm. 13 und die Pflicht der Obrigkeit, das Schwert zu führen, eingeschränkt durch Apg. 5, Gott sei mehr zu gehorchen als den Menschen. Dem Banndekret des Papstes sei daher nicht zu folgen. Gott aber zeige sich in der Heiligen Schrift, nicht in den Traditionen oder Pseudopropheten.[95] Die Situation von 1521 spiegelt sich in dieser Behandlung des Problems des Magistrats, sowohl in seiner Verantwortung für die Kirche, als auch in der Möglichkeit, in einzelnen Aspekten, etwa im Hinblick auf das Wormser Edikt, Befehlen der Obrigkeit nicht Folge zu leisten.

Die Bearbeitung des Problems des Magistrats von 1543, die fast unverändert in die „Loci communes" von 1559 übernommen wurde, ist dagegen viel umfangreicher.[96] Die evangelische Sache war in den gut zwei Jahrzehnten mit dem Aufbau eigener Kirchentümer, mit der Bekämpfung der Wiedertäufer und schließlich mit der gegebenenfalls nötigen Verteidigung gegen eine Vollstreckung des Wormser Ediktes seit 1529/30 konfrontiert gewesen. Der Bauernkrieg und die Auseinandersetzung mit den Wiedertäufern einerseits, die Verteidigung des Glaubens gegen eine mögliche Bedrohung durch Kaiser und katholische Stände andererseits hatten das Problem des Gehorsams gegenüber der Obrigkeit immer wieder thematisiert. Gegenüber den Bauern und gegenüber dem Täuferreich war auf Gehorsam zu bestehen, gegenüber dem Kaiser auf der Möglichkeit der Entlassung aus dem Gehorsamsgebot zu beharren. Beides war zu vereinba-

---

[94] Vgl. *Frank*, Reason of Acting (wie Anm. 67); *Kuropka*, Melanchthon (wie Anm. 79); *Matz*, Der befreite Mensch (wie Anm. 77); *Sachiko Kusukawa*, Lutheran Uses of Aristotle. A Comparison between Jacob Schengk and Philip Melanchthon, in: Constance Blackwell/Sachiko Kusukawa (Eds.), Philosophy in the Sixteenth and Seventeenth Centuries. Conversations with Aristotle. Aldershot 1999, 169–188; *Charlotte Methuen*, The Teaching of Aristotle in Late Sixteenth Century Tübingen, in: ebd. 189–205; *Isabelle Deflers*, Lex und ordo. Eine rechtshistorische Untersuchung der Rechtsauffassung Melanchthons. Berlin 2005.
[95] *Philipp Melanchthon*, Loci Communes rerum Theologicarum seu Hypotyposes Theologicae, 1521, in: ders., Werke (wie Anm. 84), Bd. 2/1, 180–182.
[96] *Melanchthon*, De Magistratibus Civilibus et dignitate rerum politicarum, in: ders., Loci Praecipui Theologici (1559), Werke (wie Anm. 84), Bd. 2/2, 689–732.

ren.[97] Die ausführlichere Behandlung des Problems des Magistrats von 1543 spiegelt diese verstärkte Bedeutung.

Bereits im Titel differiert der Text von 1543 von der Version von 1521. Es ist nicht mehr allein vom Magistrat die Rede, sondern auch von der „dignitas rerum politicarum". Ebenso wie in der Bewertung der Leidenschaften ergab sich auch hier die Bereitschaft, dem Einsatz für das weltliche Gemeinwesen, freilich in der beschränkten Weise, in der das allein für die evangelischen Theologen möglich war, einen eigenen Platz zu gewähren. Es wäre jedoch völlig verfehlt, und das zeigte sich insbesondere auch an Melanchthons Vorgehensweise, nun zu folgern, dem weltlichen Fürsten sei ein Plazet zum Handeln gegeben worden. Melanchthon setzte sich zunächst kritisch mit den vom Teufel eingegebenen „falschen" Lehren zum politischen Gemeinwesen auseinander, nämlich denen, die ewiges Heil und weltliches Gemeinwesen nicht sauber trennten. Er wies weiter auf die legitime Unterscheidung weltlicher Gesetze in verschiedenen Gemeinwesen hin.[98] Der Berufung der weltlichen Obrigkeit zum Schutz der Kirche entsprach es, die Kirche gegen solche Auswüchse zu schützen. Die Sicherung der Predigt des Wortes Gottes steht im Zentrum der obrigkeitlichen Pflichten. Die Magistrate sind auch „custodes disciplinae".[99] Während die Einrichtung des *ordo politicus* von Gott sei, seien zahlreiche Herrscher nicht von den damit gegebenen Zielen beseelt gewesen, wie beispielsweise Caligula, Nero „et alia pestes" (pestis im Sinne von Scheusal), und diese seien nun von Herrschern wie David, Salomon, Iosias, Cyrus, Constantinus, Theodosius und Carolus zu unterscheiden. Die Blüte des Gemeinwesens wird mit Blick auf David und Augustus auf die gute Regierung des Herrschers bezogen, das gemeinsame Leben der Menschen aber auf das ihnen von Gott eingepflanzte Naturrecht (*notitia legum naturae*), dessen Erkenntnis durch den Sündenfall be-, aber nicht verhindert ist.[100] Hier bezieht sich Melanchthon explizit auf den scholastischen Theologen Petrus de Palude, um den *ordo politicus* als basierend auf der *notitia legum naturae* zu beschreiben, die ein Zusammenleben der Menschen, und dieses wiederum eine Ordnung unter den Menschen, notwendig mache. Eben darin unterschieden sich die Menschen von den Tieren.[101] Auf dieser Grundlage verurteilt Melanchthon nun einerseits die Wiedertäufer, aber auch beispielsweise Karlstadt[102], indem er wiederholt darauf hinweist, daß

---

[97] Vgl. nur jüngst die Beiträge von *v. Friedeburg*, Widerstandsrecht (wie Anm. 33); *Hans-Jürgen Goertz/James M. Stayer* (Hrsg.), Radikalität und Dissent im 16. Jahrhundert – Radicalism and Dissent in the Sixteenth Century. Berlin 2002.
[98] *Melanchthon*, Werke (wie Anm. 84), Bd. 2/2, 690f.
[99] Ebd. 693.
[100] *Strohm*, Zugänge zum Naturrecht bei Melanchthon (wie Anm. 67), 342–344.
[101] *Melanchthon*, Werke (wie Anm. 84), Bd. 2/2, 699, 701. Vgl. *Scheible*, Unterscheidung (wie Anm. 83), 96.
[102] *Melanchthon*, Werke (wie Anm. 84), Bd. 2/2, 703f.

Magistrate Teil der von Gott eingesetzten und gewollten Ordnung seien.[103] Andererseits wird auf die Bindung der Magistrate an göttliches und natürliches Recht hingewiesen. Diese an sich banale Bindung wird jedoch inhaltlich durch den Hinweis auf das Eigentum der Bürger (*civium proprium*) konkretisiert und die Bindung des Fürsten an die Unverletzlichkeit des Eigentums durch den Hinweis auf 1. Sam. 8 *und* 11 untermauert.

Die bekannte Ansprache von Samuel an das Volk, das einen König forderte, führte in 1. Sam. 8 die Taten des dann eingesetzten Königs auf, darunter die Wegnahme von Söhnen, Töchtern, Feldern und Vieh. Diese in der Deutung des Spätmittelalters bereits kontroverse Stelle wurde bei Ptolemaeus von Lucca, wie wir insbesondere seit den Studien von Ulrich Meier wissen, als Beleg für die Präferierung eines *regimen politicum*, eines Wechsels aus Herrschern und Beherrschten gebraucht.[104] Melanchthon hebt nicht auf diese Argumentation ab – ebensowenig wie der größere Teil der späteren protestantischen Jurisprudenz im Reich, auch nicht die ständefreundliche, wie etwa Johannes Althusius.[105] Ein steter Wechsel, wie er von Ptolemaeus am Beispiel der italienischen Stadtrepubliken und vor allem der römischen Republik als gewinnbringend für das Gemeinwesen und seine Regierung gepriesen wird, hätte den Verhältnissen im Reich sicher nicht entsprochen. Aber er hebt mit Blick auf 1. Sam. 11, die Aufforderung des Richters an das Volk, zu Unrecht eingezogene Güter zu benennen, um diese restituieren zu können, auf die Bindung jeglicher Obrigkeit an Recht und Gesetz, auf den „contractus" ab. Dieser wird unter den später folgenden *definitiones* als „mutua et honesta consensio duorum vel plurium de re aliqua legitimo modo transferende vel quoad dominium vel quoad suam vel quoad obligationem divinitus oridinata" verstanden, erläutert durch Lev. 19,35: „Non facite inequalitatem in iudicio, in regula".[106]

---

[103] Ebd. 725: Die Begründung der Obrigkeit aus dem naturrechtlich im einzelnen Menschen angelegten Trieb zum Zusammenleben und der damit folgenden Notwendigkeit einer Ordnung einerseits und einer von Gott eingesetzten Ordnung wechseln im Nachdruck der Argumentation.
[104] *Annette Weber-Möckl*, „Das Recht des Königs, der über euch herrschen soll." Studien zu 1. Sam.8, 11 ff in der Literatur der frühen Neuzeit. Berlin 1986; Besprechung durch *Horst Dreitzel*, in: Zeitschrift für Historische Forschung 17, 1990, 108–111. *Ulrich Meier*, Mensch und Bürger. Die Stadt im Denken spätmittelalterlicher Theologen, Philosophen und Juristen. München 1991, Anm. 149. Vgl. speziell zu Lucca und seiner Verbindung eines Lobes des Papsttums und der städtischen Bürgerkommune *Charles T. Davis*, Roman Patriotism and Republican Propaganda. Ptolemy of Lucca and Pope Nicolas III, in: Speculum 50, 1975, 411–433.
[105] Vgl. *Robert von Friedeburg*, Widerstandsrecht, Untertanen und Vaterlandsliebe. Die Politica des Johannes Althusus von 1614 und ihre Rezeption in einem ständisch-fürstlichen Konflikt 1647–1652, in: Dieter Wyduckel (Hrsg.), Althusius. Werk und Rezeption. Berlin 2004, 261–286.
[106] *Melanchthon*, Werke (wie Anm. 84), Bd. 2/2, 731, 803.

Melanchthon stand mit solchen Überlegungen zur Bindung der Obrigkeit an das positive Recht keineswegs allein. Der bei der Kirche von Rom verbleibende und auch von der protestantischen Jurisprudenz, beispielsweise von Johannes Oldendorp, hochgeschätzte Jurist Ulrich Zasius äußerte sich ebenso zur rechtlichen Bindung jeglicher Obrigkeit. In einem Votum von 1525 im Rahmen eines Rechtsstreites vor dem Reichskammergericht bestritt Zasius die Möglichkeit eines Fürsten, in das geltende Recht einzugreifen oder jenseits des geltenden Rechtes zu handeln. Verträge seien auch durch den Fürsten einzuhalten, die *plenitudo potestatis* des Fürsten entbinde nicht von dieser Pflicht, es sei denn, er handele in besonderen Fällen zugunsten der *utilitas publica*. Aber auch in solchen Fällen bleibe der Fürst allzeit an Natur- und Völkerrecht gebunden. Zasius bezog sich in seiner Argumentation durchgängig auf das römische Recht und insbesondere auf Baldus de Ubaldis, ebnete aber die dort im Rahmen der Terminologie von *majestas, imperium* und *princeps legibus solutus* zugestandene Machtfülle der römischen Kaiser völlig durch die Wahl seiner Argumente ein.[107] Entsprechend nutzte er auch seine Abhandlung „In usus feudorum epitome" zu der Behauptung, das Lehnsrecht habe sich aus dem römischen Klientenrecht entwickelt und die Bindung beider Seiten an gegebene Absprachen fortgeführt.[108]

Es ginge zu weit, die Konzessionen, die den Bauern im Anschluß an den Bauernkrieg von Obrigkeiten in oberschwäbischen Kleinterritorien gemacht wurden, um Übelstände abzustellen, unmittelbar mit diesen Überlegungen in Zusammenhang zu bringen, galt diese Form der Konfliktlösung zwischen Untertanen und Obrigkeiten doch insbesondere für das „oberschwäbische Kernland" des Bundes, nicht aber für größere reichsfürstliche Territorien.[109] Zasius selbst stellte in seinem Consilium XI beispielsweise fest, innerhalb eines als „territorium" definierten Herrschaftsgebietes habe der Magistrat ein Herrschaftsrecht über die Untertanen. Verschiedene Ausübungen der Religion kämen in einem derartigen Territorium nicht in Frage, ebensowenig konkurrierende Gewalten.[110] Andererseits reklamierten Zasius und Melanchthon die im Rahmen solcher Herrschaftsbeziehungen kraft „Vertrag und Recht" an Schranken des positiven Rechts gebundene Macht der Obrig-

---

[107] *Ulricus Zasius*, Consilium X, Consilii lib. II, in: Opera Omnia. Hrsg. v. Johann Ulrich Zasius u. Joachim Münsinger von Frundeck. Lyon 1550, Ndr. Aalen 1966, Bd. 6, 408–429. Vgl. hierzu *Rowan*, Zasius (wie Anm. 68).
[108] *Ulricus Zasius*, In usus feudorum epitome, hervorgegangen aus seinen Vorlesungen zum langobardischen Recht von 1518/19 und 1535 erstmals publiziert (siehe *Rowan*, Zasius [wie Anm. 68]), in: ders., Omnia Opera (wie Anm. 107), Bd. 4, 243–342, hier 244f.
[109] Siehe *Carl*, Landfriedensordnung und Ungehorsam (wie Anm. 33), 111f.
[110] *Zasius*, Consilium XI, Consilii Lib II, in: ders., Omnia Opera (wie Anm. 107), Bd. 6, 430–442, hier 431: „quod magistratus eius loci intra eos fines terrendi, id est, submovendi ius habet". Ferner ebd. 436f.

keit, die das Eigentum ihrer Untertanen zu respektieren und zu schützen habe, für jede Obrigkeit schlechthin. Wohlgemerkt, weder ging es bei den oberschwäbischen Verhältnissen um eine direkte oder allgemeine politische Partizipation der Untertanen, noch ist hier von modernen vertragstheoretischen Konstruktionen die Rede, noch sollten die Hinweise von Melanchthon und Zasius zur allgemeinen rechtlichen Gebundenheit der Obrigkeit im Reich etwa die Genese eines modernen Rechtsstaats heraufbeschwören. Der untersuchte Schwäbische Bund war ein Bund von Obrigkeiten, nicht von Untertanen. Aber die Obrigkeiten ließen den Untertanen doch Klagemöglichkeiten und den Schutz ihres Eigentums in rechtsförmigen Verfahren zu. Die Obrigkeit stand daher keineswegs allein unter den Bindungen des natürlichen und göttlichen Rechts, sondern blieb auch durch positive Satzungen gebunden. Das eben reklamierten Zasius und Melanchthon für jede legitime Obrigkeit im Reich.

Auf der entstehenden territorialen Ebene spiegelt das Regentenhandbuch von Johannes Ferrarius, einem Berater Philipps des Großmütigen, der die Universität Marburg mit aufbaute, die Einbindung des Fürsten in die Rechtsordnung des Gemeinwesens. Seine „Respublica bene instituenda" erschien 1556 in Basel und wurde für die englische Königin Elisabeth zu ihrem Regierungsantritt ins Englische übersetzt (1559). Ferrarius bezog sich vor allem auf Ciceros „De Officiis" als wichtigste Quelle. Im Zentrum seiner Betrachtungen standen aber nicht etwa Pflichten und Ethik des Fürsten, und schon gar nicht des niederen Adels, sondern die fürstlichen Beamten. Diese *officials* trügen ihren Namen, weil allein auf sie im Territorium zuträfe, was Cicero von denen erwarte, die allein ihren Pflichten nachkommen könnten, nämlich diejenigen, für die sich Pflicht und Eigeninteresse gegenseitig ergänzten und bestärkten (Buch III, c I, 31). Für sie seien *imperare, coercere, iubere* Ziele des guten Leben sui generis (III, c 7). Hier sind die Wurzeln jener Beamten- und Räteethik zu finden, die in deutschsprachigen Landen noch eine wichtige Rolle spielen sollte und für die es meiner Bewertung nach nur wenige vergleichbare Entwicklungen außerhalb des Reiches gibt.[111] Weder dem Adel noch dem Fürsten wurde die entscheidende Rolle im Land zugesprochen, sondern den Räten als Ausführenden einer Herrschaftsordnung, die keineswegs allein oder in erster Linie auf den Fürsten zulief. Sicherlich hören wir hier ein Echo der Forderungen Andlaus nach einer privilegierten Rolle der – juristisch promovierten – Räte. Nun jedoch wurde ihnen auch noch das *officium in rempublicam* zugesprochen.

---

[111] *Hermann Weber* plant hierzu eine umfassende Forschungsmonographie.

IV.

Es ging hier weder um die Rechtsgleichheit in der ständisch gestuften Gesellschaft noch um die Partizipation von Untertanen, aber eben auch nicht um die fürstliche Allmacht, sondern um rechtliche Gebundenheit von Herrschaft und ihre Legitimität als Ausdruck gottgewollter und funktionaler Notwendigkeit. Wir stehen hier nicht vor einer radikalen oder grundsätzlichen Alternative zwischen unterschiedlichen politischen Ordnungsvorstellungen, etwa im Sinne einer von Untertanen getragenen Ordnung gegenüber einer absoluten Monarchie. Aber die später auftretenden Vertreter der absoluten Monarchie insbesondere in England und Frankreich und noch später auch im Reich sollten die einschlägige Samuel-Stelle ganz anders deuten. Für sie, etwa für den prominentesten Vertreter des Absolutismus im späten 16. Jahrhundert, für den schottischen und englischen König Jakob VI./I., wurde die Rede Samuels (1. Sam. 8) ohne Hinweis auf das Restitutionsversprechen in 1. Sam. 11 gedeutet, nämlich als Recht des rechtmäßigen Königs, alles zu nehmen.[112] Die von Jakob sowohl im „True Law of Free Monarchies" als auch in seinem für seinen ältesten Sohn Heinrich verfaßten „Basilicon Doron" immer wieder unterstrichene Vertreterschaft Gottes[113] kam für lutherische Autoren ohnehin so nicht in Frage.[114] Die zeitgebundene Konzentration der Forschung seit den 1920er, erst recht seit den 1970er Jahren, auf die aktive politische Partizipation der Untertanen hat die gewichtigen Unterschiede verdunkelt, die in der Legitimation weltlicher Obrigkeit im Reich durch protestantische und katholische Juristen – von einer Minderheit im 17. Jahrhundert einmal abgesehen – als rechtlich gebundener Herrschaft mit materiellen Rechten für die Untertanen in deutlichem Gegensatz zur Legitimation der absoluten Monarchie in England oder in Frankreich bestanden.

Die Stellung der Obrigkeit erfuhr ganz ohne Zweifel im Gefolge der Reformation im Reich eine deutliche Akzentuierung. Daraus läßt sich aber keineswegs folgern, die protestantische Jurisprudenz habe umstandslos dem

---

[112] *James VI and I*, Selected Writings. Ed. by Neil Rhodes et al. Aldershot 2003, 259–280, hier 262f. Überdies deutete James das Naturrecht als Grundlage der Übernahme väterlicher Herrschaft über die Untertanen. Vgl. ebd. 262: „By the law of nature the king becomes a naturall Father to all his Lieges at his Coronation […]".

[113] Vgl. edb. 261: „Kings are called gods by the propheticall king David, because they sit upon GOD his Throne on the earth"; *ders.*, Basilicon Doron, in: ebd. 199–258, 200: „God gives not Kings the stile of God in vaine […]".

[114] Zur insbesondere von reformierten, im Gegensatz zu lutherischen, Autoren konzipierten Einheit von Kirche und Staat und der sich daraus ergebenden erdrückenden Rolle für weltliche Magistrate siehe *Dreitzel*, Althusius (wie Anm. 93), 56, vor allem zu Zwingli und *Heinrich Bullinger*, De testamento seu foedre Dei unico et aeterno. Zürich 1534. Siehe auch *Scheible*, Unterscheidung (wie Anm. 83).

Territorialabsolutismus das Wort geredet. Schließlich muß daran erinnert werden, daß die von der lutherischen Reformation in erster Linie ins Auge gefaßte Fürstengesellschaft der Landesväter sich auch und gerade in der Praxis überwiegend einer zwar „betont patriarchalischen", aber eben auch „konsensorientierten Repräsentations- und Regierungsweise bediente".[115] Auf diese Gruppe, in die sich gegen Ende des Jahrhunderts in der Tat Figuren wie Moritz von Hessen kaum einfügen lassen, war bereits Gottlob von Polenz' Diktum von 1860 gemünzt. Im Zusammenhang mit seiner Rückkehr nach Wittenberg von der Wartburg schrieb Luther 1522 an den Kurfürsten: „Ich wolle EKFG mehr schützen, denn sie mich schützen könde [...] wer am meisten glaubt, der wird hie am meisten schützen [...]. Wenn EKFG gleubte, So würde sie Gottes herrlichkeit sehen, Weil sie aber nicht gleubt, hat sie auch noch nichts gesehen". „Allein zu einem solchen Schreiben", bemerkte Polenz, „gehörte nicht bloß ein deutscher, ein gemüthlicher und zugleich ein kindlicher Schreiber, sondern auch ein deutscher, gemüthlicher und landesväterlicher Leser und wenn Calvin auch jener Schreiber gewesen wäre, wo hätte er unter Gewaltigen und Großen [in Frankreich, R. v. F.] diesen [...] finden können?"[116]

Dabei obliegt es gar keinem Zweifel, daß die Obrigkeit erheblichen Handlungsspielraum besaß und diesen faktisch auch in Kirchensachen, insbesondere im Falle der Auseinandersetzungen unter den Theologen, geltend machte. Das galt selbst für städtische Obrigkeiten, wie insbesondere die Konflikte in der Stadt Magdeburg und die Rechtfertigung der Räte zur Ausweisung von mißliebigen Predigern zeigen. Der Konflikt stand im Zusammenhang mit dem Streit um die Deutung der Rechtfertigungslehre zwischen Georg Maior und Nikolaus von Amsdorf. Daraus entwickelte sich in Magdeburg ein Streit um die konkurrierende Verantwortung der Prediger und der weltlichen Obrigkeit um die Regelung der Predigt und um die Handhabung des Strafamtes der Prediger auch gegen die eigene Obrigkeit.[117] Der

---

[115] Vgl. *Manfred Rudersdorf*, Die Generation der lutherischen Landesväter im Reich. Bausteine zu einer Typologie des deutschen Reformationsfürsten, in: Anton Schindling/Walter Ziegler (Hrsg.), Die Territorien des Reichs im Zeitalter der Reformation und Konfessionalisierung. Land und Konfession 1500-650. Bd. 7: Bilanz, Forschungsperspektiven, Register. Münster 1997, 137-70, hier 167.
[116] *Gottlob von Polenz*, Geschichte des französischen Calvinismus. Bd. 3. Gotha 1860, Ndr. Aalen 1964, 64f. Vgl. zu den Rahmenbedingungen der Rückkehr nach Wittenberg und zur Lage 1522/23 *Eike Wolgast*, Die Wittenberger Theologie und die Politik der evangelischen Stände. Studien zu Luthers Gutachten in politischen Fragen. Gütersloh 1977, 95.
[117] Vgl. *Schorn-Schütte*, Evangelische Geistlichkeit (wie Anm. 61), Kap. VII: Die Geistlichkeit zwischen Obrigkeit und Gemeinde, 390-432, zu Hesshusius 402; *Inge Mager*, Tileman Heshusen (1527-1588). Geistliches Amt, Glaubensmündigkeit und Gemeindeautonomie, in: Heinz Scheible (Hrsg.), Melanchthon in seinen Schülern. Wolfenbüttel 1996, 341-359.

Prediger Tilman Hesshusius, ein Anhänger von Amsdorfs, hatte durch eine 1561 in Magdeburg veröffentlichte Schrift „Vom Ampt und Gewalt der Pfarherrn" in diese Auseinandersetzung zugunsten der Rechte der Prediger eingegriffen. Die „Bürgermeister und Rathmänner" der Stadt Magdeburg setzten in diesen Auseinandersetzungen die ihnen genehme Deutung in der Lehrstreitigkeit gegen Hesshusius[118] durch und verweigerten Hesshusius den Druck einer Schrift gegen Maior. Ein Mitstreiter von Hesshusius flocht daraufhin in seiner Predigt, folgt man Hesshusius' Darstellung des Konfliktes, eine „Christliche Warnung und Vermahnung" an den Rat ein. Gott solle es den „Regenten aus Gnaden verzeihen", daß sie einzelne Prediger an der Veröffentlichung ihrer Meinung gehindert und einen anderen eingesperrt hatten. Hesshusius griff die Bürgermeister und Räte in seiner „Nothwendigen Entschuldigung und Verantwortung wider den Bericht des Raths der Stadt Magdeburg" darüber hinaus öffentlich als „gottlose Juristen" an.[119] Der Rat reagierte mit der Ausweisung der opponierenden Prediger aus der Stadt und zugleich mit der öffentlichen Rechtfertigung seiner Politik gegenüber den Bürgern der Stadt, den Untertanen. Rat und Bürgermeister begründeten ihre Handlungsweise mit dem Hinweis auf das ihnen von Gott auferlegte Amt als Obrigkeit, ihre Verantwortung für die „erste Tafel der zehn Gebote" und ihre Pflicht, „auffsehenshalben auff der Kirchen/ die inn unsere Stadt Ringmauer und Bothmäßigkeit begriffen sind, gebührende und habende Amtsgerechtigkeit Gott und unserer hohen Obrigkeit zu ehren und aller Kirchen zum besten und zur Notdurft/ nach unserer Amtspflicht Erforderung zu üben und zu halten". Hesshusius wolle mit seinen öffentlichen Angriffen „Unser Amt als uns von Göttlicher Majestät aufferlegt [...] unter die Füsse treten und vernichten". Er möge meinen, sein Urteil sei das des „Heiligen Geistes [...] und uns mit Gewalt einbilden, als könt ein Prediger nimmer irren". Tatsächlich spreche jedoch „nicht allwege der Heilige Geist sondern offt der Teufel selbst aus den Predigern." Die öffentlich opponierenden Prediger verglich der Rat mit Müntzer. Auch Müntzer habe „den gemeinen Mann, ja auch wohl verständige Leute verführet". Die Sündhaftigkeit von Rat und Stadt stellte der Rat nicht in Abrede. Aber die Deutungsautorität über einzelne Begebenheiten, so den plötzlichen Tod einer Frau in der Stadt, dürfe nicht allein bei einem Prediger liegen. Sie, die Bürgermeister und Ratsleute, dürften und brauchten „ihr Gewissen" dem Urteil solcher „köstlichen Zeloten und ernstlich eiffrigen" nicht „zu unterwerfen", weil sie als „Weltli-

---

[118] Vgl. *Schorn-Schütte*, Evangelische Geistlichkeit (wie Anm. 61), 217-219.
[119] Vgl. Tilemani Hessui nothwendige Entschuldigung und gründliche Verantwortung wider den Bericht des Raths der Stadt Magdeburg. O. O. 1562. Dazu jetzt auch *Chang Soo Park*, Die Politica christiana und politische Kommunikation in der zweiten Hälfte des 16. Jahrhunderts am Beispiel Bremen, in: Luise Schorn-Schütte/Sven Tode (Hrsg.), Debatten über die Legitimation von Herrschaft. Politische Sprachen in der Frühen Neuzeit. Berlin 2006.

che Stadtregierung [...] nach göttlicher Ordnung" diesen Predigern nicht unterworfen seien. Vor den Augen der Magdeburger Stadt nahmen die Räte dann explizit zur öffentlichen Auseinandersetzung um ihre Autorität Stellung. „Und ob dann wol Tilemann inen geschwinden griff gebraucht das er sich auff unsere Gemeine reserviert, villeicht der fröhlichen Hoffnung und Zuversicht, uns unsere Gemein also vorzubilden, als ob wir ganz übel mißgehandelt so mögen wir aber dennoch mit Gott, Warheit und allen Rechten und demnach auch mit gutem Gewissen" behaupten, daß das Stadtregiment keine „Tyrannei wider treue Lehre" sei, sondern „gegen Tilemann und seinen Anhang unser Amtpflicht geübt [...] daß wir alle gegen Gott und unserer Gemein zu Ehren und besten gemeinet". Zu den Pflichten des Amtes, das Rat und Bürgermeister „von Gottes, unserer hohen Obrigkeit" besaßen, gehöre eben auch die Fürsorge für die Stadt und ihre „notdurft". Rat und Bürgermeister beanspruchten damit das Amt des Richters auch über theologische Streitigkeiten für sich.[120]

V.

Die Reformation gab der territorialstaatlichen Umformung des Reiches zweifellos einen nachhaltigen Schub.[121] Besonders nach 1945 geriet die Formierung des Territorialstaats im Jahrhundert der Reformation in den Sog der Perhoreszierung von Herrschaftsverhältnissen. Die Vereinnahmung des fürstlichen Territorialstaates des 16. Jahrhunderts durch die borussische Schule des späteren 19. Jahrhunderts wurde dabei nicht in Frage gestellt, die Bewertung des Territorialstaats aber nun mit negativen Vorzeichen versehen. Überdies geriet die Frage nach der Partizipation der Untertanen seit den 1970er Jahren zunehmend in das Zentrum der Forschung. Dabei trat die Frage der rechtlichen Bindung von Herrschaft in den Hintergrund. Forschungsstrategische Dichotomien wie die zwischen „Kommunalismus" und „Absolutismus" haben diese Entwicklung eher befördert.

Der Reformation ging es jedoch um nichts weniger als die Loslösung fürstlicher Herrschaft aus rechtlichen Bindungen. Daß das Evangelium nicht von den Gesetzen entbinde – *evangelium non tollit leges* – zählte zu den Kernüberzeugungen der Reformatoren. Die Fürsten blieben jedoch nicht allein in den Konzeptionen der Reformatoren und der Juristen, sondern auch tatächlich in der Realität des Reiches dessen Rechtsordnung unterworfen, an die die Stände mit Erfolg appellierten. Die Entwicklung des Territorial-

---

[120] Nothwehr des Rats und Syndici auch etliche Pastoren und Prediger der Alten Stadt Magdeburg [...]. Magdeburg 1562.
[121] Zur Frage der Bedeutung des landesherrlichen Kirchenregiments vor der Reformation vgl. *Heckel*, Ius Reformandi (wie Anm. 49), 85f.

staates als Gehäuse der verschiedenen Konfessionen stellt sich daher als ausgesprochen innovative Entwicklung dar, die zu Recht als Ausgang des Weges zum „modernen Staatskirchenrecht im konfessionellen Zeitalter beschrieben wird".[122]

Diese Feststellung ist an sich alles andere als ‚neu'. Entschlackt von der sachfremden Hypostasierung des Territorialstaates der Reformation als Wiege des bürgerlichen Nationalstaates des 19. Jahrhunderts und der ebenso sachfremden Perhorheszierung obrigkeitlicher Herrschaft in der frühen Neuzeit als autoritärer Sonderweg gilt es aber, gerade auch für den europäischen Vergleich, an sie zu erinnern, um die Reformation im Reich und die durch sie ermöglichten politischen Innovationen sachgerecht bewerten zu können.

---

[122] *Heckel*, Ius Reformandi (wie Anm. 49).

„La Grande Cassure": Violence and the French Reformation

By

Mark Greengrass

What makes the French Reformation distinctive? At the beginning of the last century, the response to that question would have been in terms of its national experience: the existence of a French „pre-reform", a Calvinist Reformation that was distinctive in its impact in France, a Huguenot political movement and party with remarkable powers of military and political organization, and finally a French monarchy that chose to demonstrate its emerging absolutism, firstly by imposing a uniquely imposed toleration at the edict of Nantes (1598), and then by abolishing it three generations later in its revocation (1685). The story was one of French exceptionalism. Move a century later and, like most of these nationally-conceived historiographies, these irreducible elements of French exceptionalism have largely been rewritten. The French „pre-reform" is now seen as part of a wider humanist engagement, seeing the renewal of the church in distinctive ways from Luther, and often leading them eventually to support the traditional church as of breaking its mould.[1] The Calvinist Reformation is studied in an international and comparative context rather than being appropriated uniquely to its French setting.[2] The Huguenot political movement, almost despite itself, expressed remarkable political aspirations – ones that often set it apart from established political structures. But it also had its feet of clay. These included a succession of conservative-minded, aristocratic leaders who understood their „duty of revolt" as being to protect the perceived and inherited values of the French nobility, and themselves as their natural representatives, as well as to advance God's cause; and who would, if the choice had been offered

---

[1] See, among others, *Guy Bedouelle*, Lefèvre d'Etaples et l'intelligence des Ecritures. Geneva 1976; *Guy Bedouelle/Bernard Roussel* (Eds.), Le temps des Réformes et la Bible. Paris 1989; *Jean-Pierre Massaut/Josse Clichtove*, L'humanisme et la réforme du clergé. 2 Vols. Paris 1968; *Jean-Pierre Massaut*, Critique et tradition à la veille de la Réforme en France. Etude suivie de textes inédits traduits et annotés. Paris 1976; *Guy Bedouelle*, Lefèvre d'Etaples et Luther. Une recherche de frontières, 1517-1527, in: Revue d'histoire et de philosophie religieuse 63, 1983, 17-31; *Michel Veissière*, L'évêque Guillaume Briçonnet (1570-1534). Contribution à la connaissance de la Réforme catholique à la veille du Concile de Trente. Provins 1986.
[2] E. g. *Menna Prestwich* (Ed.), International Calvinism, 1541-1715. Oxford 1985; *Philip Benedict*, Christ's Churches Purely Reformed. A Social History of Calvinism. New Haven/London 2002.

them, have preferred royal favour to making themselves hostages to fortune in rebellion.[3] Its military strength depended on foreign backers and a financial basis that was largely inadequate to the task of defeating the French monarchy, temporarily weakened though the latter was by the civil wars.[4] That monarchy was not responsible for introducing „toleration" to France, a word with pejorative connotations which never saw the light of day in the so-called edicts of toleration of the period. Instead, it brokered a „co-existence" of the kind that was attempted many times with varying degrees of success during the hostilities of the later sixteenth century from the edict of Romorantin (1560) onwards. The justifications for that pluralism, the arguments advanced for it, were based on those developed for similar „simultanea" elsewhere in Europe, not least upon those of the German Reich, and in its principalities, in the peace of Augsburg (1555).[5] But it was a „coexistence" within a framework of „intolerance" and the revocation of the edict of Nantes, too, can now be understood as a late example of the state-building forces of the French monarchy aligning themselves unambiguously with an emergent catholic confessional identity, though whether it was accompanied by the pressures for „social discipline" that the „ideal-type" of the confessionalisation model, at least in its „strong" form, would require, remains a matter for debate.

Not much, then, is left of French exceptionalism in the protestant Reformation: save violence. A century ago, historians were not talking about it. Now, in the shadow of world events to which it has an obvious relevance, it is the focus of our attentions; a social and cultural distinctiveness, rather than a national one. In 1973, the American historian Natalie Zemon Davis published an article entitled „The Rites of Violence in the French Wars of Religion".[6] It has done much to change the parameters with which we view the subject. Davis focused on the grim, bizarre, terrifying episodes of popular religious violence in the French wars of religion. The documentation had always been there, but it offended, and still offends, liberal sensibilities. Some of the descriptions of individual brutality and collective carnage are undeni-

---

[3] *Arlette Jouanna*, Le devoir de révolte: la noblesse française et la gestation de l'état moderne, 1559-1661. Paris 1989; *Kristin Neuschel*, Word of Honor: Interpreting Noble Culture in Sixteenth-Century France. Ithaca 1989.
[4] *Mark Greengrass*, Financing the Cause: Protestant Mobilisation and Accountability in France (1562-1589), in: Philip Benedict/Guido Marnef/Henk van Nierop/Marc Venard (Eds.), Reformation, Revolt and Civil War in France and the Netherlands, 1555-1585. Amsterdam 1999, 233-254.
[5] *Olivier Christin*, La paix de religion. L'autonomisation de la raison politique au XVIe siècle. Paris 1997, esp. ch. 1; *David El Kenz/Claire Gantet*, Guerres et paix de religion en Europe, 16e-17e siècles. Paris 2003.
[6] *Natalie Zemon Davis*, The Rites of Violence. Religious Riots in Sixteenth-Century France, in: Past and Present 59, 1973, 51-91; reprinted in: *idem*, Society and Culture in Early Modern France. Stanford 1975, 152-188.

ably gruesome. And there are questions to be asked about what constitutes the appropriate degree of objectivity towards the surviving evidence, just as there are about the descriptions which abound of more recent ethnic cleansing in the Balkans or terrorist outrage in the Middle East.[7] Historians have a habit of ignoring the evidence that they cannot make sense of; and in the case of the violence of the French wars of religion, these episodes seemed senseless and sad. Natalie Zemon Davis offered, for the first time, a rationale, an explanatory framework for it. She explained how the participants in these events used a pre-existent vocabulary of ritualised, popular violence, „rites" which gave shape, form and explanatory power to what was happening. All violence is, in some sense or other, „predetermined". In these instances, the 'predetermination' was religion, viewed as a cultural vocabulary. The cultural vocabulary was, she argued, asymmetric. There was a difference between the „ritual massacral space" afforded by the traditional religion and the relative paucity of objectives for ritual attack, destruction or derision afforded by the reformed religion. She cites the „Histoire ecclésiastique" (of which more in a moment) as asserting that „those of the Reformed Religion made war only on images and altars, which do not bleed, while those of the Roman religion spilled blood with every kind of cruelty".[8] As she put it, „when all this is said, the iconoclastic Calvinist crowds still come out as the champions in the destruction of religious property" whilst „in bloodshed, the catholics are the champions".

One of the incidental, and certainly unintended, consequences of Natalie Davis' article has been to highlight a tautology: that the wars of religion were about religion.[9] They were not a cloak by which social groups dressed up their aspirations. They were not the vehicle for expressing social or economic grievances, even though both emerged in due course and as a result of the prolonged hostilities, and to an extent that we have almost certainly understated.[10] They were not merely the tragic outcome of the „triple whammy" that afflicted the French monarchy at more or less the same time in 1559–1562: undeclared bankruptcy, royal minority, and aristocratic factionalism. Religion – not in the sense of a set of confessionally determined beliefs, but in the sense of the „sacred" (as opposed to the „profane") – lay at the centre of the conflict. Her explanatory framework had coherence because it

---

[7] The issues of „scientific neutrality" and „critical distance" in relation to the phenomena of extreme violence and massacre is raised in an article, reflecting on a 1999 Paris colloquium on the subject by *Jacques Sémelin*, In Consideration of Massacres, in: Journal of Genocide Research 3.3, 2001, 377–389.
[8] *Davis*, Rites (note 6), 173.
[9] Highlighted by the review article by *Mack P. Holt*, Putting Religion back into the Wars of Religion, in: French Historical Studies 18, 1993, 524–551.
[10] And emphasised in *Henry Heller*, Iron and Blood: Civil Wars in Sixteenth-Century France. Montreal 1991.

rested upon the insights of social theorists, especially Emile Durkheim and cultural anthropologists, especially Mary Douglas.[11] But it was a coherence which lacked much by way of a dynamic framework. It explained a phenomenon in terms of its cultural meaning, rather than in terms of a process. Chronology played little part in it.

The article begins chillingly with two scenes. Let us consider them both in greater detail, since they will inform our discussion later on. The first comes from that famous „Histoire ecclésiastique des églises réformées de France", published in 1580 and generally catalogued under the name of Théodore de Bèze although, in reality, it was a collaborative work, constructed from testimonies collected over twenty years from the French protestant churches, in which Claude Goulart probably had the greatest hand.[12] It is written with a studied air of objectivity, although how far it was based on personal testimony we shall, for most of the provincial sections of it, never know. The date is 3 May 1562; the place, Gien in the Gatinois. The civil war was not a month old, and Louis, prince de Condé, having set up headquarters of the revolt at Orléans, issued commissions to his captains to recruit soldiers for the cause from far and wide. Capitaine La Borde [var: La Borderie], an Auxerrois, was despatched to Gien, where there was a small protestant church established whose pastor was a young man with a long and illustrious future in Geneva ahead of him: Lambert Daneau. What happened on 3 May 1562? The protestant congregation assembled (as it was legally allowed to do after the edict of January 1562) outside the town walls for a catechism class.[13] It began with a reading from the Bible: Dt. 12, „où il est parlé de la destruction des autels & images".[14] The passage is the deuteronomic injunction to destroy images, as direct an incitement to violence as any Taleban could want to hear.[15] Capitaine La Borde was there too. The churches were an important recruiting ground for protestant troops in the early civil wars. News had just arrived of

---

[11] In particular, *Emile Durkheim*, Formes élémentaires de la vie religieuse. Paris 1912; *Mary Douglas*, Purity and Danger: an Analysis of the Concepts of Pollution and Taboo. New York 1966. The influence of the latter upon her writing at this time is confirmed in: *Natalie Zemon Davis*, L'histoire tout feu tout flamme. Entretiens avec Denis Crouzet. Paris 2004, 69f.

[12] *G. Baum/Ed. Cunitz* (Eds.), Histoire ecclésiastique des églises réformées du Royaume de France. 3 Vols. Paris 1883–1889, facsimile reprint Nieuwkoop 1974.

[13] Ibid. Vol. 2, 537–539.

[14] „where the destruction of altars and images is spoken of".

[15] Dt. 12, 1–3. The text in the French Geneva Bible has more impact than it does in English: „Voici les ordonnances et droits que vous garderez, pour les faire en la terre que le Seigneur le Dieu de tes peres t'a donnee pour la posseder, tous les iours que tu vivras sur la terre. Vous destruirez tous lieux esquels les gens que vous possederez auront servis à leurs dieux, sur les montagnes haustes et sur les costaux, et sous tout bois verd. Aussi vous demolirez leurs autels, et desromprez leurs statues, et bruslerez au feu leurs bois. Vous despecerez les images de leurs dieux et perdrez leur nom de ce lieu."

the destruction of religious icons in Orléans itself. La Borde and his new recruits, fresh from their catechismal class, set out for the centre of Gien to do the same, „à ruiner temples & autels, n'oublians pas aussi de se saisir de ce qui sert à la messe".[16] The results of their day's work are no longer to be seen in the parish church at Gien. It would be rebuilt in 1686, partly with masonry from the abandoned protestant „temple", and consecrated as the „Eglise de Saint-Louis" by the bishop of Auxerre in 1689.[17] The „pieds nuds de Bourges" („The Bare-footed of Bourges"), as La Borde's company came to be known, also left their mark in the churches round about, including that of Saint-Brisson-sur-Loire, where they not only smashed the images but also ransacked the belongings of the priests.[18] In the name of religion, religious objects are being smashed: religious violence.

Our text is manifestly embarrassed by what it is describing. It is, above all, anxious not to inculpate its by now distinguished Genevan colleague Lambert Daneau, from whom I suppose the information for this passage may well have come, in anything seditious or illegal. The story points the finger everywhere else but towards him; he was not preaching, the congregation present that day had no hand or knowledge in what was about to happen. Capitaine La Borde, the outsider, takes most of the blame: „sans conscience [...] tresmal complexionnés, & disposés seulement à voler le calice sous ombre de la religion".[19] But, to further exculpate the protestants of being a „violent" group in society, the account sets the context more deeply. The countryside around Gien had already demonstrated its hostility towards the new protestant community. There was bad blood over the issue of images, going back well before 1562. At Ouzouer-sur-Trézée, for example, a community of vine-cultivators, peasant farmers and labourers some 14 kilometres from Gien, the villagers had begun to take the law into their own hands. Under the pretext of „protecting their religion and their images" they had begun to rob and set about suspected protestants from Gien as they passed to and fro. They refused to pay rents on the agricultural lands that they owned; and they set fire to their barns and farms too. So it is not surprising that some protestants in Gien, we are to infer, wanted to hold their meetings inside the town itself for fear of reprisals, or that a prime target on La Borde's iconoclastic list, was Ouzouer. There were scores to settle, as well as God's cause to carry through. It was religious violence: but there were other things mixed up in it too. These are complex events with a large „hinterland".

---

[16] „to desecrate temples and altars, not forgetting also to seize all the objects for saying mass".
[17] *L.-A. Marchand*, Histoire de la ville, des seigneurs et du comté de Gien. Orléans/Gien 1885, 35f.
[18] Ibid. 47.
[19] „without conscience [...] psychopathic, and disposed only to steal the chalice under the cover of religion".

Mixed up in it as well were those in and around Gien who had not quite decided which side they were on. We must not forget them. They included the parish priest of St-Brisson who had his belongings ransacked and his life threatened. He was half way towards being a protestant, according to the „Histoire ecclésiastique": „il faisoit la cours à l'Evangile".[20] Brave man, he had preached in the Gatinois countryside that the mass was a blasphemy, and was using a book of protestant prayers, psalms and a catechism with which to instruct his flock. Perhaps shopped by some of his villagers, shocked by their turn-coat priest, he found himself vulnerable from all sides when La Borde's troops came to town. It took one of its sergeants to negotiate for the return of his belongings. Not surprisingly, given the experience, he had learnt a hard lesson and was next heard of occupying a canonry in Gien. He knew which side he was on after May 1562. Religious violence determined people's confessional identities, for better or worse, forcing them to decide whose side they were on, and to justify it. It was part of a process.

Now for the second source and incident cited by Natalie Zemon Davis. This time it is the authentic voice of a catholic priest as recorded in his memoirs: his name, Claude Haton. Writing in the later 1570s, by which time he was in his forties, he was sometimes a bit confused about some of the events earlier in his life. The son of a *laboureur*, he spent most of his life, so far as we know, in and around Provins, where he was priest-in-charge, chaplain of the local hospital, and vicar at various parishes in the surrounding neighbourhood. But he had contacts at the royal court, which he visited on several occasions, and also in Paris, where he had friends among the clergy.[21] This time we are in early April 1568, in the wake of a rapid stream of political and military events that did as much as any to poison the atmosphere at the French court and create the conditions for the assassination of the Admiral Gaspard de Coligny and the subsequent massacre of St Bartholomew in 1572. The protestant military high command held a series of top-secret meetings in the autumn of 1567 at Valéry (one of Condé's châteaux, not far from Sens) and Châtillon-sur-Loing (Coligny's principal residence) to decide their strategy in the face of what they believed to be an attack. In La Noue's account, they opted (not without much internal discussion) for a preemptive strike, and one aimed at the heart of royal authority, the court itself and its Swiss guards.[22] The result was the „Surprise of Meaux" of 26-28 September 1567. It was a high-risk strategy, and it failed disastrously. Charles IX, Henri duc d'Anjou (his brother and the future king), Catherine de Médicis, and

---

[20] „he paid court to the Good News".
[21] *Laurent Bourquin* (Ed.), Mémoires de Claude Haton. 2 Vols. Paris 2001/2003, Vol. 1, xi-xiv.
[22] *François de La Noue*, Discours politique & militaires. Ed. by E. Sutcliffe. Geneva 1967, 682.

others at court would never forget this „infâme entreprise", „n'y allant de rien moings que de la perte de cest Estat et du danger de noz vies" as the queen mother wrote on 28 September.[23] Having failed to capture the court, Condé and Coligny rallied their forces to menace the capital, seizing Saint-Denis, the mausoleum of the kings of France, on 1 October 1567. Smelling their fields and mills burning in the distance and seeing the flames in the sky, Parisians feared the worst. The rumour went around that protestants in their midst were collecting wood and materials to set light to the whole city. The local watch and ward, in a state of high readiness to defend the city against the possible, imminent attack, swung into action to seek out the suspects and eliminate them, believing that they had official permission to do so. An anonymous Latin source from Paris records on the night of 1 October that „they found in the street the skin of a man who had been flayed, which terrified pious souls. If someone said a word in favour of the authors of the rebellion, it was permitted to kill him, which was the fate of many".[24] Flayed skin: the ineluctable Christian reference point is St Bartholomew, the martyr who was skinned alive. Etienne Pasquier, a Paris lawyer, records that, those who did not carry a white cross on their hat in early October 1568, risked being summarily assassinated on the streets of the capital. The same Latin source says (almost certainly misinformed, but the misinformation is itself instructive) that a royal edict required all catholic men and women to display the sign of the cross prominently about their person „otherwise they would be put to death on the spot". October 1568 was, as Barbara Diefendorf has said, a „„dress-rehearsal" for the events of St Bartholomew's Eve, August 1572.[25] At the great battle of Saint-Denis (10 November 1567), the result was indecisive, though the larger royal army held the field. In the early months of 1568, the royal administration of Charles IX made a supreme effort, deploying 72,000 men in the field, perhaps having as many as 100,000 military men in garrisons and elsewhere on its pay-roll. It was by far the largest mobilization of the early civil wars. But protestant reinforcements continually flowed up from the west and south to join Condé's and Coligny's forces in the Loire; and 6,000 German *reîtres* and 3,000 *lansquenets* joined them from the Palatinate, led by Duc Casimir. With the odds tremendously high, the French monarchy decided, as it generally would in the wars of religion, that caution was the better part of valour. It negotiated a peace, signed at Longjumeau on

---

[23] „directed at nothing less than the loss of this State and to endanger our lives", *Hector de La Ferrière/Gustave Baguenault de Puchesse* (Eds.), Lettres de Catherine de Médicis. 9 Vols. Paris 1880–1905, Vol. 3, 59.
[24] *Henri Hauser*, Un récit catholique des trois premières guerres de religion. Les Acta tumultuum gallicanorum, in: Revue historique 108, 1911, 304 – cited in the translation given in: *Barbara B. Diefendorf*, Beneath the Cross. Catholics and Huguenots in Sixteenth-Century Paris. New York/Oxford 1991, 80.
[25] *Diefendorf*, Beneath the Cross (note 24), 81.

23 March 1568, „la meschante, petite paix, pire que la guerre", as La Noue contemptuously dismissed it.[26] The views were not much different among catholics, combattants and observers alike. Politics, in short, was in and around the violence of the civil wars at every turn. We cannot write about violence without it.

This is where we rejoin our source, Claude Haton. He was in touch with his friends in Paris, the *curés* in the numerous parishes of the capital. It was Lent, the preaching season, and they took the opportunity to say exactly what they thought of the recent peace. Their anger was directed, fair and square, towards the monarchy: king, queen mother and council. „Et disoient à haulte voix que Dieu feroit vengence de Sa Majesté et dudit Conseil, et que Sadite majesté dès ce monde endureroit punition et adversité en son esprit et en sa vie qui ne seroit longue, laquelle seroit accélérée et hastée devant son temps par lesditz huguenotz [...]".[27] The preachers used, Haton said, Old and New Testament scriptures to prove their point: Charles IX was King Ahab, Catherine de Médicis was Jezabel and the Book of Kings told, in graphic detail, what happened to them – arguably the bloodiest bits of the Bible.[28] But Haton, too, was embarrassed by what he was saying, anxious to give an alibi to his friends in Paris, „nostre maistre d'Ivollé" [Pierre Dyvolé, *curé* at St-Etienne du Mont], Jacques Hugonis, the great Franciscan preacher of his day in Paris, Simon Vigor and others. „Ces docteurs deffendoient tousjours au peuple qu'il ne se esmeut et qu'il ne fist sedition aucune contre l'estat du roy et le repos public de la patrie".[29] Protestant houses were ransacked; those Huguenots who dared to take advantage of the peace and return to the city were assaulted. There were assassinations on a main thoroughfare in Paris, the rue Saint-Antoine, in broad daylight, despite armed guards and heavy security. And many, miscellaneous revenge killings: „more have been murdered since the publishing of the peace than were all these last troubles" recorded the English ambassador in Paris grimly on 7 August 1568.[30] Although he disculpated the Paris preachers of encouraging it, Haton did not condemn this collective, „extreme" violence. He wanted us

---

[26] „the wicked, little peace, worse than war", *La Noue*, Discours (note 22), 712.
[27] „And they said out loud that God would have his vengeance on His Majesty and those of his Council, and that, so long as he should be in this world, he would be punished and would suffer adversity in his mind and in his life, which would not last long, and that his death would be hastened and brought forward from its due date by the said Huguenots", *Bourquin*, Haton (note 21), Vol. 2, 223.
[28] E. g. 2 Kings 9: 32–33 (again in the French Geneva Bible): „Ausquels il [Iehu] dit, Iettez-la [Iezebel] en bas. Et ils la jetterent: tellement qu'il y avait du sang d'icelle espandu à la paroy, et contre les chevaux, et la foulerent aux pieds [...]".
[29] „These doctors always forbade the people to undertake any uprising or sedition against the state of the king or the public repose of the patria", *Bourquin,* Haton (note 21), Vol. 2, 528.
[30] Calendar of State Papers Foreign (1568). London 1906, 516 (Norris to Elizabeth I).

to understand that he held the monarchy itself to blame for it. Catherine de Médicis and Charles IX, and with them the whole monarchical enterprise, were implicated in violence by the wars of religion, and (we should note) well before the terrible events of St Bartholomew's Eve, 1572.

Two testimonies of the phenomenon of violence in the French Reformation, briefly analysed – two among thousands. Before we return to the historiography, we should note an important reality about the contemporary histories of religious violence. They are asymmetric, just as Natalie Davis' understanding of the violence itself is asymmetric. We have next to no personal testimony from the perpetrators of religious violence, a total silence, apart from the occasional reported comment from someone in their cups. What we hear is mediated through the „I heard say" and (as in the case of the Claude Haton extract above) the „this is what happened elsewhere". From the victims of religious violence, too, the personal testimony is also thin. Some people were doubtless too traumatised to confront their experiences and commit them to paper. When they did, it was generally (a common experience for victims of „extreme violence" in other periods of history) a generation after the events when they had had time to put some perspective on what had happened.[31] In addition, as I have argued elsewhere, their relative silence was doubtless also because the fragments of personal experience which they had endured did not make up a comprehensible narrative that would answer the important, big, underlying questions in their minds – why had it happened? how many had perished? who had started it all?[32] Also, the civil wars were punctuated by periodic pacifications (1563; 1568; 1570; 1576; 1577; 1598) which granted an amnesty from prosecution for most crimes committed during the periods of hostility.[33] So there is no criminal record attesting to violence in the civil wars, and no truth and reconciliation commission afterwards either. Indeed, the pacifications without exception imposed upon the warring parties an obligation not to discuss, write about, document and remember, the traumatic events of the recent past. The celebrated first article of the edict of Nantes (but it is replicated in the earlier edicts) runs: „Que la

---

[31] For the problematic concept of „extreme violence" see *Jacques Sémelin*, Extreme Violence: can we Understand it?, in: International Social Sciences Journal 54, 2002, 429–431; also *Omer Bartov*, Extreme Violence and the Scholarly Community, in: ibid. 509–518.
[32] *Marc Greengrass*, Hidden Transcripts: Secret Histories and Personal Testimonies of Religious Violence in the French Wars of Religion, in: Mark Levene/Penny Roberts (Eds.), The Massacre in History. New York/Oxford 1999, 69–88. The argument is derived from *Denis Crouzet*, La Nuit de la Saint-Barthélemy: Un rêve perdu de la Renaissance. Paris 1994.
[33] For the issue, see *Marc Greengrass*, Amnistie et Oubliance: Un Discours Politique autour des Édits de Pacification pendant les Guerres de Religion, in: Paul Mironneau (Ed.), Paix des Armes, Paix des âmes. Paris 2000, 113–123.

mémoire de toutes choses passées d'une part et d'autre, depuis le commencement du mois de mars 1585 [...] demeurera éteinte et assoupie, comme de chose non advenue".[34] In 14 of its remaining 92 articles, the edict returned to the theme, seeking to prevent individuals from „refreshing the memory, attacking, injurying, provoking one another with reproaches for things past, no matter what the pretext or cause, disputing, contesting, quarrelling, taunting or offending one another by word or deed". The absolute monarchy sought to rewrite memory itself. So – and here is where the asymmetry in the written record appears – although the personal testimonies are few and far between, the „metahistory" of violence is two-a-penny-armchair pundit with an axe to grind, only too ready with comprehensive and comprehensible explanations for why religious violence had occurred. It was the fault of someone (the Guises; Catherine de Médicis: the wicked Italians: the Spaniards). It demonstrated that French society and institutions were corrupt and needed reform from top to bottom. And someone could tell you precisely how many had died in each locality and how many bodies had floated down the rivers.[35] The historical evidence is shaped in a curious way. It is, in truth, very unsatisfactory for the purposes of explaining religious violence, given that (as our two brief examples show) we are dealing with complex events, freighted with enormous „baggage".

Let us return now to the historiography because, although historians have readily agreed that religion provides a framework of explanation, they then disagree about how that framework actually works. And behind those disagreements lies a big underlying question about how our understanding of French religious violence explains its exceptionalism in the wider, comparative history of the European Reformation. Natalie Davis' explanation is in terms of religion equalling „cultural meaning". Since culture is concerned in part with symbols and meanings, violence is explained by the *religious meaning* of objects (buildings, texts, books, clothes, parts of the body, people ...) and behaviour (ways of expressing approval and disapproval, laughing with and against, sacralising and desacralising ...). The difficulty with an explanation dependent on religion as cultural meaning is that it conflates the question whether the violence is being *manifested* in religious terms, or whether it is being *caused* by religion.[36] It is a question of what kind of explanation we are being offered. And the question becomes still more delicate when one

---

[34] „That the memory of all things happening on both sides since the beginning of the month of March 1585 [...] will rest expunged and anaesthetized, as a non-event."
[35] The „somebody" in question is „N. Froumenteau", author of „Le secret des finances de France, descouvert et départi en trois livres [...]" (1581), the pseudonym being often attributed to the Dauphinois physician Nicolas Barnaud.
[36] The point is made in the context of the violence of the French Revolution period by *Claude Langlois*, De la violence religieuse, in: French Historical Studies 21, 1998, 113–123.

considers that what constitutes „religion" was itself the subject of change in the sixteenth century. That introduces into the equation a dynamic which has been used by other historians to help to „explain" the violence in the French context. One way in which historians have understood that change has been inspired by John Bossy's encapsulation of it. Catholics tended to see religion as a „body of believers", a worshipping community, invested with meaning by historic place, by its structural role within a traditional world order.[37] Describing Paris on the eve of the wars of religion in terms of its „fabric" of catholic processional rituals, Barbara Diefendorf describes the city as „the body social, the body politic, and the body of Christ [...] so closely interwined as to be inseparable".[38] Explaining the significance of the famous „Affair of the Placards" of 1534, Mack Holt emphasizes the social implications of an attack on the sacramental character of the mass, an attack not simply on the cultural meaning of the mass but on its functioning, structural reality as a focus of communal reconciliation and social embodiment.[39] Protestants, by contrast, evolved into seeing religion as a „body of beliefs", a „credal community" that did not necessarily map onto any pre-existent social entity. The protestant social entity laid claim to meaning and relevance to its adherents with reference to God's word and the activity of God's providence in the world. That body of beliefs created a different sense of community, disjoined from the past, a new Jerusalem (Geneva?) with a stronger sense of social discipline – all components of a distinctive structural solidity. The violence of the French civil wars becomes a confrontation between two different ways of understanding belief. This explanatory pattern has the advantage of being a *dynamic* explanation, dependent on religion as *cultural structure* rather than *cultural meaning*.[40] A cultural structure is one in which coherent patterns of culture have causal social significance – as Max Weber argued almost a century ago – an underlying cultural „logic" in which events parallel one another and play out in dramas at different times and places, but with similar plots, creating a cultural phenomenon that we are justified in regarding as an ideal type (in this instance: „religious violence").

Another approach to understanding this „logic" has been to apply the more modern notion of „ideology". The French protestant Reformation is a case-study of the „beginnings of ideology" for Donald Kelley, reverse-engineering the „end of ideology" arguments of American political theorists of

---

[37] *John Bossy*, Christianity and the West. Oxford 1985, 170f.
[38] *Diefendorf*, Beneath the Cross (note 24), 48.
[39] *Mack P. Holt*, The French Wars of Religion, 1562–1629. Cambridge 1995, 19f.
[40] I draw the distinction from *John R. Hall*, Cultural Meanings and Cultural Structures in Historical Explanation, in: History and Theory 39, 2000, 331–347, and implicitly, too, from *John R. Hall/Philip D. Schuyler/Sylvaine Trinh*, Apocalypse Observed: Religious Movements and Violence in North America, Europe and Japan. New York 2000.

the 1950s and 1960s.⁴¹ He began his book by pointing out that the word „ideology" was first coined in English by John Adams, Vice-President of the new United States, reflecting on the French Revolution through the „model" of a similar situation in the historical past afforded by the wars of religion.⁴² He then proceeded to provide a model of the dynamic formation of ideology as a „cultural structure", from the moment of conception through growing outward concentric circles of sociability, creating and reinforcing a distinctive „consciousness" as it grows. The last stage is the creation of a party to defend the ideological „cause", with all the divisive and violent consequences that were witnessed in the wars of religion.

If the French Reformation was about ideology, Calvin was its ideologue. Donald Kelley's book rather side-steps the huge „problem" of Calvin. What is the Calvin „problem"? Why are we still struggling – the recent crop of historical studies and biographies witness to it – with Calvin?⁴³ It is not an absence of relevant material; after 1536 we are superabundantly provided for by Calvin himself in his writings, sermons, commentaries, correspondence and, of course, „The Institutes of the Christian Religion". He tells us, and in detail, about his anxieties, his aspirations, his methods, his views on every subject under (and including) the sun. It is partly that Calvin's patterns of thought and methods of exposition are not those of an ideologue. His major work is like a highway under permanent construction – growing and evolving its shape over a period of over twenty years until its final rewriting in the published version of 1559. Calvin explicitly draws on humanist pedagogical traditions. There are many fundamental questions to which we, as humans, have no ultimate answer – beyond those which God has given us, and which we must accept on trust. „Docta ignorantia" is hardly the by-line for an ideologue. Telling people the answer is not the answer either. They must be „persuaded" of the truth – by all the human arts of rhetoric and persuasion, „led" to it by clear, delineated paths in which the labyrinths of confusion (and sin) into which human beings so readily fall can be avoided. So the „Institutes of the Christian Religion" have a remarkable chameleon-like quality. They can be read as a „confession of faith" – which is how they had begun life – some rudiments of the true faith, offered humbly to François I, king of France. But they can also be read (as Calvin intended them to be read) as a „sure guide",

---

[41] *Donald R. Kelley*, The Beginning of Ideology. Cambridge 1981.
[42] Ibid. 1f.
[43] Major biographical studies, by no means agreeing in their interpretation and approach but tending to nuance the received, austere picture of Calvin, over the past fifteen years include (the list is inevitably arbitrary): *William J. Bouwsma*, John Calvin. A Sixteenth-Century Portrait. New York 1988; *Bernard Cottret*, Calvin. Paris 1995; *Olivier Maillet* (Ed.), Calvin et ses contemporains. Geneva 1998; *Denis Crouzet*, Jean Calvin: vies parallèles. Paris 2000.

of „utility" to Christians precisely because they contain an orthodoxy. This was how Calvin put it in the 1541 edition:

„car, en ce faisant, je leur monstreray le but auquel ilz devront tendre et diriger leur intention en le lisant. Combien que la saincte Escriture contienne une doctrine parfaicte, à laquelle on ne peut rien adjouster, comme en icelle nostre Seigneur a voulu desployer les Thrésors infiniz de sa Sapience, toutesfois une personne qui n'y sera pas fort exercité[e] a bon mestier de quelque conduicte et addresse pour sçavoir ce qu'elle y doibt chercher, à fin de ne [s']egarer point ça et là, mais de tenir une certaine voye, pour attaindre toujours à la fin où le Sainct Esprit l'appelle."[44]

Calvin the pedagogue (and his preoccupation with the necessity for a visible church, with powers to discipline its community of believers was another facet of his pedagogy: the church as schoolroom) disguised Calvin the ideologue within a structure of thought that was deliberately anti-systematic. Calvin, we might say, was an *ideologue caché*.

What has Calvin to say about violence? He was, of course, opposed to it. It had no limits or boundaries. It opened the door to the abyss of human iniquity. It represented human passions uncontrolled by reason and the workings of the soul. It undermined legitimate authority, itself created by God in order to cement the boundaries and limits of human sin. But that was hardly the end of the matter. In Geneva, Calvin faced criticism for using the „violence" of the state against tender consciences – specifically the conscience of Sébastien Castellion.[45] And, if it was a question of state violence, then what about those who were willing to die in its prisons and on its gibbets for their beliefs? Calvin was in a perpetual dialogue from 1541 through to 1560 with them.[46] He willingly drew on the hagiographical traditions of the early church to call them „martyrs" for the faith. Suffering for the faith occupied a central place in the French protestant Reformation. Already in the first edition of the *Institutes*, Calvin had exhorted the faithful, reflecting the language

---

[44] „For, in doing this, I shall show them the purpose to which they ought to bend and direct their intention whilst reading it [Calvin's book]. Although Holy Scripture contains a perfect doctrine, to which one can add nothing, since in it our Lord has meant to display the infinite treasures of his wisdom, yet a person who has not much practice in it has good reason for some guidance and direction, to know what he ought to look for in it, in order not to wander hither and thither, but to hold to a sure path, that he may always be pressing toward the end to which the Holy Spirit calls him"; *Jean Calvin*, Institution de la Religion chrestienne. Ed. Jacques Pannier. 4 Vols. Paris 1936, Vol. 1, 3–4. For the English translation, see *J. T. McNeill/F. L. Battles* (Eds.), Institutes of the Christian Religion. 2 Vols. London 1961, Vol. 1, 6.
[45] See the interesting recent study of the Castellion affair by *Stefan Zweig*, originally published in German, but which I know through its French translation: Conscience contre violence ou Castellion contre Calvin. Bègles 1997.
[46] Brilliantly analysed in *David El-Kenz*, Les Bûchers du roi: la culture protestante des martyrs (1525–1572). Paris 1997, ch. 4–5.

of the Pauline epistles, that „ce pendant qu'ils habitent en terre, soyent comme brebis destinées à la boucherie, à fin d'estre faictz conformes à leurs Chef Jesus Christ".[47] In its pages, he offered a means by which they could live through these earthly tribulations and win the assurance of being one of the elect. In the last chapter of the original edition of the „Institutes", entitled „De la vie chrestienne", Calvin explored the paradox that God had placed us on this earth, but with a desire to be reunited with Christ. We live with two lives, one „entombed" here on earth, which we must suffer; the other being a life promised us in heaven, but which we can scarcely conceive of, let alone grasp. Martyrdom was an extreme form of living that paradox. In his occasional writings, mostly destined for a French audience, Calvin dwelt on suffering as a way by which members of the true church were to be distinguished from the false church. He tended to avoid the use of the word „martyr". Exile was a Christian response to unholy power. But so too was passive resistance. Through it, the faithful would discover that poverty was power; that spiritual courage was not sedition; that nicodemism (those who wanted to have it both ways, to outwardly conform but inwardly be one of the true church) was no answer; and that persecution had to be accepted as part of God's mysterious providence. In his copious surviving correspondence with those in France the martyr was evoked increasingly not as an abstract and distant conceptual device but as a real and present actuality, which (by the late 1540s) they most certainly were. In the famous letters exchanged with the martyrs of Lyon (1553), Chambéry (1555) and the rue Saint-Jacques in Paris (1557), intended initially for scribal publication only, but published for the first time by Jean Crespin in successive editions of his „Livre des Martyrs", Calvin had no hesitation about using the words „martyr", or indeed that of „tyrant". By 1559, in a letter addressed „To the Faithful in France", Calvin wrote:

„Apprenez donc, mes frères, que c'est la vraye saison de vous escrire, quand le feu des persécutions est allumé, et quand la pauvre Eglise de Dieu est alarmée jusques au bout. Nous voyons que les bons martyrs ont eu ceste coutume entre eux, d'estre d'autant plus vigilans à s'inciter par sainctes admonitions, selon qu'ils voyoient que les tyrans faisoyent tous leurs efforts pour ruyner la chrestienté".[48]

---

[47] „so long as they inhabit the earth, they should be as sheep destined for the slaughter, in order that they be made conformable to their Head, Jesus Christ", *Calvin*, Institution (note 44), Vol. 4, 287 [Bk 4, ch. 17].

[48] „Learn then, my brethren, that this is the true time to write to you, when the persecution fires have been kindled, and when the poor Church of God has been thoroughly shaken. We see then that the good martyrs of old held this custom, to be still more vigilant to sustain one another with holy admonitions, in accordance with what they saw as the tyrants bending all their efforts to bring Christianity to ruination." *Jules Bonnet* (Ed.), Lettres de Jean Calvin, recueillies pour la première fois et publiées d'après les manuscrits originaux par Jules Bonnet. Lettres françaises. Paris 1854, Vol. 2, 298f.

Calvin was not in favour of violence; but passive resistance was a means of demonstrating the violence of others – in this instance, the judicial state of Valois France. That demonstration „inverted", to use the language of David El-Kenz, the judicial state by questioning its fundamental *raison d'être*: that royal justice was not in the image of God, that it was a pseudo-justice. Garnering the stories from those arriving in Geneva and their contacts as best he could, Crespin set about making his martyrology a series of dubious arrests, illegal imprisonments, dramatic court-room scenes and, finally, indelibly described and moving death-scenes.[49] The image of Christ was not on the bench, but in the dock. Here is Crespin's description of the interrogation of Aymon de La Voye, a protestant who was tortured before the investigating magistrate in order to reveal his accomplices. Exhausted, La Voye borrowed the words of Christ on the Cross: „Seigneur, Seigneur, pourquoi m'as-tu laissé?"[50] The magistrate recognized what was happening and replied, in Crespin's account: „Meschant Lutherien, c'est toi qui as delaissé Dieu".[51] But La Voye has his reply ready: „Hélas, messieurs, pourquoi me tourmentez-vous tant? Seigneur, veuilles leur pardonner, car ils ne savent ce qu'ils font".[52] There was a profound subversion at work here; a delegitimation of justice. The condemned criminal (and royal edicts had increasingly equated heresy with criminality) was transformed into a suffering hero. The invitation was to condemn the monarchy itself. For justice was in the king's name and Henri II, king of France (1547–1559) had made sure that he was associated at every level with the pursuit of heresy, even attending an *auto-da-fé* of a protestant in Paris on 4 July 1549. And the last great protestant show trial before the civil wars was the most controversial of all; the trial of a sovereign court judge at the Parlement of Paris in 1559, Anne du Bourg. In the latter's speech in his own defence, printed in 1560, Anne du Bourg openly invited the judges to assume their role as enforcers of justice, even against the king himself:

„Et vous, accordez avec eux, ô Messieurs! C'est pour quoy nous ne voulons point vous obeir, et si par ce moyen nous vous obeissons. Or que pour cela vous nous condamniez d'estre rebelles à nostre Prince, aucunement vous ne pouvez ne devez ainsi inferer. Car

---

[49] For the subversion by protestants of the rituals of spectacles of suffering, the commonplace of sixteenth-century judicial execution, see *David Nicholls*, The Theatre of Martyrdom in the French Reformation, in: Past and Present 121, 1988, 49–73.
[50] „Lord, lord, why hast thou forsaken me?"
[51] „Wicked Lutheran, it is you who has deserted God".
[52] „Alas, Sirs, why do you thus torment me? Lord, have mercy on them, for they know not what they do"; *Jean Crespin*, Histoire des Martyrs persecutez et mis a mort pour la verité de l'Evangile, depuis le temps des apostres jusques a present. Ed. par Daniel Benoît et accompagné de notes par Matthieu Lelièvre. Reedition of the Geneva, P. Aubert edition of 1619, being the work of Jean Crespin, continued by Simon Goulart. 3 Vols. Toulouse 1885–1888, Vol. 1, [book III], 349.

qui a fait Roy nostre Prince, et qui luy a baillé auctorité sur tant de peuple? N'a-ce pas esté le grand Seigneur de tous les Roys? L'auroit-il placé en un tel lieu pour luy contrevenir, l'exemptant de garder ce qu'il a commandé à toutes les nations, au ciel et à la terre? Par cela je conclus que le Roy nostre Prince est subjet, et tous les siens, aux commandements du souverain Roy, et commet luy mesme crime de lese majesté, s'il determine quelque chose contre la volonté de son Roy et le nostre, et par ainsi coulpable de mort, s'il persiste en une erreur qu'il devroit condamner".[53]

It was exactly these sentiments that inspired the Regicides a century later to do exactly as he said, and put to death the „man of blood", Charles Stuart, king of England in the course of another „war of religion", at least as some historians have seen it. But we should note in passing that Anne du Bourg's speech, if this was indeed what he had said, was too strong for the stomachs of the protestant publicists. As David El-Kenz shrewdly noticed, Pierre de La Place edited that part of it out when he came to publish it in his „Commentaires sur l'estat de la Religion et République" in 1565; and Crespin, probably not aware of the omission, also cited it without that passage. There is a strong tension in the surviving printed material from the wars of religion between what it dares to tell us, and what is being thought, talked about on the streets, and had been experienced in people's lives. We must work from the assumption that the violence about which we hear is only a fraction of what was perpetrated, and that was only a fraction of what was thought.

The search for an underlying cultural „logic" to religious violence in the French wars of religion led Denis Crouzet to the thesis underlying his remarkable two-volume work: „Les Guerriers de Dieu (The Warriors of God)", published in 1990.[54] In this work, Crouzet argued that religious violence must be viewed as the expression of a deep apocalyptic anxiety in French culture, a collective fear of the end of the world that had developed decades before the violence actually manifested itself.[55] He started by exploring the mental world of „traditional" catholic France, locating the notion that the world would shortly come to an end in a structure of belief in which

---

[53] „And you [my fellow judges], you agree with them [these persecutors], O Sirs, this is why we do not want to obey you, and thus, by this means, we obey you [all the same]. Since, for that [disobedience] you will condemn us to be a rebel to our prince, something which cannot and ought not to be inferred at all. For, who made the King our Prince, and who gave him such authority over so many people? Was it not the great Lord of all the Kings? Would he have placed him in such an office to contradict him, exempting him from the obligation to keep his commandments, imposed upon all the nations, in heaven and in earth? By that, I conclude that the King, our Prince, along with all his servants, is subject to the commands of the sovereign King of Kings, and commits the crime of high treason if he decides something contradictory to the King of King's will, and thus should face the death penalty if he persists in an error which should be condemned".

[54] *Denis Crouzet*, Les guerriers de Dieu: la violence au temps des troubles de religion vers 1525 – vers 1610. 2 vols. Paris 1990.

[55] For a summary in English of Crouzet's arguments, see *Marc Greengrass*, The Psychology of Religious Violence, in: French History 5, 1991, 467–474.

holy power was immanent, engaged mystically and prophetically in a struggle against the forces of darkness. Looking back to the period before the protestant Reformation – to around 1480 – he identified a renewed concern (to the point of collective obsession) with divine judgement and the Last Days. It was expressed in non-political and political modes and ran in self-sustaining cycles in which preachers and the new printing medium acted as critical points in the spiral. We may take a rough analogy to the process which he envisages in the heightened fear of crime in many contemporary western societies (despite the fact that the crime statistics suggest that the reality does not justify the apprehensions), fears which are fed and channelled by tabloid journalism and media sensationalism and lead to greater criminalisation with, as a consequence, a greater level of crime. The analogy has to be adapted, though, because people were conditioned to think of themselves as under, and responsible for, God's judgment. Judicial astrology, popularized in printed almanacs and prognosticons, miracle pamphlets and prodigy literature, published sermons and speeches advertising the cosmic significance of the Turkish menace, the Black Arts of witchcraft and necromancy, the advent of syphilis in Europe provided exempla for which the only appropriate response was abject penitence (the contemporary antonym of „extreme violence"). The coming of the new protestant heresy was simply a summative fear, a fear embracing all fears. They were the false prophets of the Apocalypse, prophets whom God commanded must be destroyed in the end time. Through it, this „conscience eschatalogique" was mobilized by a „littérature panique", exemplified for Crouzet by the writings of the excitable Parisian preachers and publicists like Artus Désiré, François Le Picart, and Claude Haton's esteemed rôle-model, Pierre Dyvolé. The result was a violence that was unchained by an inescapable logic, an inextricable fear, a violence which liberated people from their fears in events, where they transgressed normal boundaries of social behaviour because they were behaving like puppets, God having sanctioned them to be his ministering angels.

This was one „logic", one way of explaining the violence. But Crouzet's account has also to take into account the rise of Calvinist Protestantism in Reformation France. This provides yet another impulsive logic, leading to another, distinctive form of violence. Calvin offered anxious believers a release from their fears by creating a new sense of a providential order. Calvin rejected judicial astrology, prognostication, divination and millenarianism. His belief system was fundamentally different. Holy power was not immanent in the world, fighting with the forces of darkness. World order came from the laws of nature, imposed by God the Curator, dictating a Providence which predestined its history and our salvation in ways that we could not hope to, and did not need to, comprehend. Calvinist theology provided a „désangoissement" from the spiral of anxiety which afflicted France in the sixteenth century. Its violence was „human", „rationalistic" and „cool". It attacked images because Calvinists did not accept the semiotics of catholic holy power. This iconoclasm spread towards other aspects of power too. Preachers were interrupted during sermons, clergy mocked in the streets, catholic processions held up to ridicule. The Roman church was portrayed as a world of „fools", „dogs", „beasts", „ravening wolves" etc. Parody, carnival, charivari were harnessed by protestants to desacralize the traditional religion and liberate people from its ruses. The priests were the inevitable victims, and the gruesome rituals of their suffering took on the gestures and images appropriate to the mocking of their animal lusts before the people.

Crouzet's thesis is a *tour de force*; an attempt at an explanation of a phenomenon of religious violence which measures up to the phenomenon, and takes account of the internal dynamics behind it. His understanding of protestant iconoclasm has been substantiated by the detailed investigations of Olivier Christin.[56] But how much has, in reality, been explained? Not, it seems, the exceptionalism of French violence. For, if the underlying tensions that he identified in the culture of France on the eve of the Reformation were as instrumental as we are told, it is implausible that similar tensions did not exist elsewhere in Europe and with a similar impact. And, indeed, they can all be readily documented from similar evidence in other parts of western Europe, including those where the Reformation had a very divisive impact. So the question becomes whether, within French culture, there was not some particular mechanism by which such tensions were highlighted. The spotlight inevitably falls upon the „dangerous vocation" of the catholic preachers and popular reactions to what they said, wrote and printed.[57] A detailed study of the surviving sermons of one for whom the evidence is most plentiful – Pierre le Picart – suggests that his undoubted popularity came from his being banished from Paris for seditious preaching in 1534, for some scarcely-veiled and sensational attacks on those at the French court who were known to favour the new ideas, and for his commitment to the reform of the church, rather than his eschatological or millenarian views.[58] Perhaps, as Luc Racaut suggests in an important recent study, it was more the power of focusing traditional stereotypes of the alien „other" in society upon the protestants, a process that involved lay and clerical input alike, that was more important than the eschatological dimensions empha-

---

[56] *Olivier Christin*, Une révolution symbolique. L'iconoclasme huguenot et la reconstruction catholique. Paris 1991
[57] The term is taken from *Larissa Taylor*, Dangerous Vocations: Preaching in France in the late Middle Ages and Reformation, in: idem (Ed.), Preachers and People in the Reformations and Early-Modern Period. Leiden 2001, 91–124.
[58] *Larissa Taylor*, Heresy and Orthodoxy in Sixteenth-Century Paris. François Le Picart and the Beginnings of the Catholic Reformation. Leiden 1999.

sised by Crouzet.[59] And, when it comes to the mobilising power of the printing press, we have to take into account the significant fact that the numbers of sermons being printed in France were in considerable decline in the years from 1530 to 1560, in comparison to the tens of thousands in the years before.[60] Only the analysis of the surviving imprints from French presses for the years from 1559–1600, currently being undertaken at the French Book Project under the direction of Andrew Pettegree, will begin to assist us in seeing whether the patterns of publication among the impressive production from catholic presses in those years give us any clues as to what was creating a spiral of violence in France that did not exist in, for example, the Netherlands in the 1560s.

That said, if we rely simply on the problem of violence as the creation of a collective psychology, we will have ignored the important political, institutional and social context in which it occurred. That context is evident to us in the example from Claude Haton's diary that we analysed above. The preachers whom Haton knew as his friends were independent-minded and voluble. They expressed themselves graphically and they were used to attacking people in high places. The Dominican Pierre Dyvollé was renowned for it. In his sermons on the Mass, delivered at Chartres in 1558, Dyvollé used the language of war, evoking the „heretics and infidels" who corrupted the faith and the invisible „devils" who do so by subtly introducing corruption from within. Satan reigned in the church, holding the world in blindness and the Great Dragon of the Book of Revelation had come upon them all.[61] When he came to preach at Advent in Provins in 1560, the news of the „Tumult" of Amboise was fresh in all their ears. Haton recalled that Dyvollé predicted an imminent, great conflict, in which the protestants would raise arms against God, the catholic religion, the king and the public peace of the kingdom, „desolant les villes, saccageant les eglises, temples et les prebstres, tascheant à abolir toute vraye religion, lois ecclesiastiques, politicques et civilles, tous sacremens et service divin; et commant, par leur orgueil, ilz prendroient les armes au poing pour exterminer le roy et son Estat, ensemble tout le peuple catholicque".[62]

---

[59] *Luc Racaut*, Hatred in Print. Catholic Propaganda and Protestant Identity during the French Wars of Religion. Aldershot 2002; cf. *idem*, Religious Polemic and Huguenot Self-Perception and Identity, 1554–1619, in: Raymond A. Mentzer/Andrew Spicer (Eds.), Society and Culture in the Huguenot World, 1559–1685. Cambridge 2002, 29–43.
[60] See *Larissa Taylor*, Out of Print: The Decline of Catholic Printed Sermons in France, 1530–1560, in: Robin Barnes (Ed.), Books Have Their Own Destinies. Essays in Honor of Robert V. Schnucker. Kirksville 1998, 121–129.
[61] *Pierre Dyvollé*, Dix sermons de la Saincte Messe et de ceremonies d'icelle. Paris 1577, 470–472.
[62] „despoiling towns, ransacking churches, temples and priests, seeking to abolish all true religion, ecclesiastical, political and civil laws, all sacraments and divine worship; and how, through their pride, they would take up arms to exterminate the king and his state, and all the catholics as well"; *Bourquin,* Haton (note 21), Vol. 1, 171f.

Moses and David had protected the people of Israel against the Philistines. Would the French monarchy do the same? With the aid of passages of the Old Testament, his voice rang out: „Maulditte soyt la terre qui a ung jeune enfant pour son roy! Mauldit soit le royaulme qui a des princes qui sont desloyaux et compaignons des larrons, et qui ne font aulcun jugement des larrons!"[63] In the congregation were the *bailli* of Provins and his *lieutenant*, representatives of the king's justice, witnesses to bare-faced provocation and incitement. But what were they to do? They were, as Dyvollé well knew, crypto-protestants themselves, intensely vulnerable to charges of belonging to those behind the Tumult of Amboise. When they tried to collect evidence against Dyvollé, no one would come forward to testify as to what he had said. The next time he rose in the pulpit it was to electrify his congregation by repeating the same words, offering to write them down with his own hand, in his own blood. But, he continued, „je voy bien que les huguenotz de ceste ville ne sont que des bestes; car s'ilz estoient sçavans, ilz trouveroient en l'Escriture saincte les parolles que j'è ditte et ne peseroient, comme ilz font, que je les eusse inventée de moy mesme".[64] The poor *bailli* sought help from the king, but he found himself humiliated by the duke of Guise. Why had he not collected any incriminating evidence against the preacher, the duke asked him in front of the king? „Tu es donc de ceux qui veulent troubler le roy et le royaume? Tu es donc huguenot? Va t'en quant tu vouldras, je te marque.' Ledit bailli fust si honteux qu'il eust volu estre entre les jambes de sa femme".[65] The point here is the politics of violence, played out on a local stage with a national backdrop, by individuals with reputations to lose and lots at stake. The French civil wars became indissociably *about* that politics, albeit politics shot through, within and without, with religious meaning.

That political context is clearest in the case of the St Bartholomew massacre itself, the epitome of extreme violence in the French wars of religion, a determining moment in French politics and for the destiny of the protestant Reformation in France itself. We shall never know what it was all about; and some of the recent debates have generated more heat than light; certainly not a great deal more evidence.[66] What we can be reasonably sure of is that

---

[63] „Cursed be the land which has a young child for its king! Cursed be the kingdom which has disloyal princes in it, with robbers as companions, whom they do not denounce"; *Bourquin*, Haton (note 21), Vol. 1, 171f.
[64] „I see clearly that the Huguenots of this town are quite stupid; for, if they were wise, they would have looked up in holy scripture the words that I pronounced and would not have thought, as they do, that I had invented them by myself".
[65] „'So you are one of those who want to trouble the king and the kingdom then? So you are a Huguenot? Be on your way, I have my eye on you.' The said *bailli* was so ashamed that he wanted to shelter between the legs of his wife."
[66] See *Jean-Louis Bourgeon*, „Les légendes ont la vie dure: à propos de la Saint-Barthélemy et de quelques livres récents, in: Revue d'histoire moderne et contempo-

the attempted assassination of Coligny had its roots in a „pratique", a „plot" in the language of French sixteenth-century aristocrats.[67] Who was behind it, and how that „pratique" went out of control is the essence of the debate; its eventual manifestation and consequences are mostly not in doubt. The French monarchy became directly implicated in violence. It had blood on its own hands; and the dream of the reconciliation of „opposites" through the operation of a neo-Platonic royal magic, if that was what Catherine de Médicis and Charles IX had been about in the years before 1572, was in tatters, a „lost dream".[68] France had to wait a generation for those with clean hands – like the king of Navarre, someone who was manifestly an unwilling witness and victim rather than a participant – to rebuild the fortunes of that monarchy.

But the violence is also about an institutional and a social context. It involved, as we have seen, the French judicial state and its judges. Their role in society was quite different from that of, say, the municipal magistrates in the Netherlands. Julian Woltjer may therefore be right to suggest that some of the difference between the Netherlands and France in patterns of violence lies in the different institutional allegiances of the judiciary.[69] Behind the institutional context lies the social context too. Here, we should return briefly to the example of the protestants of Gien, caught up in the social tensions of a small town with a rural hinterland of *vignerons* who hated the townies. There *were* social tensions in the violence of the French wars of religion, and they are not simply the consequences of the civil wars. They go back before the wars – to urban factionalism and the dispute over who paid *taille* in the case of the Carnival at Romans that turned very nasty in 1580, to the suppression of the Vaudois and a nobility that came back from Italy determined to blame someone and change things in the case of Provence on the eve of the civil wars, to a deep-seated anti-seigneurialism in the south-west in the case of the famous and much-advertised assassination of the baron de Fumel, again on the eve of the civil wars.[70] Woltjer may be correct to suggest

---

raine 34, 1987, 102–116; *Jean-Louis Bourgeon*, L'assassinat de Coligny. Geneva 1992, and the resulting controversy.
[67] For the „form" and curious ways by which a court „pratique" manifested itself, see the important new work by *Xavier Le Person*, „Pratiques" et „Pratiquers". La vie politique à la fin du règne de Henri III (1584–1589). Geneva 2002.
[68] This is the challenging interpretation of *Crouzet*, La Nuit de la Saint-Barthélemy (note 32), by far the best account of the massacre that we have.
[69] *J. J. Woltjer*, Violence during the Wars of Religion in France and the Netherlands: a Comparison, in: Nederlands Archief voor Kerkgeschiedenis 76, 1996, 26–45.
[70] See *Emmanuel Le Roy Ladurie*, Le Carnaval de Romans. De la chandeleur au mercredi des Cendres, 1579–1580. Paris 1979; for Provence, see *Woltjer*, Violence (note 69); for the Baron de Fumel, the recent thèse d'habilitation at the University of Paris-I of Professor Serge Brunet (December 2003) provides important evidence to place the affair in the anti-seigneurial conflicts of the region.

that one of the key differences between the Dutch and French context for religious violence in this period lay in the greater adaptability of the Dutch urban environment, its magistrates with great authority to mediate conflicts before they grew out of hand. Violence, like a chameleon, wore the colours of its surroundings. In the case of the French Reformation, there is a long and respectable tradition, stretching back to Henri Hauser at the beginning of the twentieth century, which has interpreted the French Reformation in terms of its underlying social tensions. Even though we find the tensions difficult to generalize about, they are there when we look at the local level.[71] And it was at the local level that the violence of the French Reformation, and what eventually contained it, has been most profitably analysed and discussed.

---

[71] For important recent studies analysing violence in a local or regional context, see *Philip Benedict*, Rouen during the Wars of Religion. Cambridge 1981; *Penny Roberts*, A City in Conflict. Troyes during the French Wars of Religion. Manchester 1996; *Mark Konnert*, Civic Agendas and Religious Passion: Châlons-sur-Marne during the French Wars of Religion, 1560–1594. Kirksville 1996; *Kevin C. Robbins*, City on the Ocean Sea. La Rochelle, 1530–1650. Leiden 1997.

Traditional Politics and Visionary Theology: the English Reformation

By

Ralph Houlbrooke

Hardly ever during the English Reformation was the vision of reforming theologians completely shared by governments motivated by more traditional political concerns. As a result, the „unofficial" Reformation of the visionary vanguard was almost always out of step with the „official" Reformation of governments. It is also difficult to see the English Reformation as the natural culmination of protracted later medieval developments. The Church in later medieval England manifested both considerable strengths and serious weaknesses. The need for renewal and reform had been felt to varying degrees within the western Church throughout the Middle Ages. It was clearly perceived in several different quarters of the Church in England in the early sixteenth century. Could the necessary changes have been undertaken within the framework of existing institutions, or was a more fundamental transformation necessary? No firm conclusions can be built on counterfactual speculation. There are however good reasons for thinking that the Catholic Church in England was capable of a considerable measure of self-reformation, given royal and papal encouragement and co-operation.

Since the fourteenth century, England had had its own heretical movement, largely inspired by the Oxford theologian John Wycliffe (d. 1384). Late fourteenth-century circumstances, notably the Great Schism, war with France, and parliamentary hostility to some aspects of papal authority, had helped to prevent the immediate suppression of Wycliffite ideas. They had indeed spread as far as Bohemia and influenced Jan Hus. They had attracted several influential English knights. Proceedings against one powerful heretical knight, Sir John Oldcastle, had provoked a rebellion in 1414. This had proved a turning point. Facing resolute royal hostility, cut off from the universities, and deprived of upper class support, the so-called „Lollard" heretics had become an underground movement of the middle and lower ranks of society. The Lollards were above all hostile to all forms of what they saw as idolatry, especially the mass and transubstantiation, sacramentals, images, relics, shrines and pilgrimages. Open access to the Bible was for them the basis of sound belief; Lollard translations of parts of the Vulgate circulated in manuscript. The Lollards were widely scattered through southern England, as the major studies by J. A. F. Thomson and Anne Hudson reveal particularly clearly, but their strategy of partial conformity makes it difficult to estimate their strength accurately. Early sixteenth-century persecutions uncovered major surviving Lollard clusters. These heretics, however, seldom revealed millenarian attitudes, much less any aspirations towards political activism. They had no discernible political influence.[1]

The evangelical Protestantism which began to influence England during the 1520s differed in important respects from Lollardy, especially in its distinctive doctrine of justification by faith. There was however sufficient overlap for evangelical preachers and books to find an audience in surviving Lollard groups. The foremost evangelical was William Tyndale (1494?-1536), an outstanding biblical scholar, whose English translation of the New Testament, drawing on the work of Erasmus and Luther, was finished and published at Worms (1526). Tyndale's theology was strongly influenced by Luther, but he also respected Wycliffe and his conception of the eucharist came to resemble Zwingli's more closely than Luther's. Evangelical ideas penetrated London and the universities as well as some areas where Lollardy was strong. Lollards and evangelicals were nevertheless far too few and lacking in powerful patrons during the 1520s to have set a national Reformation in train.[2]

Catholicism enjoyed strong support at every level of English society on the eve of the Reformation, as has recently been demonstrated by the work of Eamon Duffy in particular. This support showed itself above all in loyalty to the parish church and in the endowment of masses and prayers for the dead. Churches all over the country were being rebuilt, extended, redecorated and re-equipped during the decades before the Reformation. The celebration of masses for the dead was either a central purpose of, or a duty linked with, a huge number of institutions, ranging from parish fraternities to schools, almshouses, hospitals and university colleges. Despite Lollard criticisms, the images and shrines of a host of saints still attracted widespread devotion. Recruitment to the ranks of the clergy was buoyant on the very eve of the Reformation.[3]

---

[1] *K. B. McFarlane,* John Wycliffe and the Beginnings of English Nonconformity. London 1952; *idem,* Lancastrian Kings and Lollard Knights. Oxford 1972; *A. G. Dickens,* Lollards and Protestants in the Diocese of York, 1509-1558. Hull 1959, London 1982; *John A. F. Thomson,* The Later Lollards, 1414-1520. London 1965; *Margaret Aston,* Lollards and Reformers: Images and Literacy in Late Medieval Religion. London 1984; *Anne Hudson,* The Premature Reformation: Wycliffite Texts and Lollard History. Oxford 1988.
[2] *J. F. Mozley,* William Tyndale. London 1937; *A. G. Dickens,* The English Reformation. London 1964, 68–82; *William A. Clebsch,* England's Earliest Protestants, 1520-1535. New Haven/London 1964; *Susan Brigden,* London and the Reformation. Oxford 1989, 82-128; *David Daniell,* William Tyndale: A Biography. New Haven/London 1994.
[3] *John J. Scarisbrick,* The Reformation and the English People. Oxford 1984, 1-39; *Eamon Duffy,* The Stripping of the Altars: Traditional Religion in England, c. 1400–c. 1580. New Haven/London 1992, 1-376; *Felicity Heal,* Reformation in Britain and Ireland. Oxford 2003, 65.

Doubtless the English Church had its weaknesses. The life of many monasteries, especially the middling and smaller ones, was stagnant. Some were in a parlous state. Many of the abler clergy in the middle and upper ranks of the Church were involved in secular as well as ecclesiastical administration. This involvement, the linked problems of pluralism and non-residence, and the inadequacy of many parochial benefices, meant that pastoral duties were all too often discharged by poorly educated and badly paid stipendiary priests. A number of churchmen, however, saw the need to improve clerical education and endowed new schools or university colleges or promoted their foundation. Christian humanism strongly influenced several outstanding members of this group. Such men readily embraced its commitment to the renewal of Christian life in the light of more dependable and better understood biblical and patristic sources. Erasmus had several friends among senior churchmen in England, including John Colet, John Fisher, and Richard Fox. Such men, Richard Rex reminds us, supported in principle Erasmus's aim of a new and trustworthy vernacular Bible, as distinct from unreliable Lollard translations. The potential for reform was illustrated in striking fashion by a man who was not himself a respected humanist, albeit an acquaintance of Erasmus. Thomas Wolsey, cardinal and legate *a latere,* issued legatine statutes for the two most important monastic orders, and later closed down nearly thirty weak religious houses and used their revenues to found a school and university college. On the eve of his fall in 1529 he received wide new powers to dissolve monasteries and convert their resources to different purposes, including the foundation of cathedrals. Wolsey's reforming credentials, sympathetically presented by his biographer Peter Gwyn, were alas all too seriously compromised by the fact that he embodied to a quite exceptional degree some of the clergy's most notorious faults, including pluralism, non-residence and unchastity. He was however (as Gwyn insists) the king's servant first and foremost, and the dominant position of this rather unsuitable man within the English church was due above all to the king's influence. Wolsey owed his unique combination of powers to the papacy's desire to retain the valued support of his royal master.[4]

Relations between the English crown and the papacy were generally good for over a century before the Reformation. Popes accepted royal nominees to bishoprics; the early Tudor kings raised far more taxation from the English church than did the papacy. Henry VIII fought his early wars as an ally of successive popes. By defending Catholic orthodoxy against Luther in his

---

[4] *David Knowles,* The Religious Orders in England. Vol. 3: The Tudor Age. Cambridge 1959; *Peter Heath,* The English Parish Clergy on the Eve of the Reformation. London 1969; *Richard Rex,* Henry VIII and the English Reformation. Basingstoke 1993, 28–59, 117–120; *Peter Gwyn,* The King's Cardinal: The Rise and Fall of Thomas Wolsey. London 1990, 265–353, 464–480.

"Assertio Septem Sacramentorum" (1521) he earned the title "defender of the faith" retained by his successors to this day. Henry VIII's break with Rome (1533/34) was not preceded by a long term hostility towards the papacy. It came out of an almost cloudless sky. True, a papal decree of 1514 denying that any layman had authority over a clergyman had helped to exacerbate disagreement *within* England over clerical privileges. In 1512 parliament had temporarily limited the clergy's immunity from prosecution in secular courts to men in holy orders. The case of Richard Hunne, a Londoner arrested on a charge of heresy and later found, seemingly murdered, in the bishop's prison, encouraged parliament to attempt to renew the 1512 statute when it met in 1515. Ill feeling between the convocation of the clergy on the one hand and parliament and the common lawyers on the other almost resulted in a major confrontation over the issue of clerical immunity, which would in turn have involved papal authority. This was averted by Henry's personal intervention, though the king took the opportunity of insisting that his predecessors had had no superior save God alone.[5]

The events of 1512-1515, with their echoes of fourteenth-century conflicts, constituted an exceptional episode in early sixteenth-century England. They did not affect the friendship between Henry and the papacy, which arguably reached its highest point around 1521. Popes continued to give Henry what he wanted, at least until the king asked for the annulment of his marriage to Catherine of Aragon, driven both by traditional political concerns about the succession and by his own conviction that the marriage was against God's Word. In seeking to escape his first marriage, Henry from the start appealed to the Bible, as Virginia Murphy demonstrates, insisting that the Pope could not override the Levitical prohibition on a man's marriage to his brother's wife. Unable, however, to persuade Clement VII or bring sufficient pressure to bear on him to force him to annul his marriage with Catherine, Henry and his advisers had instead to find means of justifying unilateral action in England. The English schism rested on three main related claims: 1) The English Church was fully competent to settle questions of spiritual law for itself; 2) The English Church was subject to the king of England as its supreme head on earth; 3) The kingdom of England was an empire absolutely independent of any external authority. These claims were supported with elements of medieval political thought, humanist scholarship, and antiquarian research. Graham Nicholson shows how they were developed from 1530 onwards. They were presented in their most eloquent guise in the Act in Restraint of Appeals, passed by parliament in 1533. Henry pursued a twofold strategy to gain their acceptance, intimidating the English Church and winning the cooperation of parliament, partly by exploiting anti-clerical grievances. Finally,

---

[5] *Heal,* Reformation (note 3), 15-42; *John A. F. Thomson,* The Transformation of Medieval England, 1370-1529. London 1983, 314-322; *Brigden,* London (note 2), 98-103.

the opportune death of the archbishop of Canterbury in 1532 enabled him to nominate Thomas Cranmer, a reliable king's man who supported Henry's marriage plans.[6]

William Tyndale provided one of the most vigorous assertions of royal supremacy over the Church in his „Obedience of a Christian Man" (1528). His exposition of Christian duty of obedience to secular rulers was written in the shadow of the German Peasants' War, which threatened to discredit the evangelical Reformation as subversive of authority. Tyndale's interpretation of scripture provided the basis for his political ideas. The king, as God's servant, and directly answerable to Him, was responsible for maintaining good order throughout his realm, and carrying out any necessary reforms in the Church. The king's authority over his subjects could not be shared. Papal claims to any part of such authority were false. If Henry's ideas owed anything to Tyndale, however (which is itself doubtful), he certainly did not admit it. Tyndale, like Luther himself, opposed Henry's repudiation of Catherine of Aragon.[7]

The royal supremacy over the Church, specifically including powers of correction and reform, was recognised by parliament in 1534. Henry and his advisers used it to carry through important changes, especially the dissolution of the monasteries (1536-1540, the subject of complementary studies by G. W. O. Woodward and Joyce Youings); the publication of an English Bible, largely based on Tyndale's work, and its distribution throughout the country (1538/39); attacks on saints' cults (1536-1538), and the gradual repudiation of the doctrine of purgatory (from 1536 onwards, traced in detail by Alan Kreider), preparing the way for the crown to seize endowments supporting prayers for the dead.[8]

Historians' views of Henry's church policies vary enormously. At one end of the spectrum are those who see them as fundamentally opportunist, varying, inconsistent and unstable. Henry was, according to David Starkey, influenced by powerful personalities with priorities of their own. Urgent needs – financial, political and diplomatic – pulled his religious agenda in different directions. No coherent justification for the destruction of the monasteries

---

[6] *Virginia Murphy*, The Literature and Propaganda of Henry VIII's first Divorce, in: Diarmaid MacCulloch (Ed.), The Reign of Henry VIII. Basingstoke 1995, 135-158; *John J. Scarisbrick*, Henry VIII. London 1968, 241-309; *G. Nicholson*, The Act of Appeals and the English Reformation, in: Claire Cross/David Loades/John J. Scarisbrick (Eds.), Law and Government under the Tudors. Cambridge 1988, 19-30; *Diarmaid MacCulloch*, Thomas Cranmer: A Life. New Haven/London 1996, 75-77, 83-84.
[7] *Daniell*, Tyndale (note 2), 201, 223-249.
[8] *Rex*, Henry VIII and Reformation (note 4); *Dickens*, English Reformation (note 2), 129-135; *Alan Kreider*, English Chantries: The Road to Dissolution. Cambridge, Mass. 1979, 93-153; *G. W. O. Woodward*, The Dissolution of the Monasteries. London 1966; *Joyce A. Youings*, The Dissolution of the Monasteries. London 1971.

was ever worked out or published. Starting on a selective basis, and justified in terms of the need to prune the weak or diseased branches of English monasticism, it soon became a process of wholesale plunder largely driven by the government's concern to secure resources for the crown. Henry was in key respects instinctively conservative in his personal religion, but his financial exploitation seriously weakened the Church. Locked into a struggle with the Pope, Henry authorised propaganda which demonised the Pope and linked popery and „superstition", a loose and flexible term. In opposing the papacy, he drew on the support of evangelicals who had more radical religious aims than his. Lacking a coherent alternative to a Catholic doctrine of salvation, Diarmaid MacCulloch argues, Henry had a „ragbag of emotional preferences". One historian, George Bernard, insists, against majority opinion, that Henry had a clear and coherent vision of an independent English church, Catholic but reformed, swept clean of superstition but never Lutheran. Henry, Bernard reminds us, always insisted not only on Christ's corporal presence in the sacrament of the altar but also on the need for penance and good works to be joined with faith. Few doubt that Henry had a conception of himself as a reforming monarch or latter day Old Testament king, but most see much self-deception in this conception. In shaping his policy, his theology, whether „visionary" or not, interacted closely with traditional political concerns. These included a secure succession, a strong and well-endowed monarchy, and an obedient and united realm. Henry's keen anxiety about the disruptive potential of „diversity in opinions" was a prominent feature of royal rhetoric and propaganda from 1536 onwards.[9]

There were various diplomatic contacts between England and German states from 1528 onwards. In 1536 English emissaries met leading Lutherans, including Philip Melanchthon and Martin Luther himself. The so-called „Wittenberg articles" were hammered out, with Melanchthon taking the leading role. This statement of faith was never adopted in England, but its language is nevertheless reflected in that of the much more conservative „Ten Articles" agreed by the Canterbury convocation the same year. Henry's closest involvement with Germany came early in 1540 with his marriage to Anne, sister of the duke of Cleves. The Anglo-German contacts of Henry's reign have been variously interpreted. Some have seen them as inspired by strong hopes on the English as well as the German side of reaching a closer confessional as well as diplomatic agreement. In this view, recently and

---

[9] *Rex*, Henry VIII and Reformation (note 4), 167-175; *David Starkey*, The Reign of Henry VIII: Personalities and Politics. London 1985, 103-145; *Scarisbrick*, Henry VIII (note 6), 384-423; *Diarmaid MacCulloch*, Henry VIII and the Reform of the Church, in: idem (Ed.), The Reign of Henry VIII (note 6), 178; *George W. Bernard*, The Making of Religious Policy, 1533-46: Henry VIII and the Search for the Middle Way, in: Historical Journal 41, 1998, 321-349; *Pamela Tudor-Craig*, Henry VIII and King David, in: D. Williams (Ed.), Early Tudor England. Woodbridge 1989, 183-206.

strongly re-stated by Rory McEntegart, Thomas Cromwell, Henry VIII's chief minister between 1532 and his downfall in 1540, was a keen promoter of Anglo-German contacts. Henry's readiness to welcome a visit by Philip Melanchthon indicates the king's own interest. According to a different opinion, however, Henry was actuated throughout these German contacts by „traditional political" concerns. He never had any intention of accepting the distinctive elements of Lutheran doctrine. Charles V posed a threat both to Henry and to the German Protestant princes. Henry hoped for cooperation based on their common political interests but consistently sought to avoid a commitment to a closer theological understanding. The attraction of the Cleves match lay precisely in the fact that Duke William, though an ally of the leading Protestant princes of the Empire, was at the time pursuing a course of conservative reform similar to Henry's. The king, George Bernard and Retha M. Warnicke insist, was in control all along. There was no attempt by Cromwell to draw Henry into a Protestant confessional alignment, let alone any possibility of his doing so.[10]

Thomas Cromwell was viceregent in spirituals from 1535 and the king's deputy as supreme head of the Church. He has appeared to some historians, notably to Geoffrey Dickens and Sir Geoffrey Elton, as an outstandingly creative reformer of church and state with evangelical leanings and an eirenic vision. Elton, while admitting that Cromwell was „never a straightforward Lutheran", points to his promotion of an English Bible largely based on Tyndale's work, his contacts with London „brethren" (traced by Susan Brigden), and his protection of reforming preachers. George Bernard, on the other hand, sees in him above all a loyal and efficient servant of the king, very much attuned to Henry's own reforming programme, and seldom if ever advancing beyond it. When Cromwell was condemned to death in 1540, the most damning charge against him was sacramentarian heresy. The kinder view of Henry's role in this process is that he was to some extent manipulated by Cromwell's enemies. The more damning hypothesis, favoured by George Bernard, is that the king ruthlessly and deliberately sacrificed his loyal and able minister in order to underline his determination to maintain his own relatively conservative church settlement and thus reassure conservative opinion at home and abroad.[11]

---

[10] *N. S. Tiernagel*, Henry VIII and the Lutherans: a Study in Anglo-Lutheran Relations from 1521 to 1547. St. Louis 1965; *Retha M. Warnicke*, The Marrying of Anne of Cleves: Royal Protocol in Early Modern England. Cambridge 2000, 63–74, 187–195; *Rory McEntegart*, Henry VIII, the League of Schmalkalden, and the English Reformation. Woodbridge 2002; *George Bernard*, Elton's Cromwell, in: idem (Ed.), Power and Politics in Tudor England. Essays by G. W. Bernard. Aldershot 2000, 119; *Bernard*, Making of Religious Policy (note 9), 341–345.

[11] *A. G. Dickens*, Thomas Cromwell and the English Reformation. London 1959; *Geoffrey R. Elton*, Policy and Police: The Enforcement of the Reformation in the Age of

Reforms in the church were expected to yield social and political benefits, a prospect most recently explored by Geoffrey Elton and Nicholas Orme. The clergy were in 1536 instructed to exhort their parishioners to give money to the poor and needy, instead of spending it on visiting and making offerings to images or relics. (An act passed by parliament earlier that year provided that chests for the safe keeping of alms for the poor should be set up in every parish.) The closure of the monasteries would, it was hoped, eradicate centres of idleness and debauchery as well as superstition. Resources wasted by monks could be diverted to more beneficial ends, especially education. (Some schools and colleges were indeed founded or re-endowed, though the total was not very impressive. Joan Simon, writing in the 1960s, took a much more optimistic view of the outcome than did the Victorian historian A. F. Leach, and at least on this point more recent accounts have tended to agree with hers.) Better education of the populace in their Christian duties was a major social benefit expected from the process of reformation. By further inculcating the obligation of obedience to the king, it would promote the goal of a more governable and orderly realm. This concern was well expressed in such works as Thomas Starkey's „The Exhortation to the People Instructing Them to Unity and Obedience" and Richard Morison's „A Remedy for Sedition", both published in 1536, and written by men favoured by Thomas Cromwell. One of the royal injunctions of 1536 required the clergy not only to admonish parents and employers to „teach or cause to be taught" their children and servants the Lord's Prayer, articles of faith, and ten commandments, but also to persuade them to provide for those young persons' proper education and training.[12]

Recent emphasis on the strengths of the English Catholic Church in the work of Eamon Duffy, J. J. Scarisbrick (both Catholics themselves) and Christopher Haigh leaves a problem of accounting for the seeming ease with which the crown achieved its major goals and the lack of opposition to its plans. There are a number of possible explanations. First, it was certainly not clear in 1532, or for many years afterwards, that the break with Rome would be followed by the triumph of Protestantism. Many seem to have believed that Henry would continue to maintain the Catholic faith, even if reformed

---

Thomas Cromwell. Cambridge 1972; *idem,* Cromwell, Thomas, in: Hans J. Hillerbrand (Ed.), The Oxford Encyclopaedia of the Reformation. New York/Oxford 1996, Vol. 1, 453–455; *Susan Brigden,* Thomas Cromwell and the „brethren", in: Cross/Loades/Scarisbrick (Eds.), Law and Government (note 6), 31–49; *Bernard,* The Making of Religious Policy (note 9), 346.

[12] *Arthur F. Leach,* The Schools of Medieval England. London 1915; *Geoffrey R. Elton,* Reform and Renewal: Thomas Cromwell and the Common Weal. Cambridge 1973, 122–126; *Joan Simon,* Education and Society in Tudor England. Cambridge 1966, 165–214; *Nicholas Orme,* Education and Society in Medieval and Renaissance England. London 1989; *Scarisbrick,* Henry VIII (note 6), 511–523.

in detail. Stephen Gardiner, able bishop of Winchester, diplomat, and propagandist for the royal supremacy, subject of a recent biography by Glyn Redworth, was the outstanding example of such trust or self-deception. Secondly, the most important stages of the Reformation were enacted by parliaments representing most parts of the kingdom. Statutes, embodying the consent of the realm and the crown, already had paramount authority as the highest form of law made in England. The crown could not wholly control parliaments, or stifle all expression of disquiet or opposition. It could however in various ways (most fully analysed by Stanford Lehmberg) influence the legislative agenda and the course of proceedings, and on occasion dissuade potential opponents from attending. Thirdly, the crown was able repeatedly to divide clergy and laity, to isolate the clergy, present them as in need of reform, and play on lay hopes of profiting at their expense, especially in the dissolution of the monasteries. Fourthly, the duty of obedience to the crown, already strongly emphasized, was driven home by effective royal propaganda. (Print, an important new medium for this purpose, was used for the first time in a mass campaign, and was far more effectively under royal control than – for example – in Germany.) Fifthly, any potential opposition to the Reformation lacked powerful leaders and organisation. Those who saw most clearly the implications of Henry's policy either limited themselves to passive disobedience, like Thomas More, or attacked it from abroad, like Reginald Pole. Conservative churchmen and lay magnates had no common programme. They preferred to try to influence royal policies by advice, persuasion and political intrigue (variously explored by Alistair Fox, John Guy, and David Starkey among others) rather than outright resistance. The upsurge of resistance in the Lincolnshire Rising and Pilgrimage of Grace of 1536 (subject of a new study by Richard Hoyle) was genuinely popular but strongly regional in character. The government was able to contain that resistance with the help of noblemen who put their duty of obedience and their hopes of reward before the defence of religion. Sixthly, Henry was utterly determined to achieve his objectives. Fortified by self-righteous conviction of the justice of his own aims, he punished without mercy those whom he saw as opponents. Faced with the risings of 1536, he reacted with a mixture of cunning, duplicity, and cold-blooded ruthlessness.[13]

---

[13] *Scarisbrick*, Reformation and the English People (note 3); *Duffy*, Stripping of Altars (note 3); *Christopher A. Haigh*, English Reformations: Religion, Politics and Society under the Tudors. Oxford 1993; *Elton*, Policy and Police (note 11); *Stanford Lehmberg*, The Reformation Parliament, 1529-1536. Cambridge 1970; *Alistair Fox/John Guy* (Eds.), Reassessing the Henrician Age: Humanism, Politics and Reform 1500-1550. Oxford 1986, 52-73, 121-147; *Glyn Redworth*, In Defence of the Church Catholic: The Life of Stephen Gardiner. Oxford 1990, 42-44, 54f., 61-68; *David Starkey*, The Reign of Henry VIII: Personalities and Politics. London 1985, 107-145; *Richard W. Hoyle*, The Pilgrimage of Grace and the Politics of the 1530s. Oxford 2001, 167-169, 371-374, 449-454.

During the reign of the boy king Edward VI (1547–1553) England's government finally embraced the Protestant Reformation. Why did this come about? How far was the change due to „visionary theology", how far to „traditional political" considerations? Thomas Cranmer, archbishop of Canterbury (1533–1555), was a considerable theologian, a fact underlined by his latest biographer, Diarmaid MacCulloch. Cranmer probably adopted a Lutheran conception of the eucharist around 1532. When Henry VIII wrote detailed criticisms of the so-called „Bishops' Book", a formulary of doctrine published in 1537, Cranmer responded with a strong (albeit private) defence of what the Book taught concerning good works and justification by faith. Henry, Diarmaid MacCulloch says, „could not have hoped to hear a clearer exposition of the once-for-all character of justification by faith, controlled by the logic of predestination, than he did in Cranmer's annotations".[14] (An increasingly strong predestinarian emphasis was evident in Cranmer's writing under Henry VIII.) The archbishop's own desire to promote Reformation was checked in the last years of Henry's reign by the king's determination to enforce acceptance of his own conservative views, especially of the eucharist and of faith and works, by means of a revised doctrinal formulary, the „King's Book" (1543), and parliamentary statutes of 1539 and 1543. Cranmer's deep conviction of the duty of obedience to the supreme head of the church, reinforced by his personal loyalty to Henry, outweighed his considerable personal misgivings, and prevented his resignation. During Edward's reign, however, he had a unique opportunity to implement his still developing vision of the Church. At no other moment during the entire English Reformation was a churchman able to shape religious policy so strongly.

Cranmer headed the list of counsellors appointed in Henry's will to govern the realm during Edward's minority, and his ally Edward Seymour, the king's uncle, soon to be duke of Somerset, was elected protector of the realm by his fellow counsellors shortly after Henry's death. The consolidation of their hold on power was facilitated by the disgrace of Henry VIII's ablest conservative counsellors, Stephen Gardiner, and Thomas Howard, duke of Norfolk, shortly before the king's death. The „Protestant Triumph" has been the subject of fundamental disagreements among historians. Wilbur K. Jordan, for example, envisaged Henry as a wise old king who recognised that an irresistible tide was pulling the nation towards Protestantism. Others see a Henrician balance upset by an unplanned factional triumph. For George Bernard, the Edwardian Reformation marked a fundamental break with Henry's consistent principles and his settlement of religion.[15]

---

[14] *MacCulloch*, Cranmer (note 6), 211f.
[15] *Scarisbrick*, Henry VIII (note 6), 458–484; *Wilbur K. Jordan*, Edward VI: The Young King. London 1968, 27–50; *Starkey*, Reign of Henry VIII (note 14), 147–167; *Redworth*, In Defence of the Church Catholic (note 14), 242–247; *Eric W. Ives*, Henry VIII's Will:

This process began with the issue of a new and greatly expanded set of royal injunctions (July 1547). One of the most important of these required every parish in the realm to purchase a book of homilies for use by the great majority of the clergy who were not competent preachers. Of these the most significant (and the most dangerous, in Gardiner's eyes) were the ones in which Cranmer set out the nature of salvation and faith, and the relationship between them. An act passed towards the end of 1547 permitted lay participation in communion under both kinds. Another act provided for the confiscation of remaining endowments designed to support prayers for the dead, whether they belonged to chantry foundations or parish fraternities. An „Order of Communion" in English, published in time for use at Easter 1548, made prior personal confession to a priest a matter of individual choice, and declared that those who received the Sacrament in penitence and faith ate Christ's flesh and drank his blood *spiritually*. Early in 1548, too, the privy council ordered the abandonment of various ancient ceremonies and the destruction of all religious images. The first phase of the Edwardian Reformation culminated in 1549 in an Act of Uniformity commanding the use throughout the realm of new orders of service in English contained in the first „Book of Common Prayer". Another act permitted priests to marry. By this point, just two years after Henry VIII's death, the last major conservative element of his idiosyncratic and theologically unstable settlement had been removed.[16]

Rejection of the mass and of all the abuses to which (the reformers believed) it had given rise was one of the foremost themes of the Edwardian Reformation. But how did the English reformers understand the eucharist? During the later 1540s, in some cases sooner, in some later, the leading reformers, including Cranmer, adopted a Reformed conception of the Communion. England moved under the theological influence of what MacCulloch has called the „Strassburg-St Gall axis". Alec Ryrie has recently argued that Henry VIII's hostility towards the Lutheranism to which many English reformers had previously been attracted served to polarise eucharistic opinions and force those individuals into outright opposition. The direction in which Cranmer's eucharistic beliefs were moving became more evident with the publication of the „Order of Communion" in 1548.[17] The first „Book of

---

A Forensic Conundrum, in: Historical Journal 35, 1992, 779–804; *Ralph A. Houlbrooke*, Henry VIII's Wills: A Comment, in: Historical Journal 37, 1994, 891–899; *Bernard*, The Making of Religious Policy (note 9), 346–349.

[16] *Jordan*, Edward VI: The Young King (note 15), 155–229; *MacCulloch*, Cranmer (note 6), 351–409.

[17] *Alec Ryrie*, The Strange Death of Lutheran England, in: Journal of Ecclesiastical History 53, 2002 64–92; *Peter Newman Brooks*, Thomas Cranmer's Doctrine of the Eucharist. 2nd Ed. Basingstoke 1992; *MacCulloch*, Cranmer (note 6), 179; *Diarmaid MacCulloch*, Tudor Church Militant: Edward VI and the Protestant Reformation. London 1999, 167–170.

Common Prayer" nevertheless attempted to win the widest possible acceptance of the changes in train by means of elements of judicious ambiguity. During the remaining years of the reign, the Church of England's Reformed understanding of the eucharist, which separated it not only from the Roman but also from the Lutheran churches, was made unambiguously clear. From 1550 onwards Communion tables replaced in English churches the altars where the sacrificial mass had been celebrated. In the summer of 1550, Cranmer published an explanatory „Defence" of his eucharistic doctrine. Revision of the first „Book of Common Prayer" was under way during 1551, and the revised order of worship was introduced by a second Act of Uniformity early in 1552, though it was to come into use only the following November, little more than eight months before the end of Edward's reign. In it, the words of administration of the eucharist told communicants to take the bread in remembrance that Christ died for them and to feed on him *in their hearts* with thanksgiving. In May 1553, the Forty-Two Articles of Religion, agreed by a group of reliable senior clergy, were published by the authority of the fifteen-year-old supreme head of the Church two months before his death. The third article rejected the notion of Christ's real and bodily presence in the eucharist, while the seventeenth, perhaps the most famous, declared that „predestination to life is the everlasting purpose of God, whereby (before the foundations of the world were laid) he hath constantly decreed by his own judgement secret to us, to deliver from curse and damnation those whom he hath chosen out of mankind, and to bring them to everlasting salvation by Christ, as vessels made to honour".[18]

Cranmer's reforming moves in the first half of Edward's reign have sometimes been portrayed as slow, cautious and even hesitant, especially by his earlier biographer Jasper Ridley. Diarmaid MacCulloch views them more convincingly as bold and decisive, even revolutionary, though their pace and presentation were largely determined by the need to persuade a still predominantly conservative country. If MacCulloch conveys the exhilaration experienced by those who were trying to turn the reforming vision into reality, Catharine Davies shows the other side of the coin: the anxieties felt by reformers all too conscious that they were in the minority, facing challenges or obstacles on all sides: superstition, radical heresy, lust and greed. They became increasingly suspicious of powerful worldly wise political opportunists who did not share their vision, and fearful that God would punish the sins of the nation by removing their young king Josiah.[19]

---

[18] *MacCulloch*, Cranmer (note 6), 454–513; *Gerald Bray* (Ed.), Documents of the English Reformation. Cambridge 1994, 294.

[19] *Jasper Ridley*, Thomas Cranmer. Oxford 1962, 258–261; *MacCulloch*, Tudor Church Militant (note 17), 57–104; *Catharine Davies*, A Religion of the Word: The Defence of the Reformation in the Reign of Edward VI. Manchester 2002.

Several prominent Edwardian Protestants, both clerical and lay, evinced their expectation that a fuller and more perfect Reformation would result in better behaviour and social renewal. The 1547 act authorising the seizure of chantry and other endowments designed to support intercessory masses anticipated their conversion to godly uses including the setting up of grammar schools, the augmentation of universities and provision for the poor. Some of the proceeds were indeed devoted to enhanced provision for „non-superstitious" purposes such as education, but by far the greater part went to support the government's current expenditure, especially on war. Local initiatives, above all by gentry and townsfolk, did nevertheless result in the foundation or re-foundation of many schools and almshouses. The most famous example of such a project was the establishment in London of hospitals, an orphanage, and a workhouse in five properties granted or sold by the crown and financed by means of individual benefactions, city taxes, and royal help. Paul Slack's recent account of public welfare in early modern England tends however to emphasize an essential continuity of purpose in sixteenth-century educational and charitable schemes, and the diversity of sources of inspiration, rather than any dramatic impact of Protestant „visionary theology".[20]

Some leading evangelical preachers and lay commentators expressed disappointment, impatience and anger when (as it seemed to them) the good results expected from Reformation were frustrated by greed and avarice. Preachers favoured at court such as Hugh Latimer, John Hooper, and Thomas Lever delivered particularly biting attacks on such vices. If any one action symbolised the supposedly adverse effects of individual greed for contemporaries it was the enclosure of arable land for conversion to pasture. Michael Bush shows that John Hales, „master-planner" of the government's commissions against enclosure, was convinced that conversion to pasture directly weakened the country by diminishing the numbers of hardy tillers of the soil who were best fitted to serve as fighting men. It was however his evangelical conviction that fuelled his fiery and provocative rhetoric against the covetous landowners whom he saw as responsible for a great social evil that in turn hampered the people's reception of the Reformation.[21]

Hales had the ear of the duke of Somerset. When in 1549 a wave of agrarian risings swept across southern and eastern England, several of the leaders claimed to be supporting the government's aims. Sometimes they used evangelical rhetoric. Norfolk men echoed the language of German peasants in

---

[20] *Wilbur K. Jordan*, Edward VI: The Threshold of Power. London 1970, 181–239; *Simon*, Education and Society (note 12), 223–244; *Paul Slack*, From Reformation to Improvement: Public Welfare in Early Modern England. Oxford 1999, 19–28.

[21] *Michael L. Bush*, The Government Policy of Protector Somerset. London 1975, 40–83; *Davies*, Religion of the Word (note 19), 6–8, 162–168.

1525 when they asked that remaining bondmen should be freed because Christ's sacrifice had made all men free. They also demanded that the clergy reside on their benefices and fulfil their duties of preaching and religious instruction. Essex rebels appealed to various scriptural texts. Ethan Shagan and Diarmaid MacCulloch have recently underlined Somerset's initial readiness to admit, with flourishes of evangelical rhetoric, the justice of many rebel complaints, and to blame the rebellions on the covetousness of the rich. These actions were bitterly resented by his fellow counsellors, and helped to bring about his downfall in the autumn of 1549. Somerset's view of the causes of the 1549 agrarian rebellions may have been sincerely held, but he had one urgent reason for avoiding armed suppression of the uprisings if possible: the need of men to fight his war to enforce the marriage of Mary Stuart, Queen of Scots, to Edward VI. He publicised this as a „godly purpose". In order to further it he gave some support to evangelical preaching in Scotland, but it was not sufficiently vigorous or sustained to make a big difference. An evangelical vision played some part in shaping social policy under Somerset, but his foreign policy, Michael Bush argues, was dominated by more conventional political concerns.[22]

Cranmer hoped that England would take a place in the vanguard of the European Reformation. During Edward's reign it became refuge for a galaxy of continental reformers. The foremost of them were a cluster of distinguished exiles from Strassburg, including Martin Bucer himself. Peter Martyr Vermigli played an important part in the development of Cranmer's eucharistic thought. Bucer's and Martyr's comments helped Cranmer's liturgical revision in 1551. Bucer set out a blueprint for the reform and re-invigoration of church government and discipline in his tract „De Regno Christi", while Martyr and Bernardino Ochino helped Cranmer in the ultimately abortive project of canon law revision. Several groups of religious exiles established their own congregations in England during Edward VI's reign. The „Stranger Church" in London, most fully studied by Andrew Pettegree, became under the supervision of the Polish reformer Jan Laski a model of Reformed liturgy and discipline.[23]

---

[22] *Anthony Fletcher/Diarmaid MacCulloch*, Tudor Rebellions. 4th Ed. London 1997, 77–80, 144–146; *Ethan H. Shagan*, Popular Politics and the English Reformation. Cambridge 2003; *Bush*, Government Policy (note 21), 21f.; *MacCulloch*, Tudor Church Militant (note 17), 43–50.

[23] *MacCulloch*, Tudor Church Militant (note 17), 77–80; *Diarmaid MacCulloch*, The Importance of Jan Laski in the English Reformation, in: Christoph Strohm (Hrsg.), Johannes A Lasco, 1499–1560. Emden 2000, 315–345; *Diarmaid MacCulloch*, Peter Martyr and Thomas Cranmer, in: Emidio Campi (Ed.), Peter Martyr Vermigli: Humanism, Republicanism, Reformation. Geneva 2002, 173–201; *C. Hopf*, Martin Bucer and the English Reformation. Oxford 1946; *Andrew Pettegree*, Foreign Protestant Communities in Sixteenth-Century London. Oxford 1986, 23–76.

Had Cranmer followed his own inclinations, he would probably have reformed liturgy more thoroughly. He was always conscious, however, of the need to preserve the unity of the Church and to carry with him more conservative colleagues. It was a particularly galling experience for him to face opposition from fellow evangelicals less inclined to compromise than he was. John Hooper had witnessed a more perfectly reformed Church during a stay in Zürich (1547-1549). Hooper's initial objections to wearing episcopal vestments, supported by Jan Laski, held up his consecration as bishop of Gloucester. They adumbrated a serious division within the Elizabethan Church. John Knox's objection to the 1552 Prayer Book's requirement that communicants kneel to receive the bread and wine was initially supported by members of the privy council. At the last moment a new declaration was inserted in the Book explaining that the requirement did not imply any adoration of the elements, or any real or essential presence of Christ.[24]

Cranmer in a solemn address to the young king Edward at his coronation emphasized his responsibility to see God truly worshipped, idolatry destroyed, and the Pope's tyranny removed. Henry VIII himself would probably have applauded the address, but he could hardly have approved of the ways in which key but vague and flexible elements of his own rhetoric and policy would be extended in his son's reign in order to justify a much more thoroughgoing reformation than he had contemplated. Edward, on the other hand, readily absorbed the evangelical vision of his godfather Cranmer and cherished his own responsibilities as supreme head. In this regard, Diarmaid MacCulloch's account of the king's outlook seems a great deal more convincing than that of the late Jennifer Loach, who argued that Edward's surviving writings show little interest in religious doctrine, as distinct from his power and authority as supreme head of the Church.[25]

Edward's opinions became a political consideration of outstanding importance after the downfall of his uncle the Protector Somerset in October 1549. His ability to win Edward's confidence by presenting himself as a convinced evangelical was crucial to the success of John Dudley (duke of Northumberland from 1551) in first gaining, and then retaining power as lord president of the privy council from 1550 onwards. On this point, Dale Hoak and Diarmaid MacCulloch agree, though MacCulloch's Edward is very far from the puppet king portrayed in Hoak's study of the privy council. Northumberland's patronage of the outspoken Scottish exile John Knox served to strengthen his evangelical credentials. In October 1551 he suggested that Knox be appointed bishop of Rochester, the next diocese to Cranmer's. This, he believed, would „whet" or sharpen the archbishop; he did not say, but may well have hoped, that Knox as bishop would be a counterweight to an

---

[24] *MacCulloch,* Cranmer (note 6), 471–484, 525–529.
[25] Ibid. 365; *Jennifer Loach,* Edward VI. New Haven/London 1999, 130–158, 180–184.

archbishop whose influence over the king he found irksome. Northumberland failed, however, to keep the confidence of Knox and other militant evangelicals among the clergy, and during Lent 1553 they preached a series of exceptionally mordant attacks on the greed, pride and ambition of great men. They resented above all the conspicuous failure to use confiscated church property for godly ends. Soon afterwards, Northumberland angrily blocked discussion in parliament of Cranmer's cherished scheme for the reform of the ecclesiastical law, which would have strengthened the church courts and given church property additional protection.[26]

One of the most ticklish problems Northumberland had to face during his period in power was the continuing celebration of mass in the house of the Princess Mary, Edward's half-sister and heiress to the crown. In March 1551, Edward insisted that Mary's immunity must be ended. According to one account he doggedly maintained this insistence in face of threats from the Emperor Charles V (Mary's nephew) and the advice of his counsellors. The king's attitude limited Northumberland's freedom of manoeuvre and helped to push the English government into seeking a closer entente with Henry II of France, concluded in July/August 1551, which was followed by further harassment of Mary.[27] Northumberland might have preferred to maintain better relations with the heir apparent to the throne, but he was now identified in her eyes with measures that she regarded as persecution. He for his part could only anticipate the prospect of her succession with some alarm. It used to be generally accepted that it was Northumberland who originated the attempt to exclude Mary from the throne in 1553. Wilbur K. Jordan's argument that the true author of the plan was the young king Edward himself initially encountered some scepticism, but has recently been accepted by David Loades and Diarmaid MacCulloch. Either way, Northumberland threw himself into it energetically. The story of his overthrow by Mary's followers, helped by a great upsurge of popular feeling in the princess's favour, is told in the Latin life of Mary by Robert Wingfield discovered by Diarmaid MacCulloch, one of the most important original sources for Tudor history published in the last twenty years. In August, a defeated and broken man, he abjured his Protestant faith. Northumberland's career symbolises more dramatically than that of any other individual during the English Reformation evangelical faith's entanglement with the serpentine coils of traditional political considerations.[28]

---

[26] D. E. *Hoak*, The King's Council in the Reign of Edward VI. Cambridge 1976, 154f., 249, 264f.; *David Loades*, John Dudley, Duke of Northumberland 1504–1553. Oxford 1996, 160f., 192–199; *MacCulloch*, Cranmer (note 6), 524–534.

[27] *Jordan*, Edward VI: Threshold (note 20), 127–146, 256–264; *MacCulloch*, Tudor Church Militant (note 17), 36–39.

[28] *Jordan*, Edward VI: Threshold (note 20), 510–520; G. R. *Elton*, England under the Tudors. 2nd Ed. London 1974, 213; *idem*, Reform and Reformation: England 1509–1558.

Mary I (1553-1558) was unique among Tudor sovereigns in that she was not only ready to subordinate political considerations to a religious vision, but also able, as an adult sovereign (unlike Edward VI) to take the lead in implementing that vision. Courage and determination enabled her to achieve England's return, first to the position of 1547, then to Rome, with remarkably little opposition in view of the magnitude of the reversal accomplished. Even Mary, however, had unwillingly to allow the new lay owners to keep the monastic lands, most of which had already been granted by Henry VIII before 1547. English historians, led by her biographer David Loades, now view Mary's achievement more positively and sympathetically than used to be the case. Christopher Haigh and Eamon Duffy have vividly described enthusiastic popular support for the re-equipment of parish churches. This required major expenditure after years of spoliation and destruction. Saints' cults and the endowment of prayers for the dead remained relatively unimportant objects of investment during Mary's short reign. Numerous doctrinal and devotional works were published. Catholic writers sought a better informed Catholic laity. Haigh sees a „mature Erasmian Catholicism" at work. Lucy Wooding emphasizes the missionary concerns of Marian bishops and writers whose preoccupation „was to expound a workable, pastoral, biblical faith". Wooding suggests that the Catholic leadership drew on the reforms of Henry VIII's reign, rather than simply trying to put the clock back to pre-Reformation times. (Her critics have however remained unconvinced by her positive appraisal of this „Henrician Catholicism".)[29]

In the past, attention has focused on the cruelty of the Marian persecution. Now we attempt to explain why, in a country so recently officially Protestant, so few died for their faith or felt compelled to flee abroad. Certainly there were few documented underground congregations; no national network to compare with that set up by the French Reformed churches around this time in a country where the monarchy had always remained Catholic. Andrew Pettegree has drawn attention to the many English „Nicodemites" who hid their Protestant convictions behind outward conformity in a fashion very common among the Lollards even before the Reformation.[30] The duty of obedience to the sovereign, to the „queen's pro-

---

London 1978, 373-375; *Loades*, Northumberland (note 26), 230-241; *MacCulloch*, Tudor Church Militant (note 17), 39-41; *Diarmaid MacCulloch* (Ed.), The Vita Mariae Angliae Reginae of Robert Wingfield of Brantham, in: Camden Miscellany 28, Camden Society, 4th series, 29, 1984, 181-301.

[29] *Elton*, Reform and Reformation (note 28), 376-396; *David Loades*, The Reign of Mary Tudor: Politics, Government and Religion in England, 1553-1558. 2nd Ed. London 1991; *David Loades*, Mary Tudor: A Life. Oxford 1989; *Haigh*, English Reformations (note 13), 203-218; *Duffy*, Stripping of Altars (note 3), 524-564; *Lucy E. C. Wooding*, Rethinking Catholicism in Reformation England. Oxford 2000, 271.

[30] *Andrew Pettegree*, Marian Protestantism: Six Studies. Aldershot 1996, 88f., 106, 154f.

ceedings in parliament", was widely recognised. On the other hand, the authorities rarely tried to investigate the private beliefs of people who maintained an outward facade of Catholic observance.

There was no effective resistance to the Marian restoration within England. Nearly three hundred men and women suffered death for their refusal to participate fully or at all in Catholic worship, above all because of refusal to accept Christ's corporal presence in the sacrament of the altar. Rejection of papal authority was quite a frequent charge against the victims of the persecution, and Thomas Cranmer denounced the Pope as Antichrist before he was burnt. Nearly all these people, however, suffered the consequences of their disobedience without any call for active resistance to secular authority. The only open rebellion against Mary's government, that of Sir Thomas Wyatt and his associates early in 1554, certainly included a number of Protestants in its ranks. Its leaders may have been prepared to depose the Queen, but their declared objective was rather to prevent her marriage to Philip of Spain. The restoration of Protestantism was an undeclared, but almost certainly important aim. David Loades, author of the only full modern account of the rebellion, played down the role of religion because he was sceptical of claims by Mary and her supporters that heresy was indeed the mainspring of the rising. It is given due weight in a succinct analysis by Anthony Fletcher and Diarmaid MacCulloch.[31]

The martyrs in England were greatly outnumbered by some 800 exiles who certainly or probably left England for religion's sake during Mary Tudor's reign. Substantial groups settled in Emden, Wesel, Frankfurt, Strassburg, Zürich (the most important host city), Aarau, Basel, and Geneva. The classic account of the exiles and listing of individual refugees by Christina Garrett remains, despite some shortcomings, the indispensable standard work. Perceptive descriptions of aspects of the exile have been written more recently by Patrick Collinson and Andrew Pettegree, but a new overall study is needed. However thorough, this is unlikely to alter the long-established impression that the chief importance of the exile lay in its future repercussions rather than its somewhat limited effects on the course of events in England at the time. The exodus was less organized than Christina Garrett thought, but the quarrels over liturgy and church order in the Frankfurt community foreshadowed important issues of controversy in the Elizabethan Church.[32]

---

[31] *D. M. Loades,* Two Tudor Conspiracies. Cambridge 1965, 47–80; *Fletcher/MacCulloch,* Tudor Rebellions (note 22), 90f.
[32] *Christina H. Garrett,* The Marian Exiles. Cambridge 1938; *M. M. Knappen,* Tudor Puritanism: A Chapter in the History of Idealism. Chicago 1939, 110–162; *Dickens,* English Reformation (note 2), 283–294; *Patrick Collinson,* Archbishop Grindal, 1519–1583: The Struggle for a Reformed Church. London 1979, 67–82; *Pettegree,* Marian Protestantism (note 30).

A stream of pamphlets attacking the Marian Church came from exile presses, especially in Emden. Only a very small minority of the exiles, however, developed resistance theories in their continental refuges. All these authors relied principally on scripture, but also invoked historical examples. John Ponet, a participant in Wyatt's rebellion, published in Strassburg his „Shorte Treatise of Politicke Power" (1556). He declared it lawful for subjects to depose an evil governor and kill a tyrant, but the target of his invective was the church hierarchy rather than the Queen herself. In his exposition of „How Superior Powers Ought to be Obeyed", published in Geneva in 1558, Christopher Goodman insisted that God must be obeyed rather than man. Rebellion and tyrannicide were justified as means of removing an ungodly ruler. A female ruler was against God's ordinance as well as nature: women were unfit to rule a family, let alone a kingdom. Mary Tudor was additionally disqualified by her illegitimate birth and her open idolatry. The latter made her worthy of death; left unpunished, her crime would call down the vengeance of God upon the whole realm.[33]

The most notorious of these three tracts was John Knox's „First Blast of the Trumpet against the Monstrous Regiment of Women", a relentlessly insistent and systematic diatribe against female rulers in general, and Mary Tudor in particular. It is now available in an excellent edition by Roger Mason which includes a very helpful introduction. The relatively late appearance of the „First Blast" was due among other things to the lack of encouragement from Calvin or Bullinger, Knox's involvement in ultimately unsuccessful efforts to persuade the English community in Frankfurt to move beyond the 1552 Prayer Book to a more thoroughly revised liturgy, and a missionary journey to his native Scotland. In 1556 Knox had addressed an appeal to the regent of Scotland, Mary of Guise. His readiness to address her in quite moderate and courteous tones was due to his experience of her then conciliatory policy towards Protestants and his hopes of persuading her to move to formal toleration. A fundamental difference, as Knox saw it, between England and Scotland, was that England had, under Edward VI, already promised to defend „Christ Jesus and His Evangel", whereas Scotland had not yet received the Reformation. In countries such as England it was the duty of magistrates and people to „punish to the death" all those who sought to subvert true religion. Failure to do so would provoke God's anger against

---

[33] *Winthrop S. Hudson*, John Ponet, 1516?–1556: Advocate of Limited Monarchy. Chicago 1942; *Barrett L. Beer*, John Ponet's *Shorte Treatise of Politike Power* Reassessed, in: Sixteenth Century Journal 21, 1990, 373–383; *Jane Dawson*, Resistance and Revolution in Sixteenth-Century Thought: The Case of Christopher Goodman, in: J. Van den Berg/P. G. Hoftijzer (Eds.), Church, Change and Revolution. Leiden 1991, 252–272; *Robert M. Kingdon*, Calvinism and Resistance Theory, 1550–1580, in: J. H. Burns/Mark Goldie (Eds.), The Cambridge History of Political Thought 1450–1700. Cambridge 1991, 194–197.

themselves. The English people ought to have resisted Mary „that Jezebel whom they call their queen" as soon as she began to suppress evangelical religion and restore Catholicism. Knox fiercely condemned the observance of human laws and ordinances when these clashed with God's evident will. He reproached England for her ingratitude and worldly legalism during the reign of that „innocent and tender king" Edward VI. „The stout courage of captains, the wit and policy of counsellors, the learning of bishops, did rob thee" (God) „of thy glory and honour. For what then was heard, as concerning religion, but the king's proceedings, the king's proceedings must be obeyed? It is enacted by parliament; therefore, it is treason to speak in the contrary."[34]

None of these three writers specifically limited the duty of curbing ungodly rulers to inferior magistrates. Ponet mentioned at an early stage of his tract institutions responsible for preventing tyranny, including English parliaments and imperial diets, but he did not develop this conception of their role. In their reluctance to limit the right and duty of resistance, as Robert M. Kingdon has pointed out, the British exiles differed from Peter Martyr Vermigli, another refugee from Marian England. In his commentaries on Romans and Judges, he asserted that the Empire's College of Electors could resist a prince who transgressed the limits of the power he had received or compel him to observe his covenants and promises. The British exiles' failure to develop a systematic resistance theory, their overriding hostility to Roman Catholicism, and the obsessive political misogyny of Goodman and Knox, seriously limited the influence of their thought in England when the accession of another queen, Elizabeth I, only a few months after the publication of Knox's „First Blast", was shortly followed by the introduction of a Protestant church settlement.[35]

After Mary died in November 1558, it was two „Nicodemites" who had stayed in England and conformed during her reign, Mary's sister Elizabeth, and William Cecil, the new queen's choice as principal secretary of state, who were the chief architects of the Elizabethan settlement. The 1559 Act of Supremacy made Elizabeth supreme „governor", not supreme „head", of the English church. The change went some way to meet the objections of those who could not accept a woman as head of the Church, but it made little difference in practice. The Act of Uniformity restored the Prayer Book of 1552, with some changes in a conservative direction. In the „Order of Commu-

---

[34] *Roger A. Mason* (Ed.), John Knox: On Rebellion. Cambridge 1994, viii-xxiv, 26, 104; *Jane Dawson*, Revolutionary Conclusions: The Case of the Marian Exiles, in: History of Political Thought 11, 1990, 257-272; *idem*, The Two John Knoxes: England, Scotland and the 1558 Tracts, in: Journal of Ecclesiastical History 42, 1991, 555-576; *Kingdon*, Calvinism and Resistance Theory (note 33), 196-200.

[35] *Kingdon*, Calvinism and Resistance Theory (note 33), 203f.; *Pettegree*, Marian Protestantism (note 30), 144-149.

nion" the words of administration of 1549 were combined with those of 1552, and the rubric containing explicit denial of the real and corporal presence of Christ inserted at the last minute in 1552 was left out. A vague and badly drafted new rubric required the retention of such ornaments of the Church and her ministers as had been used by parliamentary authority in the second year of Edward VI (1548/49).[36]

The compilation of a comprehensive statement of doctrine could not be undertaken in 1559. The two convocations were dominated by clergy of conservative sympathies, and most of the bishops appointed in Mary's reign had yet to be replaced with Protestants. Eleven articles approved by Archbishop Parker in 1559 or 1560 served as a stopgap. They upheld the authority of the supreme governor and the fitness of the new Prayer Book and condemned various Roman Catholic doctrines and practices as superstitious, but did not attempt positive definition of distinctively Protestant doctrines. A „semi-official" „Apologia Ecclesiae Anglicanae", the work of John Jewel, bishop of Salisbury, was published in 1562. Designed especially for a continental readership, Jewel's work emphasized the underlying unity of the Protestant churches rather than the issues that divided them. Scripture, interpreted in the light of the Holy Spirit, and complemented by the writings of the early fathers and the practice of the primitive Church, was the basis of doctrinal authority.

The Canterbury provincial convocation of the clergy accepted in 1563 a revised version of the forty-two articles of 1553. The unequivocal denial of 1553 that the body of Christ could be in more than one place at a time was left out, though the modified article concerning the Lord's Supper still insisted that the body of Christ was given, taken, and eaten in the supper only after a heavenly and spiritual manner. Between 1563 and 1571, when the articles received statutory approval in parliament, one article, asserting that the wicked, and those without sufficient faith, did not share in Christ when they received the sacrament, was by royal command left out of published editions of the articles.

The last major element in the later Edwardian programme, Cranmer's project for the reform of ecclesiastical law, was never officially revived. The hierarchical organisation of the church (archbishoprics, bishoprics, archdeaconries), was retained, together with cathedrals. England ended up with an order of worship which combined traditional, evangelical and Reformed elements; articles of belief which while showing the clear influence of Reformed Protestantism on crucial points (notably predestination), were sometimes ambiguous, and a church medieval in its administrative structure.

---

[36] *John E. Booty,* John Jewel as Apologist for the Church of England. London 1963; *W. M. Southgate,* John Jewel and the Problem of Doctrinal Authority. Cambridge, Mass. 1962.

Exactly how and why the settlement took its distinctive shape are questions which have proved impossible to answer with certainty. Sir John Neale's claim, which appeared strikingly original and persuasive when first published, that Elizabeth wanted an even more conservative settlement, but was pushed further than she wished to go by a puritan House of Commons, no longer convinces historians. It does however seem certain that Elizabeth's choice at the outset of William Cecil as principal secretary of state and her most trusted counsellor had a decisive influence on the settlement. Cecil had been personally involved in the work that produced the second Edwardian Prayer Book. It was natural for him, as Winthrop S. Hudson points out, to take as his starting point the church settlement left by the previous Protestant monarch Edward VI. This was probably modified as a result of three main influences: 1) unexpectedly strong conservative resistance in the House of Lords and desire to placate moderate Catholic opinion (emphasized especially by Norman Jones); 2) Elizabeth's strong personal preference for a less precisely-defined, more inclusive, and evangelical Protestantism over a sharp-edged, more exclusive, Reformed Protestantism (underlined by Diarmaid MacCulloch, and David Starkey, though the interpretations of these scholars differ in detail); 3) the government's wish, discussed by H. Horie, to facilitate co-operation with the Lutheran states, which may account in particular for the blurring of Reformed eucharistic doctrine in both the Communion service and, later on, in the articles of faith.[37]

The Elizabethan settlement represented to a large extent the triumph of political concerns (inclusiveness, the avoidance of conflict) over visionary theology. The reforming thrust and dynamism of Edward's Reformation were checked and diminished by Elizabeth's own vision and preferences: Protestant, certainly, but within that spectrum very conservative. Attached to the church's remaining ornaments and ceremonies as signs of unity, Elizabeth also shrank from attempts at precise definition of the holy mysteries of predestination or the eucharistic presence. She refused to move beyond the settlement that she regarded as essentially complete in 1563.

The resolute non-cooperation of the surviving Marian bishops, all but one of whom refused to accept the royal supremacy, was almost certainly a disappointment for Elizabeth. She had to rely more heavily than she may have wished on strongly committed reformers. The best account of the early Elizabethan episcopate is now to be found in a new study by Brett Usher. Eliza-

---

[37] *J. E. Neale*, The Elizabethan Acts of Supremacy and Uniformity, in: English Historical Review 65, 1950, 304–332; *Winthrop S. Hudson,* The Cambridge Connection and the Elizabethan Settlement of 1559. Durham, N. C. 1980, 85, 99–105; *Norman L. Jones,* Faith by Statute: Parliament and the Settlement of Religion, 1559. London 1982, 185–189; *MacCulloch,* Tudor Church Militant (note 17), 186–195; *David Starkey*, Elizabeth: Apprenticeship. London 2000, 275–288; *H. Horie*, The Lutheran Influence on the Elizabethan Settlement, 1558–1563, in: Historical Journal 34, 1991, 519–538.

beth chose as her archbishop of Canterbury Matthew Parker, one of her mother's chaplains, a moderate evangelical, who, like Elizabeth herself, had remained in England during Mary's reign. The majority of sees, including most of the greater and more important ones, went to former exiles. John Knox, however, was *persona non grata*. His ill-timed attack on female rule had not only completely ruled out his own subsequent preferment in England but, as Andrew Pettegree has emphasized, played a crucial part in turning Elizabeth decisively against Geneva and its influence.[38]

Most of Elizabeth's bishops agreed that the massive task of evangelisation was their prime responsibility. The ideal instrument for its accomplishment was a preaching and teaching ministry, but the necessary transformation of the clergy took decades to accomplish. Meanwhile, dissatisfaction with the „wrong signals" transmitted by the conservative elements in the liturgy, and doubts generated by the unsatisfactory ornaments rubric of 1559 caused much anxiety, anger, and waste of energy. In autumn 1559 Elizabeth had a silver crucifix and candles restored to the communion table in her own chapel only weeks after commissioners carrying out an ecclesiastical visitation of the whole country in her name had ordered the destruction of crosses in parish churches. Some of the bishops were sufficiently distressed by this restoration to remonstrate with the queen in writing. Interpretations of the incident of the crucifix have differed widely. The Spanish ambassador thought at the time that the gesture was intended to appease English Catholics; several historians concluded that it was designed to smooth the courtship of Elizabeth and Archduke Charles of Austria. William P. Haugaard's conclusion that it represented Elizabeth's settled preference seems more convincing than Winthrop Hudson's suggestion that the queen acted out of pique because the ornaments had been removed without her formal consent.[39]

Plans for liturgical reform continued to receive episcopal support after this incident. David Crankshaw's detailed analysis of papers written in preparation for the Canterbury provincial convocation of 1563 shows that Archbishop Parker himself and Bishop Grindal of London read and envisaged further discussion of proposals to end the use of vestments and organs along with „Curious Singinge" in church. A paper written during Convocation and associated with Bishop Sandys of Worcester suggested the abolition of the sign of the cross in baptism. All these points appeared in a set of pro-

---

[38] *Diarmaid MacCulloch*, The Later Reformation in England, 1547–1603. 2nd Ed. Basingstoke 2001, 27f.; *Patrick Collinson*, The Elizabethan Puritan Movement. London 1967, 61–63; *Ralph Houlbrooke*, The Protestant Episcopate, 1547–1603: the Pastoral Contribution, in: Rosemary O'Day/Felicity Heal (Eds.), Church and Society in England, Henry VIII to James I. Basingstoke 1977, 78–98; *Brett Usher*, William Cecil and Episcopacy, 1559–1577. Aldershot 2003; *Pettegree*, Marian Protestantism (note 30), 144–149.
[39] *W. P. Haugaard*, Elizabeth and the English Reformation. Cambridge 1968, 185–200; *Hudson*, Cambridge Connection (note 37), 137–142.

posals put forward in the lower house of Convocation and narrowly defeated there. The preparatory work by the bishops shows that these proposals were not, as many historians have hitherto thought, conceived by radical reforming activists without any official encouragement.[40]

One issue above all divided the Church in the 1560s: the clergy's dress. Their diversity of practice annoyed the Queen, who demanded uniformity, but left the disagreeable task of imposing it to her hapless archbishop. In the „Advertisements" he issued early in 1566 Parker required every minister conducting church services to wear a surplice with sleeves. Only in cathedrals and collegiate churches was the principal minister required to wear a cope when ministering holy communion. This was less rigorous than the ornaments rubric might have suggested. The surplice (together with the square cap also prescribed for clerical use) nevertheless became a potent symbol of continuity between the sacrificing Catholic priesthood and Elizabeth's half-reformed ministry. The cause of widespread unease among the clergy themselves, it was, as Patrick Collinson has emphasized, even more fiercely disliked and mocked by many staunchly Protestant layfolk, who often stiffened their ministers' resolve not to conform. The 1566 „Vestiarian Controversy" and the efforts to enforce the „Advertisements" resulted in the deprivation of several London ministers and the creation of secret conventicles whose members came to listen to non-conforming preachers of their choice. The Controversy generated enormous bitterness. Some bishops who had their own doubts about the surplice were offended by the harsh and angry language of uncompromising opponents of the hated vestment and impatient with what seemed to them unnecessary fuss about things indifferent. Around this time religious conservatives coined the word „puritan" as an abusive nickname for members of the Protestant vanguard.[41]

The bishops' failure to achieve liturgical reform and the participation of some of their number in the imposition of the surplice induced a mood of disillusionment with episcopal leadership among the more militant English Protestants. In 1570, the recently appointed Lady Margaret Professor of Divinity at Cambridge, Thomas Cartwright, lecturing on the first two chapters of the Acts of the Apostles, concluded that the government of the Church of England differed from the apostolic model. He called for parity of ministers, the abolition of the office of archbishop, the restriction of bishops to purely spiritual functions, and the government of the church on what were in effect presbyterian lines. Deprived of his professorship, Cartwright went to Geneva. There, Théodore de Bèze, Calvin's successor, was moving away from

---

[40] *David Crankshaw,* Preparations for the Canterbury provincial Convocation of 1562-63: a question of attribution, in: Susan Wabuda/Caroline Litzenberger (Eds.), Belief and Practice in Reformation England: A Tribute to Patrick Collinson from his Students. Aldershot 1998, 60-93.

[41] *Collinson,* Puritan Movement (note 38), 66-97; *idem,* Grindal (note 32), 176-180.

Calvin's qualified acceptance of bishops. His hostility not only reinforced Cartwright's ideas, but also influenced a fellow Englishman, Walter Travers, and the Scotsman Andrew Melville. The time was ripe for the assertion and propagation of what Patrick Collinson characterised as the „new dogma" of presbyterian government of the church.[42]

Between 1568 and 1571 a series of challenges created a new sense of beleaguerment in the Elizabethan régime. The flight of Mary Stuart into England (1568) was followed by a quarrel with the government of the Netherlands (from 1568), the rising of the Catholic northern earls (1569), Pius V's excommunication of Elizabeth I (1570), and the Ridolfi Plot to put Mary Stuart on the English throne with Spanish help (1571). The growing apprehension of internal and external danger not only made more severe measures against Catholic exiles and priests seem necessary, but also increased support for Protestant reform. In the 1566 parliament the queen had vetoed a bill, supported by the bishops, to confirm the thirty-nine articles, and several other reforming bills had failed. (Sir John Neale had seen these latter bills as part of a puritan programme; Sir Geoffrey Elton argued, persuasively, that they were much less controversial.) In 1571 the thirty-nine articles gained statutory confirmation and two other bills concerning the clergy were passed, while the Canterbury convocation approved a substantial body of canons designed among other things to improve order and discipline, recently published in a new edition by Gerald Bray. William Strickland's bill to reform the Book of Common Prayer, incorporating proposals already put forward in Convocation in 1563, had some support in the Commons, but its progress was checked when the privy council forbade Strickland's further attendance.[43]

The parliament of 1572 was summoned in response to the Ridolfi Plot and, supported by the privy council, sought the execution of Mary Stuart or at the very least her exclusion from the succession to the throne. Elizabeth refused to accept these requests, and intervened to prevent the Commons from further considering a bill that would have authorised bishops to allow clergy to omit parts of the Book of Common Prayer or use orders of service devised by more fully reformed churches. It was probably this check that provoked the publication by the radical activists John Field and Thomas Wilcox of „An Admonition to the Parliament", printed together with „A View of Popish Abuses yet remaining in the Englishe Church". These tracts made a scathing attack on the government, discipline and liturgy of the

---

[42] A. F. Scott Pearson, Thomas Cartwright and Elizabethan Puritanism. Cambridge 1925, 1–46; Collinson, Puritan Movement (note 38), 101–121.
[43] G. R. Elton, The Parliament of England, 1559–1581. Cambridge 1986, 205–211; N. L. Jones, Religion in Parliament, in: D. M. Dean/N. L. Jones (Eds.) The Parliaments of Elizabethan England. Oxford 1990, 122f.; Gerald Bray (Ed.), The Anglican Canons 1529–1947. Woodbridge 1998, xlviii–l, 172–209.

Church of England and called for thoroughgoing reform or replacement of all three: the installation of presbyterian government and discipline, and the purging of all „popish" survivals from the Book of Common Prayer. Field and Wilcox were imprisoned for a year, but treated with remarkable leniency, given the vituperative nature of their criticisms. It was left to their supporter Cartwright (back in England in 1572/73, then once again in exile) to debate the issues raised by the „Admonition" with John Whitgift, rising star of the establishment, in a lengthy exchange of voluminous tracts. The central issue was whether scripture clearly prescribed a form of government for the Church. Cartwright insisted that it did; Whitgift denied this. Meanwhile, in 1574, Walter Travers published at La Rochelle his „Ecclesiasticae Disciplinae [...] Explicatio", published in an English translation by Cartwright the same year. Travers set out not only the scriptural foundations of presbyterian church government, but also a blueprint for its establishment in England. His work had a lasting influence.[44]

The result of Elizabeth's inflexible opposition to liturgical and vestimentary reform had been to drive a wedge between the bishops and their militant brethren who could not accept that „popish abominations" were „things indifferent". Her mistrustful attitude towards evangelical preaching, which was central to the conceptions of reformation held by both bishops and their militant critics within the Church, precipitated the most dramatic confrontation of her reign. This time, however, the protagonists were the Supreme Governor and her own archbishop. Edmund Grindal succeeded Matthew Parker at Canterbury late in 1575. Many bishops had encouraged or ordered groups of clergy in their dioceses to gather for regular „exercises" (or „prophesyings" from the Zürich term for clergy training) in order to discuss or hear sermons about previously assigned passages of scripture. Laymen sometimes attended these exercises. Elizabeth, suspecting that the prophesyings might generate undesirable controversy and even mask subversive puritan activity, ordered first Parker and then Grindal to suppress them. She informed Grindal she thought three or four preachers were enough for each county, and told him to limit the number of licensed preachers. Parker had done little to implement the command; Grindal, faced with orders so directly contrary to his beliefs, felt he had little choice but to make a stand. After consulting the bishops about the exercises in their dioceses, he expressed his pained surprise at Elizabeth's desire for so few preachers, defended the good effects of the exercises, and finally politely but firmly refused to carry out the order, urging the queen to refer to her churchmen all matters concerning the church's doctrine or discipline. This was not wise. Patrick Collinson asks

---

[44] *Elton,* Parliament (note 43), 214–216; *Collinson,* Puritan Movement (note 38), 118–121; *Peter Lake,* Anglicans and Puritans? Presbyterianism and English Conformist Thought from Whitgift to Hooker. London 1988.

whether Grindal had taken his stand „on a robust churchmanship which had emancipated itself from politics". Furious, Elizabeth would have liked to deprive Grindal. Procedural difficulties prevented this outcome, but his powers were severely curtailed.[45]

John Whitgift, who succeeded Grindal as archbishop in 1583, was of all her archbishops the most congenial from Elizabeth's point of view. Whitgift was determined to eliminate liturgical nonconformity and check any real or imagined movement towards Presbyterian organisation within the Church. His principal weapons were three articles for subscription by the clergy, the most important of which was a declaration that neither the Prayer Book nor the Ordinal contained anything contrary to the Word of God. He followed this up with twenty-four articles of enquiry on which suspected „puritan" ringleaders were to be questioned on oath. This, the most ambitious campaign to impose uniformity since the making of the Elizabethan settlement, took place (as the earlier vestiarian controversy had not) against the background of especially serious developments at home and abroad. Cumulatively more threatening than those of 1568–1571, these included rebellion in Ireland (1579–1583); the Spanish conquest of Portugal and the arrival of the first Jesuit missionaries in England (1580); renewed political uncertainty in Scotland following the execution of the earl of Morton (1581); the steady progress of the duke of Parma's reconquest of the southern Netherlands from 1582 onwards; renewed plotting on behalf of Mary Stuart (1583), the assassination of William of Orange, and an alliance between Philip II and the French Catholic League (both in 1584).

Whitgift's efforts provoked counter-measures by the „puritan" clergy, especially those organized in „conferences" which had grown up in various parts of the country during the previous decade, and their lay supporters. Patrick Collinson's classic account of their campaign has never been superseded. The puritans lobbied the 1584/85 parliament intensively, supporting their campaign with surveys of the scandalous state of the clergy in many counties and accounts of their own sufferings. The Commons considered sympathetically petitions from various counties on behalf of the puritan ministers and drew up a petition of their own. Eventually, however, Elizabeth forbade further discussion of ecclesiastical matters. In both this parliament and that of 1586/87 bills were introduced by puritan MPs calling for the introduction of a Genevan liturgy and presbyterian church government. In 1584/85 the Commons refused leave for the bill to be read; in 1587, Elizabeth prevented a reading by in effect confiscating the bill.[46]

---

[45] *Collinson,* Grindal (note 32), 233–278.
[46] *Collinson,* Puritan Movement (note 38), 243–316; *Patrick Collinson/John Craig/Brett Usher* (Eds.), Conferences and Combination. Lectures in the Elizabethan Church: Dedham and Bury St Edmunds 1582–1590. Woodbridge 2003.

There were two principal lessons to be drawn from the crisis of 1583–1587. The first was that Whitgift's heavy-handed and overbearing methods not only aroused considerable sympathy for the clergy who were victims of his campaign, but also resentment on the part of gentry who had used their powers of patronage to place puritan clergy, and hostility towards him and his episcopal associates. The second lesson, however, was that there was negligible support in parliaments for the introduction of presbyterianism or a Reformed liturgy. In 1587 Sir Christopher Hatton argued, persuasively, that plans to instal presbyterian government threatened the gentry's ecclesiastical patronage, would have to be financed out of former church property in their hands, and implicitly challenged the established hierarchy not only in the church but also in the state. His masterly speech was largely written for him by Richard Bancroft, the rising star among the anti-puritan clergy, and ultimately Whitgift's successor at Canterbury. Bancroft's rhetoric underlines what many lay property owners stood to lose through the implementation of presbyterian reforms. Within the still medieval organisational structure of the Church, the Reformation had brought about a massive transfer of formerly monastic patronage and assets to the nobility and gentry. The upper class control of appointments to a large proportion of parishes was not only a counterweight to the authority of the bishops but also a barrier to presbyterian aspirations.[47]

The late 1580s saw the end of hopes for substantial changes in either the liturgy or the government of the Church of England during Elizabeth's lifetime. The puritans lost in 1588 their leading organizer, John Field, and their most powerful lay patron, Robert Dudley, earl of Leicester. They were weakened by splits in their ranks, as some separatists moved outside the Church of England altogether. Eventually, the leading would-be reformers of church government, including Cartwright, were thoroughly intimidated by being tried for conspiracy in 1591, even though they were in the end released. Meanwhile, the worst of the dangers seemingly facing England in the 1580s had passed with Mary Stuart's execution in 1587 and the defeat of the Spanish Armada in 1588.[48]

The more militant puritans had measured the Church of England by the yardstick of scripture and found it wanting. Their grievances and their ambitions for reform had fuelled a well-organised political campaign. With the benefit of hindsight, this has sometimes seemed both precocious and formidable. Sir Christopher Hatton's claim that an attack on hierarchy in the church implicitly challenged the secular order too can look remarkably pre-

---

[47] *MacCulloch*, Later Reformation (note 38), 44–46; T. E. Hartley (Ed.), Proceedings in the Parliaments of Elizabeth I. Vol. 2: 1584–89. Leicester 1995, 333–338.
[48] *Collinson*, Puritan Movement (note 38), 403–431; *MacCulloch*, Later Reformation (note 38), 47–49.

scient in the light of the crisis that was to engulf England fifty years later. Here, one might say, „traditional politics" were truly being re-shaped by „visionary theology". Sir John Neale, author of the classic account of „Elizabeth I and her Parliaments" asserted that „through the plottings of the godly brotherhood and their organised group of Parliamentary agents, Queen Elizabeth was menaced with revolution in church and state". Subsequent appraisals of the puritan challenge have been more cautious. Patrick Collinson gives an unrivalled picture of puritan hopes and fears and of feverish political activity on the eve of the parliaments of the mid-1580s. His very thorough examination also shows, however, that effective puritan organisation covered only a minority of counties and that puritans varied greatly in their militancy and their commitment to the goals of reformed church government and liturgy. The records of the Dedham conference, best documented of all the local conferences of the puritan clergy, recently published in a new edition by Patrick Collinson, John Craig, and Brett Usher, also indicate the sturdy independence of ministers and congregations unwilling to be ruled either by the conference or the „high command" in London. In a recent survey, Diarmaid MacCulloch has pointed to the puritans' very limited success in winning county seats, with their large electorates, in the fiercely contested election of 1584, and the antagonism their survey of allegedly inadequate ministers probably aroused among the many lay patrons who had presented such ministers to their benefices. Presbyterians in England never came anywhere near matching in organisation, militancy or distinctiveness of identity the Huguenots in France. For all its faults, the Church of England gave them scope to pursue, if not always to achieve, their most important pastoral objectives within its capacious, rambling, and complex structure.[49]

Elizabeth's resolutely firm resistance ensured the defeat of proposals for sweeping reforms of church order and liturgy. Arguably, however, the fact that they had been formulated in the first place was largely due to her inflexible hostility towards moderate nonconformity and piecemeal revision of the Book of Common Prayer. By screwing down the safety-valve of dissent she had probably provoked the build-up of a more powerful head of steam than would otherwise have existed. Was this a price worth paying for the imposition of Elizabeth's own liturgical preferences? What else was gained? Elizabeth may have wished to avoid upsetting religious conservatives within England. It is a moot point whether the relatively conservative outward face of the Elizabethan Church did indeed secure the adherence of a substantial body of clergy and laity who might otherwise have remained

---

[49] *J. E. Neale,* Elizabeth I and her Parliaments. Vol. 2. London 1957, 156; *Collinson,* Puritan Movement (note 38), 277-282, 303-307, 317-329; *Collinson/Craig/Usher* (Eds.), Conferences and Combination (note 46); *MacCulloch,* Later Reformation (note 38), 43f.

loyal to the mass and re-joined the Roman Church when they had the opportunity. Certainly it did not prevent the formation of an English recusant community.

Elizabeth's religious policy was not however shaped by domestic considerations alone. She had to take account of the international situation. The „traditional political" goals of security and freedom of diplomatic manoeuvre dictated efforts to reassure foreign opinion, whether Catholic or Lutheran, especially in the early years of the reign. Anticipated Lutheran reactions almost certainly influenced the formulation and presentation of the Church's eucharistic doctrine in 1563. Susan Doran has suggested that Elizabeth's marriage negotiations with the archduke Charles of Austria, and her consequent concern that the Church of England should present an appearance of orderly uniformity, help to explain the 1560s drive against vestiarian nonconformity. Elizabeth's retention of a crucifix in her chapel was noticed in Spain and Rome. Philip II's minister Guerau de Spes, in a draft address he prepared for delivery to Elizabeth towards the end of 1568, praised her conspicuous moderation „in sustaining the churches and preserving to the clergy their ecclesiastical vestments, as well as maintaining a large portion of the Catholic observances, the veneration on the altar of the figure of the cross on which our Lord died, and the checking of the mad and furious insolence of those unhappy men, vulgarly called ministers, but who really are coarse clowns and charlatans". (De Spes's rhetoric was designed to persuade Elizabeth to return to the Catholic Church.)[50]

Elizabeth was well aware of the unpredictable disruptive force of confessional hostilities, and sought to limit their potentially destabilising effects on her own country. The intentions of a heretic queen were however viewed with suspicion by the Catholic powers from the start, and the proximity of Protestant England to the Habsburg Netherlands was a source of particular anxiety. From the 1560s onwards, mutual suspicions were enhanced by the presence in England of substantial colonies of refugees from the Netherlands, and in Louvain (Brabant) of a small group of English Catholic exiles. Elizabeth disliked the idea of helping rebels, especially religious rebels, but in practice frequently did so. William Cecil, her principal secretary of state, was the chief driving force for intervention in Scotland in 1559–1560 in face of the queen's own doubts and hesitations. In helping the Lords of the Congregation, he used a shared language of evangelical commitment. His chief aims, however, were the maintenance of English influence in Scotland, and the exclusion of the French. Soon, too, as Stephen Alford and John Guy have recently underlined once again, he became almost obsessively con-

---

[50] *Horie*, Lutheran Influence (note 37), 531–534; *Susan Doran,* Monarchy and Matrimony: The Courtships of Elizabeth I. London, 1996, 76; *Martin A. S. Hume* (Ed.), Calendar of State Papers, Spanish, 1568–1579. London 1894, 87.

cerned with the threat posed (in his eyes) by Mary Stuart, by birth the strongest potential rival claimant to Elizabeth's throne. Through kindred and religion and by virtue of her personality and ambitions Mary appeared the most serious potential source of division within Britain. Cecil worked hard to eliminate this danger by trying to persuade Elizabeth to settle the succession, to exclude Mary from it, and ultimately by seeking Mary's death.[51]

England's Catholic neighbours were unreliable. Cecil saw no point in gratuitously provoking them. After the failure of the Huguenots to oust the Guises from power in the Conspiracy of Amboise in 1560, for example, he firmly opposed the idea of entering into the „bottomless pit" of intervention in France with no support beyond „a devotion popular upon opinions in religion". On the other hand, he was ready to exploit an existing resistance in order to prevent the complete triumph of hostile Catholic forces as a prelude to their possible intervention in the British Isles. Thus he was prepared to support intervention in France in 1562. Early in 1569 he sketched that nightmare of Elizabethan policy makers, an alliance of the Spanish government of the Netherlands with militant Catholics in France. Anticipating such a development, he advocated the encouragement of rebels in both countries by all means short of war, and a firm alliance with other Protestant powers. A statesman who was prepared to support Elizabeth's marriage negotiations with the Archduke Charles of Austria in the 1560s and the duke of Anjou in the late 1570s can however hardly be regarded as a hardline advocate of the „Protestant cause". His paramount concern was the security of the realm, and in 1579 he saw the marriage negotiations with the duke of Anjou as the best means of preventing co-operation between the Catholic powers. Cecil also grew more cautious as he grew older.[52]

Stronger promoters of the Protestant cause there certainly were, especially Sir Francis Walsingham (principal secretary of state, 1573-1590) and Robert Dudley, earl of Leicester (though he was not entirely consistent). These men and their allies and supporters were the most persistent advocates of intervention in the Netherlands. Bruce Wernham characterised Walsingham in particular as a man who „spoke so often of ‚God's glory and next the Queen's safety,‘ always in that order". Elizabeth herself was ready

---

[51] *R. B. Wernham*, The Making of Elizabethan Foreign Policy 1558-1603. Berkeley/Los Angeles 1980; *Laura H. Yungblut*, Strangers Settled Here Amongst Us: Policies, Perceptions & the Presence of Aliens in Elizabethan England. London 1996; *David J. B. Trim*, Protestant Refugees in Elizabethan England and Confessional Conflict in France and the Netherlands, 1562-c. 1610, in: R. Vigne/C. Littleton (Eds.), From Strangers to Citizens. Brighton 2001, 68-79; *Stephen Alford*, The Early Elizabethan Polity: William Cecil and the British Succession Crisis, 1558-1569. Cambridge 1998; *John Guy*, My Heart is My Own: A Life of Mary Queen of Scots. London 2004.

[52] *R. B. Wernham*, Before the Armada: The Growth of English Foreign Policy 1485-1588. London 1966, 265, 299, 359; *Doran*, Monarchy and Matrimony (note 50), 73-98, 154-194.

to invoke religion when it served her purpose. „Her letters", says David Trim, „not only to the Condés and Navarres, but to William of Orange and to the German princes and the Scandinavian kings, are full of references to the common cause and the need for them to act together against the Papacy." But in practice Elizabeth refused to allow her policy to be determined by militant Protestantism. Only when a seemingly inexorable Spanish reconquest of the Netherlands was well under way, and the 1584 Treaty of Joinville had brought closer the realisation of the nightmare of co-operation between the Catholic powers, did she agree to send substantial help to the Netherlands. Even then she acted unwillingly, and in hope of inducing Philip II to enter negotiations.[53]

David Trim has emphasized the important part played by numerous English volunteers in Protestant armies in France and the Netherlands, giving as a particular instance the participation of members of the Champernowne family of Devon in the second and third religious wars in France and in assistance to beleaguered La Rochelle in 1572. Henry Champernowne died fighting in the third civil war. His personal ensign bore, on a black ground, a head uttering the words „My death is virtuous". Many volunteers were inspired by religion and the hope of renown. Others however were actuated by profit as well as Protestantism. The prospect of plunder was a powerful inducement to take part in the *guerre de course* in which Huguenot, Dutch and English sailors preyed on Catholic shipping, especially around 1570, and in England's later privateering war against Spain.[54]

The authors of the 1572 „Admonition to the Parliament" believed that England belonged in the vanguard of a Reformed cause whose dramatic early successes held out the hope of international victory. „Is a reformation good for France? and can it be evyl for England? Is discipline meete for Scotland? and is it unprofitable for this Realme?" But the most powerful uniting force for many, perhaps most English Protestants, was a common awareness of what they were *against*, rather than of any positive goals. Antipopery became a potent element of English politics, even – despite the survival of the persecuted Catholic community within England itself – an important strand of the dominant idea of English identity. The transformation of the papacy into a dark and sinister „other" and powerful force of evil had already gone a long way during Henry VIII's reign. The 1536 „Act extinguishing the authority of the bishop of Rome" charged the Pope with distorting

---

[53] *Wernham*, Making of Foreign Policy (note 51), 45, 48; *David J. B. Trim*, The „Secret War" of Elizabeth I: England and the Huguenots during the Early Wars of Religion, 1562-77, in: Proceedings of the Huguenot Society 27, 1999, 197.
[54] *Trim*, The „Secret War" (note 53), 195; *idem*, The Context of War and Violence in Sixteenth-Century English Society, in: Journal of Early Modern History 3, 1999, 253-255; *Wernham*, Before the Armada (note 52), 302, 307-309; *K. R. Andrews*, Elizabethan Privateering. Cambridge 1964.

and obscuring the meaning of Scripture in order to establish his own dominion over the souls, bodies and goods of Christian people, and with robbing the king of his rightful pre-eminence, spoiling the realm of treasure, and seducing his subjects into superstitious and erroneous opinions. The statute complained that „divers seditious and contentious persons", „imps" of the bishop of Rome, were still trying to maintain his authority. This shadowy multitude „whispering in corners" was in different guises to be an enduring feature of the English imagination. To the already long indictment of Rome was added, as a result of Mary Tudor's Catholic restoration, merciless persecution of God's people. This charge was exhaustively documented in John Foxe's „The Actes and Monuments of the English Martyrs", first published in 1563. Foxe's was one of many books of martyrs produced in different countries during the Reformation. It was international in scope, as V. Norskov Olsen has emphasized, rightly qualifying William Haller's more Anglocentric account. It provided a record of all the most notable persecutions since the time of Christ, and grew out of a Latin work published at Strassburg in 1554. The long climax of the „Actes and Monuments" was however the story of how the English Church had been tried by fire under Mary before its miraculous delivery through Elizabeth's accession to the throne. The sheer weight of testimony gathered by Foxe helped to obscure the more inglorious aspects of the English reaction to Catholic restoration, including the conformity of the great majority and the considerable extent of active cooperation. It encouraged English people to be proud of their martyrs, while stiffening their determination never again to fall prey to the Romish Antichrist. At the same time, the identification of persecution as one of the distinctive marks of popery militated against the rigorous and systematic repression of religious dissent in a way that benefited even the hard pressed Catholic community. England's form of anti-popery was to be an enduring product of her Reformation. It was a complex mixture whose ingredients certainly included elements of visionary theology and long-standing political claims and grievances, but much else besides.[55]

England escaped a religious war in the sixteenth century above all because the centre held. The legitimacy of the monarch was hardly ever seri-

---

[55] *W. H. Frere/C. E. Douglas* (Eds.), Puritan Manifestoes: a Study of the Origins of the Puritan Revolt, with a Reprint of the Admonition to the Parliament, etc. London 1907. 2nd Ed. 1954, 19; *G. R. Elton*, The Tudor Constitution: Documents and Commentary. 2nd Ed. Cambridge 1982, 365–367; *William Haller*, Foxe's Book of Martyrs and the Elect Nation. London 1963; *V. Norskov Olsen*, John Foxe and the Elizabethan Church. Berkeley 1973; *David Loades* (Ed.), John Foxe and the English Reformation. Aldershot 1997; *idem* (Ed.), John Foxe: An Historical Perspective. Aldershot 1999; *John Bossy*, The English Catholic Community, 1570–1850. London 1975; *Christopher Haigh*, Revisionism, the Reformation and the History of English Catholicism, in: Journal of Ecclesiastical History 36, 1985, 394–406; *MacCulloch*, Later Reformation (note 38), 126.

ously challenged, and the privy council always included leading magnates who represented a variety of opinions. Civil war came closest in 1553, when the succession was disputed between the Protestant Jane Grey and the Catholic Mary Tudor. The crisis was cut short by the swift victory of Mary, the more popular candidate as well as the one with the better claim. Elizabeth faced only one remotely convincing potential rival, Mary Stuart. Mary's alien birth, association with France, political ineptitude, and, for nearly the last twenty years of her life, virtual imprisonment by Elizabeth, limited her power to do harm. Nor did Elizabeth face an overmighty male relative with hopes of succeeding to the throne who might have presumed to press his advice on her. The puritans never matched in militancy or organisation the Reformed churches in France. Impatient with Elizabeth though they might be, most of them knew that her continued rule offered the best guarantee of security for English Protestantism. In an England threatened by enemies on all sides, it was crucial to avoid capsizing the boat. Elizabeth's government blocked the demand for Presbyterian reform in the 1580s, but only a tiny fraction of the puritans thought it necessary to separate from the Church of England.

The Catholic recusants also had much to lose. As Englishmen, most of them disliked the prospect of a foreign succession. The persecution of the Catholic laity was haphazard, often half-hearted, and increasingly aimed at raising revenue rather than extinguishing the Catholic community altogether. The main brunt of persecution was borne by the clergy; the Catholic nobility were largely exempt. A small minority of Catholics plotted for Mary Stuart's succession, but the majority remained loyal to Elizabeth, trying to separate their religious allegiance to the Roman Church from their political allegiance to the English crown – a point emphasized by Arnold Pritchard in particular. From abroad, William Allen and Robert Parsons defended resistance to a heretic monarch by reference to papal authority or the common good, but these ideas had little influence in England.[56]

Although many conservatives and Protestant activists remained dissatisfied with the Elizabethan church settlement, historians such as Judith Maltby and Christopher Haigh believe that in time it came to attract positive support from a growing proportion of the population.[57] The Book of Common Prayer offered services which called for lay understanding and participation within a formal framework which still included some ceremony. The church's liturgy and articles allowed some room for varieties of belief about the eu-

---

[56] *Peter Holmes,* Resistance and Compromise: The Political Thought of the Elizabethan Catholics. Cambridge 1982; *Arnold Pritchard,* Catholic Loyalism in Elizabethan England. London 1979.
[57] *Haigh,* English Reformations (note 13), 285-295; *Judith Maltby,* Prayer Book and People in Elizabethan and Early Stuart England. Cambridge 1998.

charist and predestination. Most of the theologically trained clergy may have seen the Church of England as properly belonging to the Reformed wing of European Protestantism, but much of their preaching, especially that of the puritans, fell on deaf ears. Erasmian and evangelical influences were still strong, even though there was as yet no clearly articulated theological alternative to the dominant Calvinism. Different styles of churchmanship could flourish.

The English Reformation in the Sixteenth Century: Major Themes and New Viewpoints

By

Martin Ingram

Ralph Houlbrooke's contribution offers a clear guide to the current state of thinking among historians on the origins and progress of the English Reformation, focusing principally on the evolution of royal policy and how this was affected by other forces, including visionary theology. This paper is intended to complement, not contradict, his account by exploring other perspectives that have emerged or are emerging in recent work on the English Reformation. The approach is therefore more explicitly historiographical. Successive sections of the paper focus on antecedents to the Henrician changes of the 1530s and the subsequent evolution of royal policy in the 1540s; the processes by which the English people became, at least in some sense, Protestant; cultural adaptations that helped to limit the shock of change and, to an extent, fostered peaceful co-existence among individuals and groups of differing religious persuasion; and the different story that emerges if what happened in England is viewed in tandem with what occurred in other parts of the British Isles.

I.

„We are also nowadays grieved of heretics, men mad with marvellous foolishness. But the heresies of them are not so pestilent and pernicious [...] as the evil and wicked life of priests."[1] For an older generation of scholars this quotation from the excoriating sermon delivered to the Convocation of 1512 by John Colet, Dean of Saint Paul's and a leading humanist scholar, encapsulated some of the circumstances that led to the English Reformation. This was the argument developed, with more subtlety than many recent critics have allowed, by the late Geoffrey Dickens. Dickens was under no illusions about the difficulties faced by Protestant reformers in the sixteenth century, and the enormous drag effect of religious conservatism, hardening eventually into stubborn recusancy, in many parts of England but especially the north. He was also well aware of contingencies, the twists of fate and political machination that helped to determine the course of religious policy. Above

---

[1] *C. H. Williams* (Ed.), English Historical Documents, 1485–1558. London 1971, 656.

all he knew that the great changes inaugurated in the 1530s owed much to Henry VIII's „great matter".[2]

Thus to characterise his model of religious change as „a rapid Reformation from below" is a caricature.[3] It is true, however, that Dickens, along with a majority of his generation, saw the Protestant Reformation as in some sense the destiny of the English people, intimately bound up with national identity. Accordingly he was more deeply impressed than might otherwise have been the case by symptoms of change before 1529, of the kind that Colet's sermon seemed to illustrate. He emphasized the native tradition of Lollard heresy, deriving from the followers of John Wyclif in the late fourteenth century and surviving as a stubborn minority in pockets mainly in southern England – in the Weald of Kent, on the Essex-Suffolk border, in the Thames Valley and points west in Gloucestershire, above all in the southern Chilterns, where in Amersham and a few other places Lollards were clustered in significant numbers. He also assumed that the failings of the pre-Reformation clergy, combined with the enormous wealth and power that the Church disposed of, had created a deep well of resentment among lay people. He linked this with the erastian tendencies of the monarchy, which had already in theory and practice achieved, at the expense of the Papacy, a great deal of power over the Church, and periodically flexed its muscles in its relations with the spiritual power within England. On this view, anticlericalism and erasmianism made Reformation, if not an easy matter, at least feasible when the crisis came in 1529–1534.

More generally Dickens assumed that the beliefs and practices of late medieval devotion, though outwardly popular and flourishing, lacked real spiritual substance. They were therefore vulnerable to the new religious ideas, inspired by European Protestantism, that gradually infiltrated from the 1520s. Many of these innovations made slow progress in the reign of Henry VIII, who never explicitly countenanced Protestant doctrines and reaffirmed key doctrines of Catholicism in the Act of Six Articles of 1539. But they had free rein under his Protestant son Edward VI, to the extent that Mary's attempt to restore Roman Catholicism faced a variety of major obstacles and some stubborn resistance, and was doomed to extinction by her failure to produce an heir and her own death after only five years on the throne. On this view the re-establishment of a Protestant settlement by Elizabeth in 1559 represented a fitting end to the story of the English Reformation. There eventually emerged a stubborn minority of Catholic recusants, who would never reconcile themselves to the national Church. There was also a tiny minority of Protestant separatists, who on other grounds but with equal finality re-

---

[2] *A. G. Dickens*, The English Reformation. London 1964.
[3] *Christopher Haigh*, The Recent Historiography of the English Reformation, in: idem (Ed.), The English Reformation Revised. Cambridge 1987, 21.

jected that Church as hopelessly corrupt. A larger group of „puritans" strove for further reform; a sub-set of this wing within the Church even campaigned, in vain, for a fundamental remodelling of Church government on presbyterian lines. But mostly the moderate Protestant settlement of Elizabeth met the needs and desires of the people, including a large section motivated by „secularism, relative indifference to religion, weariness of doctrinal contentions, obsession with peace and security". Thus England escaped the religious strife that rent France and the Netherlands in the same period.[4]

Some elements of this account were always open to question, and the interpretation of particular incidents such as the Pilgrimage of Grace of 1536 (apparently evidence of powerful popular resistance to the first phase of the dissolution of the monasteries and other changes of the Henrician Reformation) or Wyatt's Rebellion of 1554 (at first sight more to do with anti-Spanish feeling than with religion) was fiercely contested in the 1960s and 1970s.[5] Thereafter there was a much more sustained assault on Dickens's narrative. In 1982 J. J. Scarisbrick asserted that „on the whole, English men and women did not want the Reformation and most of them were slow to accept it when it came". In support of this viewpoint he surveyed the rich variety of lay religious practice on the eve of the Reformation, expressed in will bequests and institutionalized in chantries, gilds, pilgrimages, and parish churches, and found them in a flourishing condition before Henry VIII, for reasons of his own, began to meddle with the status quo.[6] A decade later a similar argument was made, but in much greater detail and „with an earlier chronological emphasis, by Eamon Duffy. His study of pre-Reformation „traditional religion" has some curious gaps – there is nothing on monasticism – but what he does describe is evoked in extraordinary depth and detail in the first two thirds of a very big book. Succeeding chapters on the „stripping of the altars" make a lean, bleak contrast.[7] Meanwhile Christopher Haigh, building on a wide range of detailed, archivally based studies (including his own on Lancashire), had mounted a more explicit attack on Dickens's arguments. Briskly he cut Lollardy down to size, endorsing Sir Thomas

---

[4] *Dickens,* English Reformation (note 2), 451.
[5] *D. M. Loades,* Two Tudor Conspiracies. Cambridge 1965; *C. S. L. Davies,* The Pilgrimage of Grace Reconsidered, in: Past and Present 41, 1969, 54–76; *idem,* Popular Religion and the Pilgrimage of Grace, in: Anthony Fletcher/John Stevenson (Eds.), Order and Disorder in Early Modern England. Cambridge 1985, 58–91; *Margaret Bowker,* Lincolnshire 1536: Heresy, Schism or Religious Discontent?, in: Derek Baker (Ed.), Studies in Church History 9: Schism, Heresy and Religious Protest. Cambridge 1972, 195–212; *Malcolm R. Thorp,* Religion and the Wyatt Rebellion of 1554, in: Church History 47, 1978, 363–380.
[6] In the Ford lectures delivered at Oxford, published as *J. J. Scarisbrick,* The Reformation and the English People. Oxford 1984.
[7] *Eamon Duffy,* The Stripping of the Altars. Traditional Religion in England, c.1400–c.1580. New Haven/London 1992.

More's observation that if anyone surveyed the English dioceses „except London and Lincoln he shall scant in any one of all the remnant find punished for heresy four persons in five years". Even in Lollard „strongholds" such as Amersham, groups of adherents were small in scale and inward-looking, with an unheroic tendency to profess their heterodox beliefs in secret or alone, and to recant under pressure; many were, to outward appearance, conforming practitioners of parish religion. While Lollard groups possessed books, including copies of the Wycliffite Bible, they were themselves intellectually moribund, devoid of new texts and fresh ideas. Haigh was equally dismissive of anticlericalism, in his view a „convenient fiction" that had deflected historians from serious thought about lay-clerical relations. In truth there was no „groundswell of discontent" with the pre-Reformation Church. If there were indeed signs of tension, they were few and the individuals and groups involved were mostly self-interested. Even the so-called anticlerical legislation of the Reformation Parliament was less substantial than often supposed, and to a great extent drummed up by the enemies of Wolsey, including the London Mercers' Company. Haigh's overall conclusion was clear. To all intents and purposes this was „a Church unchallenged". It was the break with Rome that was to cause the decline of Catholicism, not the other way round.[8]

What provided the „dynamic of change" was politics. Henry's initial moves to secure an annulment of his marriage with Katherine of Aragon led on to the dissolution of the monasteries and other changes, and the pace quickened under Edward VI, when chantries (and with them prayers for the dead) were abolished, the catholic mass and the traditional liturgy were replaced by a Protestant communion service in English, and explicitly Protestant doctrines were promulgated in the Forty-Two Articles of 1553. But, Haigh urged, there was nothing pre-ordained in this sequence of events. On the contrary, change was uncertain and halting under Henry; as far as was possible most of the changes of the previous twenty-five years were reversed under Mary; and the Elizabethan reversion to a Protestant settlement was a fudged affair. What made English people – or rather, *some* English people – Protestant was an always incomplete process of evangelical conversion extending over generations. „So England had blundering Reformations, which most did not understand, which few wanted, and which no one knew had come to stay."[9]

Inherent in this situation was the danger of religious strife. Some historians have argued that, if things had gone awry – for example, if Elizabeth,

---

[8] *Christopher Haigh*, English Reformations. Religion, Politics and Society under the Tudors. Oxford 1993, 23, 28, 53–55; *idem*, Anticlericalism and the English Reformation, in: idem (Ed.), English Reformation Revised (note 3), 56.
[9] *Haigh*, English Reformations (note 8), 14, 20.

with no undisputed heir, had died prematurely or suffered assassination in the 1560s, '70s, or '80s – there might have been a succession war that must, in the circumstances, have become in part a war of religion. As it was, England witnessed religious strife in the form of major popular rebellions in 1536 (the Lincolnshire revolt and the Pilgrimage of Grace), 1549 (the Western or „Prayer Book" rebellion), 1554 (Wyatt's rebellion, which, it is now generally agreed, did have religious overtones), and 1569 (the revolt of the northern earls of Northumberland and Westmorland). But engrained habits of obedience to the crown, which successive governments reinforced by a constant stream of propaganda and a string of penal measures, held violence in check.[10]

Of course politics was important, as has always been recognized. But the account offered by Haigh is unduly simplified. This theme is pursued by Ralph Houlbrooke, who emphasizes the large measure of conviction politics seen in the reign of the strongly Protestant Edward VI as well as of his conservative half-sister Mary, and develops the theme of Tudor theories of obedience and other reasons why, in his apt phrase, „the centre held". But what of the other elements of the so-called „revisionist" arguments that have been reviewed here?

II.

In the light of the work of Scarisbrick, Haigh and Duffy, and indeed of others such as Burgess, Rosser and Kümin, it is incontrovertible that many elements of popular devotion were flourishing right up until the 1530s.[11] What people actually believed and what they thought can never be known, but it is plain that they were prepared to invest large amounts of money, time and energy in the rebuilding and adornment of churches, the cult of saints and, above all, in the endowment of prayers for the dead; and that these practices were associated with an extraordinarily complex set of religious ideas that

---

[10] C. S. L. Davies, Peace, Print and Protestantism, 1450-1558. St. Albans 1977, 320-321; Anthony Fletcher/Diarmaid MacCulloch, Tudor Rebellions. 4th Ed. London/New York 1997.
[11] Scarisbrick, Reformation and the English People (note 6), 3, 6, 34; Haigh, English Reformations (note 8), ch. 1; Duffy, Stripping of the Altars (note 7), ch. 1–10; Clive Burgess, „By Quick and by Dead": Wills and Pious Provision in Late Medieval Bristol, in: English Historical Review 102, 1987, 837-858; idem, „A Fond Thing Vainly Invented": an Essay on Purgatory and Pious Motive in Later Medieval England, in: Susan J. Wright (Ed.), Parish, Church and People. Studies in Lay Religion 1350-1750. London 1988, 56–84; Gervase Rosser, Communities of Parish and Guild in the Late Middle Ages, in: ibid. 29–55; Beat A. Kümin, The Shaping of a Community. The Rise and Reformation of the English Parish, c.1400–1560. Aldershot 1996.

were capable of being, and indeed were, articulated in varying degrees of sophistication from the very simple to the highly learned. As Duffy's preference for the term „traditional" rather than „popular" religion suggests, many of these ideas and practices were not confined to the poor or ignorant but were (with variations) the common property of all ranks, orders and degrees of men and women, whether layfolk or clergy, peasants, townsmen, gentry, nobles, or courtiers. However, as much could be said for other areas of Europe that felt the force of Reformation; and to emphasise unduly the flourishing state of popular piety begs the question of how religious change occurs. It cannot be assumed that what was popular and flourishing in the early decades of the sixteenth century was bound to remain so. Religion is part of culture, and hence subject to sometimes dramatic and sudden transformations; and the culture of the sixteenth century was particularly mutable as a result of the accelerating impact of the printing press. Religious practice is also subject to fashion, which is no less fickle in this area of human life than in others. The term „traditional religion" has the disadvantage that it can suggest an age and persistence that are not warranted; while surveys of religious practice extending over a century or more, or defined by some vague chronological term such as „pre-Reformation" or „late medieval", can obscure the processes of and potential for change. Ronald Hutton has emphasised that practices such as Hocktide customs – when, to raise money for the church, groups of men seized and ransomed women and, much more lucratively, groups of women likewise seized men – had not existed from time immemorial but had identifiable, often quite recent origins. Moreover, Haigh and Scarisbrick concede that there are signs of changing fashion in the decades preceding the breach with Rome; for example, it appears that in London and some other towns the impetus to endow prayers for the dead had peaked before 1500.[12] Haigh emphasises the attraction around 1530 – but presumably only among literate people of reasonable substance – of vernacular guides to pious living, of which Richard Whitford's *Work for householders* (1530) is the outstanding example.[13] Yet he does not consider the potential of such an austere, quasi-monastic regimen of lay piety to shift tastes away from the more extravagant elements of „traditional" ritual observances. As is well known, contemporary humanist observers roundly condemned what they saw as the ignorant or superstitious abuses of such practices; and while there is no reason to believe these criticisms had much immediate impact, they were the sign of shifting religious tastes that could, in time, have had far-reaching effects.

---

[12] Ronald Hutton, The Rise and Fall of Merry England. The Ritual Year 1400–1700. Oxford 1994, ch. 2; *Scarisbrick*, Reformation and the English People (note 6), 33f.; *Haigh*, English Reformations (note 8), 37.

[13] *Haigh*, English Reformations (note 8), 25–28.

Setting such speculations aside, it is a matter of fact that many elements of popular piety, apparently so vibrant, proved extremely vulnerable to attack and collapsed quite rapidly from the 1530s onwards. The Royal Injunctions of 1538 instructed parishes to extinguish all lights in the church except those on the altar, in the rood loft and before the Easter sepulchre, ordered the removal of images that had been „abused with pilgrimages and offerings", and forbade the veneration of relics. While the impact was regionally patchy, there was undoubtedly an immediate effect in many parishes, and expenditure on new images practically ceased. Because lights were, in many regions, the single most common expression of mortuary piety, the injunctions also contributed to a decline in bequests for intercessory prayers and the gilds and chantries associated with them.[14] A more direct attack on prayers for the dead was in any case already in train. In 1534 purgatory had been identified as a controversial topic on which preaching was banned; two years later the Ten Articles mentioned purgatory only to cast doubt on its existence; while the King's Book of 1543, in many respects a conservative document, referred to the doctrine in contemptuous and dismissive terms.[15] Evidence from parishes indicates that bequests for intercessory prayers rapidly declined; gilds and fraternities, „numerous and healthy" up to the early 1530s, ran into difficulties thereafter; and increasingly chantry property and endowments were expropriated by laymen and put to other uses. The trickle of expropriations became a flood between the act of 1545, which authorized the king to confiscate chantry property in certain circumstances, and that of 1547, which suppressed all chantries and related institutions on the grounds that the doctrine of purgatory was a „vain opinion" rooted in „blindness and ignorance".[16] Duffy finds „surprising" the fact that there were few revivals of these institutions under Mary. As will be seen, the destruction of the cult of the dead was driven partly by financial incentives, and there were both monetary and practical difficulties about re-erecting chantries. But what the rapid extinction of this set of institutions and practices primarily seems to show is their vulnerability to an authoritative statement that they were, contrary to what had been believed for generations, simply unnecessary for salvation. „A rotten structure crumbles when kicked": rightly, Duffy evokes this image only to dismiss it. But Dickens may not have been far wrong when he surmised that by the time of the dissolution of the chantries many people had effectively

---

[14] *Duffy*, Stripping of the Altars (note 7), 407–410; *Caroline Litzenberger*, The English Reformation and the Laity. Gloucestershire, 1540-1580. Cambridge 1997, 51f.
[15] *George Bernard*, The Making of Religious Policy, 1533-1546: Henry VIII and the Search for the Middle Way, in: Historical Journal 41, 1998, 324, 334; *Duffy*, Stripping of the Altars (note 7), 393, 443.
[16] *Scarisbrick*, Reformation and the English People (note 6), 34-36, 65-68, 85-99.

„ceased to believe in the doctrine of intercessory masses for souls in purgatory".[17]

The religious houses were another set of institutions that had proved remarkably vulnerable. In a sense this is less surprising, and the idea of expropriation has a longer history. It is agreed that some communities, notably the Carthusians and Brigettines, still maintained extremely high standards of monastic piety, while many other religious houses served useful social and economic functions. Yet many others – if not the dens of iniquity purportedly exposed by the visitations of the smaller monasteries in 1535/36 – were uninspiring at best, while even in terms of numbers and wealth some were scarcely viable. There was a more basic problem. Monasteries served to offer prayers and masses for their founders and benefactors; but new foundations were by the early sixteenth century impossibly expensive and, in any case, the monastery as a purgatorial institution was out of fashion even before Henry's government began to attack the doctrines that upheld them. Money was flowing instead towards the provision of intercessionary prayers for a limited period, and towards the foundation of colleges, almshouses and hospitals with practical social as well as intercessory functions. Educational foundations were especially fashionable.[18]

There was, as a result, much sympathy among churchmen and pious lay people for the idea that small, unsatisfactory, or simply redundant houses might usefully be dissolved and their endowments transferred to more desirable ends. This practice had begun well before 1500 and was continued in the early sixteenth century not only by Wolsey but also by such unimpeachably dedicated churchmen as Archbishop Warham and Bishops Fox of Winchester and Longland of Lincoln. The houses so suppressed were invariably small, if not unsatisfactory in other respects. But the core principle of pious recycling was appealed to in the act of 1539 that stated that ex-monastic assets might be „turned to better use [...] whereby God's word might the better be set forth, children brought up in learning, clerks nourished in the universities, old servants decayed to have livings, almshouses for poor folk to be sustained in, Readers of Greek, Hebrew and Latin to have good stipends, daily alms to be administered, mending of highways, exhibition of ministers of the Church [...]".[19]

However, there was an alternative set of ideas in favour of expropriation, and one that was more in accord with the uses to which the spoils of the monasteries were eventually put – that is, to swell the king's coffers, especial-

---

[17] *Duffy*, Stripping of the Altars (note 7), 478, 495; *Dickens*, English Reformation (note 2), 292.
[18] *Felicity Heal*, Reformation in Britain and Ireland. Oxford 2003, 45–59; *R. W. Hoyle*, The Origins of the Dissolution of the Monasteries, in: Historical Journal 38, 1995, 276f.
[19] *Joyce Youings*, The Dissolution of the Monasteries. London/New York 1971, 85.

ly his war chest, and, eventually, to augment the resources of the lay aristocracy. This tradition is particularly interesting in suggesting evidence of Lollard influence, at least indirectly, on Henry's actions. It is, of course, the case that the later Lollards were defined by their heretical doctrines and unorthodox practices, notably a reliance on the vernacular scriptures and (often) a denial of transubstantiation. Though some were literate, in terms of contemporary educational hierarchies they counted as unlearned folk; and, though recent research has shown that some were quite wealthy and prominent in their local communities, compared to those with real influence in early Tudor England their social station was decidedly humble. They had no access to the powerhouses of learning and political influence, the universities, the court, or the households of the great. Their impact on the king was therefore non-existent, save in the negative sense that Henry knew that Lollards existed and disapproved of them strongly. In particular, he abhorred the sacramentarian heresy as a fundamental threat to right order in the Christian world.[20]

But there had been another strand in early Lollard opinion – one that had appealed to men like John of Gaunt and a number of knights in the royal entourage in the late fourteenth century. This was the idea of expropriating ecclesiastical wealth for a dual purpose: to remove from the body of the Church a corrupting influence, and thus to help it to purify itself for its mission in the world; and to apply the Church's lands and goods to the crown's urgent needs in fighting its just war against France, to the maintenance of knights and noblemen whose assistance the king urgently needed, and to the endowment of almshouses. In the event these schemes had come to nothing. Wyclif's eventual rejection of transubstantiation had tainted the movement with execrable heresy. The usurper Henry IV had found it more expedient to support the ecclesiastical status quo than sponsor radical reform, and hence, after some hesitation, had turned firmly away from the Lollards; Henry V, casting himself in the role of most pious Christian prince, a veritable „defender of the faith", had rejected Lollardy even more emphatically, especially after his support for proceedings against Sir John Oldcastle had provoked

---

[20] *A. G. Dickens*, Lollards and Protestants in the Diocese of York, 1509–1558. Hull 1959; *John A. F. Thomson*, The Later Lollards, 1414–1520. London 1965; *Margaret Aston*, Lollards and Reformers. Images and Literacy in Late Medieval Religion. London 1984; *Andrew Hope*, Lollardy: The Stone the Builders Rejected?, in: Peter Lake/Maria Dowling (Eds.), Protestantism and the National Church in Sixteenth Century England. London 1987, 1–35; *Anne Hudson*, The Premature Reformation. Wycliffite Texts and Lollard History. Oxford 1988; *Derek Plumb*, The Social and Economic Status of the Later Lollards, in: Margaret Spufford (Ed.), The World of Rural Dissenters, 1520–1725. Cambridge 1995, 103–131; *Margaret Aston/Colin Richmond* (Eds.), Lollardy and the Gentry in the Later Middle Ages. Stroud/New York 1997; *Richard Rex*, The Lollards. Basingstoke 2002.

rebellion in 1414 – an event that indelibly stained the Lollard movement with sedition and deprived it of virtually all upper-class support.[21]

It would appear, however, that Lollard plans for expropriation were revived under Henry VIII, as Richard Hoyle has shown. A paper roll associated with the parliament of 1529 combines two texts: a copy of a Lollard petition to Henry IV in 1410, calling for a partial disendowment of the clergy; and a petition of 1529, likewise calling for disendowment and linking this to the twin objectives of reforming the clergy and undertaking a crusade against the Turks. Some of these themes are anticipated in a memorandum drawn up by Thomas Lord Darcy in July 1529, and Hoyle may well be right to argue that the document emanates from the circle of Darcy and, perhaps, Cardinal Wolsey's other aristocratic critics, including the Dukes of Norfolk and Suffolk. Admittedly this was not a blueprint for the dissolution of the monasteries as it actually happened. Though likely, it is not certain that the 1529 petition was presented to Parliament; and though some of its concerns were reflected in the legislation of that year, the proposals as such were not enacted. Moreover, the thrust of the document is reform of the clergy, not wholesale destruction of the monasteries.

What seems to have happened is that ideas countenancing a certain degree of expropriation for beneficial purposes, current around 1530, were radicalized out of all recognition in succeeding years. In 1534, in the context of the king's desperate need for money and the escalation of Kildare's rebellion in Ireland, a paper entitled „Things to be moved for the kings highness for an increase and augmentation of his most royal estate and for the defence of the realm, and necessary to be provided for taking away the excess which is the great cause of the abuses in the church", proposed much more far-reaching changes. Not only were monastic houses to be disendowed, but in addition the bishops were to lose their lands and to be put on stipends. It is even less certain that these proposals were put to Parliament, nor is it altogether clear that they represented government policy; if they did, the measures that threatened the bishops' lands foundered. But policy with regard to the monasteries stiffened. On the basis of visitations that purported to reveal the ill-discipline, immorality and superstition of the religious, the lesser monasteries were dissolved by statute in 1536. Since this act conceded that the greater monasteries still maintained satisfactory standards, it appeared to preclude further dissolutions. But the confiscation of the property of the larger religious houses was, in fact, achieved by the simple expedient of sending royal commissioners to persuade them, one by one, to surrender to the king. The act of 1539 merely tidied up a *fait accompli*. The dissolutions must therefore be seen in a dual

---

[21] *Margaret Aston*, Lollardy and Sedition 1381–1431, in: Past and Present 17, 1960, 1–44; *Jeremy Catto*, Religious Change under Henry V, in: G. L. Harriss (Ed.), Henry V. The Practice of Kingship. Oxford 1985, 97–115.

light. As they actually happened they were sudden and startling; but underlying them was „an idea awaiting its time" that had long been in circulation.[22]

The events leading up to the dissolution of the monasteries have a bearing also on impulses to church reform that predated the breach with Rome, on the issue of anticlericalism, and, of course, on the origins of the royal supremacy. Again these are areas where, as recent research has shown, a degree of chronological perspective is desirable. It is certainly true that the breakdown of relations with the Pope, and its radical outcome, was quite against the trend of royal-papal relations and arose out of the immediate crisis of the king's great matter. The relationship between the crown and the Church within England was a rather different issue. As has been said, the first two Lancastrian kings rejected the role of church reformers and instead championed religious orthodoxy, while Henry VI – who was either simple-minded or in other respects completely unsuited to the position of monarch – immersed himself in conventional piety. The Yorkist usurper, Edward IV, likewise chose to support the status quo, though the charter that confirmed the liberties of the Church in 1462 had little effect in practice. Henry VII was rather more aggressive. Support for Christian renewal was one element of Henry's royal ideology, but the forms it took, though highly fashionable, were wholly conventional.[23] However, his reign saw determined efforts to restrict „benefit of clergy" (protection from the penalties of the secular law in cases of felony) and rights of sanctuary. Moreover, in response to the pleas of litigants his judges began to police the borders between royal and ecclesiastical jurisdiction more rigorously, especially in the areas of litigation over debt (handled by the church courts in the guise of suits for perjury or breach of faith) and defamation concerning temporal crimes such as theft. The weapons used by the royal courts were writs of prohibition and, more importantly, prosecutions under the statutes of *praemunire*. The latter threatened individuals who were found to have unlawfully exercised spiritual jurisdiction with fearsome penalties, in theory extending to confiscation of all goods and perpetual imprisonment. In the decades after 1500 these moves began to have a perceptible effect on the pattern of ecclesiastical court business, which both contracted in scope and, it would seem, declined in volume. Even if, in the short term, these manoeuvres amounted to no more than small-scale turf wars between the spiritual and temporal courts, they did show ecclesiastical institutions could be cowed. The threat of *praemunire* proceedings was to be Henry VIII's most effective weapon in securing the submission of the clergy.[24]

---

[22] *Hoyle*, Origins of the Dissolution of the Monasteries (note 18), 275–305.
[23] *R. N. Swanson*, Church and Society in Late Medieval England. Oxford 1989, 108, 184; *Anthony Goodman*, Henry VII and Christian Renewal, in: Keith Robins (Ed.), Religion and Humanism. Oxford 1981, 115–125.
[24] *John A. F. Thomson*, The Early Tudor Church and Society, 1485–1529. London/New York 1993, 91–105; *R. H. Helmholz*, Roman Canon Law in Reformation England. Cam-

Various other events have a bearing on the eventual emergence of the Royal Supremacy. It is sometimes suggested that at the beginning of his reign Henry VIII modified the coronation oath to express a more exalted view of royal power, but it seems more likely that the alteration was made in the 1530s. In 1515, however, in the wake of the alleged murder in episcopal custody of the London merchant Richard Hunne, and the controversy over Henry Standish's subsequent assertions of royal authority, Henry had declared that „the kings of England in time past have never had any superior but God alone". In its context the significance of this statement was plainly limited: of far more importance for the development of the ideas on which the Royal Supremacy was based was the „Collectanea satis copiosa" compiled by Edward Foxe and Thomas Cranmer in 1530. But this early statement is indicative of currents of thought that could, under the intense pressure of the king's demand for a solution to his matrimonial problems, be developed with extremely radical effect.[25]

A related issue is the apparent vulnerability of the clerical estate in 1529–1532. While Haigh and others are doubtless right to reject the idea of anticlericalism as a widespread and powerful force, it does seem that something was amiss. One thread in this is the issue of clerical immorality. If, as has been suggested, few priests were actually guilty of illicit sexual relations and lay complaints were few and muted, why should a document like the supposed parliamentary petition of 1529 lay so much emphasis on clerical lechery: „who is there known more lecher[ous] than priests hath been known of late days or who is there that shall hear a temporal man tell so bawdy a tale or speak of lechery openly without shame than priests and for keeping of men's wives or men's servants or daughters contrary to the commandment of Almighty God more than priests?"[26]

Haigh and others have downplayed the issue; indeed Loades has gone so far as to state that parishioners „normally accepted that a man needed a woman, and as long as he treated her decently and provided for his children, they were not disposed to be critical".[27] Recent work indicates that this is wide of the mark. Lay people were deeply scandalized by clerical immorality

---

bridge 1990, 25–27, 30–34, 56–58; *John Guy*, Henry VIII and the *Praemunire* Manoeuvres of 1530–1531, in: English Historical Review 97, 1982, 481–503.

[25] *Guy*, Henry VIII and the *Praemunire* Manoeuvres of 1530–1531 (note 24), 497; *idem*, Thomas Cromwell and the Intellectual Origins of the Henrician Reformation, in: Alistair Fox/John Guy (Eds.), Reassessing the Henrician Age. Humanism, Politics and Reform, 1500–1550. Oxford 1986, 151–178; *G. W. Bernard*, The Pardon of the Clergy Reconsidered, in: Journal of Ecclesiastical History 37, 1986, 262.

[26] *Hoyle*, Origins of the Dissolution of the Monasteries (note 18), 303 (spelling modernized).

[27] *Haigh*, English Reformations (note 8), 41f.; *David Loades*, Anticlericalism in the Church of England Before 1558: an „Eating Canker"?, in: Nigel Aston/Matthew Cragoe (Eds.), Anticlericalism in Britain, c.1500–1914. Stroud 2000, 5.

for several reasons. They were concerned about the corruption of wives and young women; they saw it as a betrayal of trust; and they feared that an impure priest would contaminate the sacraments and perhaps render them inefficacious. Particular horror was felt at the thought that the hands that consecrated the sacrament might before or afterwards have „handled a whore's arse". It is true that clerical immorality was not rampant. Concubinage was not widely practised, as it was in some parts of the continent; and in any year, in any jurisdiction, probably fewer than 5 per cent of priests were brought in question for sexual incontinence.[28] But the cumulative impact of such figures was greater than appears at first sight. Conclusions derived solely from visitation materials are misleading. When the full range of ecclesiastical court records survive for comparison, it emerges that visitation presentments were not the main source of detections for this kind of offence. The reasons are obvious. The clergy were themselves often present at visitations, and churchwardens and their fellow „inquisitors" must often have been reluctant to accuse them face to face. It was also advantageous for the church authorities to receive accusations privately, so that scandal could be avoided as much as possible. The corollary, however, was that cases were often handled secretly. Moreover, convictions were hard to achieve. Even when priests were found guilty, they were sometimes enjoined discreet forms of penance, such as fasting or going on pilgrimage; they were thus spared the penalties of public exposure. Stipendiary priests were sometimes dismissed from their posts, or encouraged to move elsewhere; but beneficed clergy were rarely deprived.[29]

That some lay people were dissatisfied with these procedures is suggested by the fact that they resorted to the criminal courts to bring immoral priests to book. The means was to indict them on charges of rape. Some such cases may indeed have involved forcible intercourse without the woman's consent. But it is plain that, in many cases, the relationship was consensual: the rape charge was used as a legal fiction to bring the matter before the secular courts. Admittedly the outcome for the priests involved was less dire than might at first sight be supposed. Most cases led to acquittals; indeed many charges were probably thrown out by the grand jury before they reached the stage of formal indictment. Priests who were convicted could plead „benefit of clergy", which freed them from the danger of hanging. It must therefore be understood that the purpose of these prosecutions was not to secure the execution of the priests concerned but to expose them publicly and put them to considerable expense and trouble, which might well include a period of pre-trial imprisonment in noisome and dangerous conditions. The practice

---

[28] *Peter Marshall*, The Catholic Priesthood and the English Reformation. Oxford 1994, 142-163.
[29] This and the following paragraph are based partly on my unpublished work in progress.

was well established by the fifteenth century and, in some parts of the country, cases occurred in significant numbers. Thus nearly one hundred parochial clergy of Norwich diocese were arraigned on charges of rape at gaol deliveries between 1423 and 1441, and additional cases were probably prosecuted in sessions of the peace. Loss of the relevant records makes it impossible to provide comparable figures for the eve of the Reformation, but it is plain both from scattered references in the courts of King's Bench, Star Chamber and Chancery and from contemporary comments that the practice continued. Sir Thomas More claimed that „men know well in many a shire how often that many folk indict priests of rape at the sessions. And as there is sometime a rape committed indeed, so is there ever a rape surmised were the women never so willing, and oftentime where there was nothing done at all [...] Ye see not very many sessions pass but in one shire or other this pageant is played".[30]

There was perhaps another reason why laymen pursued charges of clerical incontinence with such alacrity. Such behaviour was so clearly forbidden by canon law that the authorities could not object when parishioners voiced well-founded accusations. In contrast, it would seem that complaints and criticisms on many other matters, and objections to rights claimed by the clergy, were muted because laymen feared that churchmen would retaliate by bringing heresy charges against them. The most famous case is that of Richard Hunne, who claimed to have incurred the wrath of the officials of the bishop of London for refusing to make a mortuary payment after the death of his young son. Analogous cases can sometimes be traced in local records. For example, in 1520 a Sussex man was prosecuted for heresy, and ordered to perform a humiliating penance, for suggesting that it was lawful to set aside seed corn before calculating tithe payments.[31] Whether or not cases occurred in any numbers, contemporary comments suggest that lay people had come to believe that churchmen were acting in this way and were fearful of the consequences. The direction of royal policy in 1529 opened up the prospect of a very different world. As the chronicler Edward Hall commented:

„These things before this time might in no wise be touched nor yet talked of by no man except he would be made a heretic, or lose all that he had, for the bishops were chancellors, and had all the rule about the king, so that no man durst once presume to attempt any thing contrary to their profit or commodity. But now when God had illumined the eyes of the king, and that their subtle doings was once espied: then men began charitably to desire a reformation, and so at this Parliament men began to show their grudges."

---

[30] R. L. Storey, Malicious Indictments of Clergy in the Fifteenth Century, in: M. J. Franklin/Christopher Harper-Bill (Eds.), Medieval Ecclesiastical Studies in Honour of Dorothy M. Owen. Woodbridge 1995, 221-240; *Frank Manley/Germain Marc'hadour/ Richard Marins/Clarence Miller*, The Complete Works of St. Thomas More. Vol. 2. New Haven/London 1990, 131 (spelling modernized).

[31] West Sussex Record Office, Ep.I/10/2, fos. 27-28, 31.

As Ethan Shagan has recently shown, a similar response is discernible in numerous local incidents – and some larger-scale regional episodes – of aggression towards members of the clergy in the 1530s and 1540s. Evidently the perception that the crown had turned against the priests could activate or intensify feelings of resentment and hostility that had previously lain dormant.[32]

III.

As Patrick Collinson has observed, recognition of the apparent vitality of pre-Reformation religious practice raises in acute form the „conundrum of compliance".[33] Admittedly, it is within limits possible to question just how great the impact of Reformation changes actually was. Christine Peters, emphasizing the strongly Christocentric nature of much late medieval devotion, suggest that this „offered the possibility of a relatively easy transition to Protestantism", since the idea of salvation by the merits of Christ's passion was equally accessible to a late medieval Catholic as it was to an early Protestant evangelical. She makes this case in the context of a discussion of the impact of the Reformation on female piety, but the argument can be extended to both genders. Christopher Marsh is also at pains to emphasize the continuities, across the Reformation divide, of many basic Christian doctrines and core religious practices, and in longer term perspective this may well have served to ease the transition.[34] On the other hand, it is undeniable that the generation that experienced the changes of the Henrician, Edwardian and Elizabethan Reformations suffered a great deal of religious dislocation. Even acknowledging the large scale and deep popular roots of the Pilgrimage of Grace and the Western Rebellion, the extent of determined opposition seems surprisingly limited, and the degree to which people went along with what happened cries out for explanation. The chief answers are summarized by Houlbrooke: the piecemeal nature of the changes, which made it difficult to identify a decisive issue and hence inhibited people from making a stand; the way royal policies, whether by accident or design, divided potential opponents; the crown's reiterated stress on the duty of obedi-

---

[32] *Charles Whibley* (Ed.), Edward Hall's Chronicle. The Life of King Henry VIII. 2 Vols. London 1904, Vol. 2, 167; *Ethan H. Shagan*, Popular Politics and the English Reformation. Cambridge 2003, 140–147.
[33] *Patrick Collinson*, The Papal State of England [Review of Duffy, The Stripping of the Altars], in: The Times Higher, 15 Jan. 1993, 23.
[34] *Christine Peters*, Women in Early Modern Britain, 1450–1640. Basingstoke 2004, 151; idem, Patterns of Piety. Women, Gender and Religion in Late Medieval and Reformation England. Cambridge 2003; *Christopher Marsh*, Popular Religion in Sixteenth-Century England. Basingstoke 1988.

ence, articulated through an elaborate propaganda campaign and backed up by its by no means unimpressive powers of coercion; above all, Henry's determination to have his way.

It has always been recognized that material gain, accruing as a result of the destruction of the monasteries under Henry VIII, the dissolution of the chantries and the stripping of churches of most of their ornaments in the reign of Edward VI, and the rich pickings that favoured lay people were able to pluck from the lands of bishops and deans and chapters under Henry, Edward and Elizabeth, was a powerful incentive. Scarisbrick and Duffy have been at pains to emphasize that some of this apparent spoliation (even cases of theft) was traditionally pious in intent, designed to save as many holy things as possible – some were set aside or actually concealed in the hope that they could be restored at a later stage – or at least to ensure that they were put to charitable use or otherwise continued to be of local benefit. Yet it has always been clear that the acquisitive impulse, if not plain greed, was much more important – a point rammed home by Shagan's detailed account of the ransacking of the fabric and fittings of Hailes Abbey by large numbers of the local inhabitants from a wide social spectrum.[35]

A more far reaching argument is made by Clive Burgess, based on a detailed study of the important town of Bristol. He emphasizes that by the sixteenth century, particularly in urban communities, the cumulative financial and administrative burden imposed by the cult of the dead was immense, but it was upheld by the „knowledge" that all would depend on the faithful discharge of the same service by others. The government's attack on purgatory was in this sense liberating: it enabled the living to renege on their predecessors and enjoy the full fruits of their possessions without incurring sin. Burgess's argument is one among a number of attempts to tease out the implications of involvement in the process of expropriation for people's religious outlook and sense of identity. Duffy himself recognizes that the stripping of monasteries and churches, for whatever reason, were „ritual acts of deep significance". They profoundly devitalized the cult of the dead simply by rupturing the sense of continuity, and in other respects changed people's expectations of the sacred and distanced them from past practice; in that sense they did indeed constitute the act of exorcism or cleansing that the reformers wanted. Similar arguments, conceived in terms of the effects of „desacralization" have been developed at greater length by Shagan.[36]

---

[35] *Scarisbrick*, Reformation and the English People (note 6), 101–106; *Duffy*, Stripping of the Altars (note 7), 484–493, 497–501; *Shagan*, Popular Politics and the English Reformation (note 32), 162–196.
[36] *Burgess*, „By Quick and by Dead" (note 11), 856–857; *Duffy*, Stripping of the Altars (note 7), 494–495; *Shagan*, Popular Politics and the English Reformation (note 32), 189–196.

Shagan also emphasizes the idea of „collaboration", but the implications of this are not confined to the issue of material gains. Rather he is thinking along the lines suggested by some anthropologists: „meaning is use"; „religious as well as other knowledge becomes important to people only when it can be used for something, only when it is connected to their experience". This is important in both a negative and a positive sense. The message of government policies and proscriptions in the reigns of Henry VIII and Edward VI was that certain beliefs, institutions, symbols, rituals and images were worthless if not dangerous. Though that message may have been resisted, and could be counteracted by contrary instructions (as in Mary's revival of Catholic practice), it was plainly a powerful one that profoundly affected attitudes. On the positive side, the ideas embodied in government policies offered new opportunities. These included not simply material rewards, but also, for example, strategic opportunities for those involved in local disputes: people could present themselves as loyal servants of the crown while denouncing their opponents for obstructing royal policy.[37]

Much more far-reaching, Shagan suggests, was what Protector Somerset offered in the reign of Edward VI. It is well established that Somerset embarked on a quite extraordinarily ambitious programme of reform and reformation in Church and Commonwealth. The religious aspects of this programme are discussed by Houlbrooke along with the social policies. On the social side, Somerset and his agent John Hales promised to remedy the evils of enclosure, rack-renting and high prices, and in other respects to address the grievances of the common people against their social superiors. It was a tacit bargain: the acceptance of the gospel and the rejection of Catholic doctrines and rituals were to be rewarded by social reform. The policy backfired spectacularly. It was ineffective in the west country, in part because of this region's innate religious conservatism, but also because the government's reforms included an innovative tax on sheep and cloth that severely harmed the economic interests of the common people of Devon. The result was the Western Rebellion. In many other parts of central and southern England, the response was too enthusiastic. In the belief that they were acting in accord with government policies, the commons became remarkably assertive and in many areas took direct action to knock down enclosures. In Suffolk and in Norfolk (under the leadership of a substantial tanner called Robert Ket) they rose in rebellion against their social superiors. Inevitably, the government responded with armed repression. But for a brief moment in 1549, large parts of England witnessed a powerful and volatile combination of visionary theology and social radicalism. It is no accident that, as many have

---

[37] *Shagan*, Popular Politics and the English Reformation (note 32), 13–17, 24f., 257–269; *Thomas Hylland Eriksen*, Small Places, Large Issues. An Introduction to Social and Cultural Anthropology. London/Sterling, Va. 1995, 212.

noticed, the demands of the forces led by Ket carried echoes of the Twelve Articles of Memmingen, including the plea that „all bond men may be made free, for God made all free with his precious blood shedding".[38]

IV.

Reiterating Scarisbrick's point that the English Reformation was unwanted and only slowly and reluctantly accepted, Haigh has written of „a premature birth, a difficult labour and a sickly child".[39] The importance of the last phrase is to emphasise the obstacles that the reformers faced, not only in the early stages of the Reformation but also in Elizabeth's reign and on into the sevententh century, in planting Protestant beliefs in the hearts and minds of the English people. For Haigh, the pre-Reformation popularity of a religion based on ritual practice implies that Protestantism, pre-eminently a religion of the Word (scriptures and sermon), could never appeal strongly to a population that was still, by the early seventeenth century, predominantly illiterate. Adopting the terminology used by Gerald Strauss in the context of the Lutheran Reformation, Haigh has recently revisited the question of the English reformers' „success and failure"; inevitably, he finds that they failed to impart a full knowledge, understanding and acceptance of key Protestant doctrines. But this is to judge by standards which may be not merely exacting, but actually unrealistic. Other historians have taken a different view. Diarmaid MacCulloch has gone so far as to say that in the long term the English Reformation was a „howling success", and it is striking that Eamon Duffy employs the hardly less positive term „a runaway success".[40] Part of

---

[38] *Ethan H. Shagan*, Protector Somerset and the 1549 Rebellions: New Sources and New Perspectives, in: English Historical Review 114, 1999, 34–63; *idem*, Popular Politics and the English Reformation (note 32), 280–286; cf. *M. L. Bush*, Protector Somerset and the 1549 Rebellions: A Post-Revision Questioned, in: English Historical Review 115, 2000, 103–112; *G. W. Bernard*, New Perspectives or Old Complexities?, in: English Historical Review 115, 2000, 113–120; *Ethan H. Shagan*, „Popularity" and the 1549 Rebellions Revisited, in: English Historical Review 115, 2000, 121–132; *Fletcher/MacCulloch*, Tudor Rebellions (note 10), 145; *Peter Blickle*, The Revolution of 1525. The German Peasants' War from a New Perspective. Baltimore/London 1981, 197f.

[39] *Christopher Haigh*, The English Reformation: A Premature Birth, a Difficult Labour and a Sickly Child, in: Historical Journal 33, 1990, 449–459.

[40] *Christopher Haigh*, Success and Failure in the English Reformation, in: Past and Present 173, 2001, 28–49; cf. *Gerald Strauss*, Success and Failure in the German Reformation, in: Past and Present 67. 1975, 30–63; *Geoffrey Parker*, Success and Failure during the First Century of the Reformation, in: Past and Present 136, 1992, 43–82; *Diarmaid MacCulloch*, The Impact of the English Reformation, in: Historical Journal 38, 1995, 152; *Eamon Duffy*, The Long Reformation: Catholicism, Protestantism and the Multitude, in: Nicholas Tyacke (Ed.), England's Long Reformation, 1500–1800. London 1998, 36.

the story was the simple passage of time. Recently Norman Jones has identified generational change as a key analytical term, but the essential point has often been made before. In Duffy's evocative words, „[b]y the end of the 1570s, whatever the instincts and nostalgia of their seniors, a generation was growing up which had known nothing else, which believed the Pope to be Antichrist, the Mass a mummery, which did not look back to the Catholic past as their own, but another country, another world".[41]

Bearing on this theme is an enormous amount of recent and not so recent work. Some of it focuses on the admittedly slow growth in numbers of committed Protestants in the early to mid sixteenth century, and on the more impressive, but still limited, expansion of the „godly" – both ministers and a substantial lay following – in the reigns of Elizabeth and her early seventeenth-century Stuart successors. These people had an influence out of all proportion to their numbers. The role of some of the earlier exponents of reform has been well researched, though the beliefs of leading court figures such as Anne Boleyn and Thomas Cromwell, and the nature of their influence on the development of policy, remain controversial.[42] The fortunes of Protestants in the last years of Henry VIII, from 1539 to the beginning of 1547, have now been ably elucidated by Alec Ryrie, who among other things stresses that the conservative reaction after 1543 forced them from an ill-defined Lutheran stance to the more radical Zwinglian position that underlay the Edwardian Reformation.[43] In the process Ryrie raises important issues about the much more obscure subject of Protestant and proto-Protestant beliefs in the clerical and lay populace at large. There remain some grounds for thinking that Lollards, small in numbers though they were, did have an influence. Certainly there were many encounters between individuals espousing continental Protestant beliefs and existing Lollard communities. The Protestants had better translations of the scriptures (Robert Barnes's sales pitch recommending Tyndale's New Testament to two Essex Lollards who visited him at the Austin Friars in London is an historical commonplace).[44] They could also offer new and more sophisticated doctrines (above all the powerful and exciting idea of justification by faith alone) and, more generally, the sense of belonging to a wide and expanding European movement. But Lollards had something to offer too: their radical and long-standing rejection of

---

[41] *Norman Jones*, The English Reformation. Religion and Cultural Adaptation. Oxford 2002, 10–32; *Duffy*, Stripping of the Altars (note 7), 593.
[42] *G. W. Bernard*, Anne Boleyn's Religion, in: Historical Journal 36, 1993, 1-20; *idem*, Elton's Cromwell, in: History 83, 1998, 596-598; *E. W. Ives*, Anne Boleyn and the Early Reformation in England: the Contemporary Evidence, in: Historical Journal 37, 1994, 389-400.
[43] *Alec Ryrie*, The Gospel and Henry VIII. Evangelicals in the Early English Reformation. Cambridge 2003.
[44] *Dickens*, English Reformation (note 2), 56-57.

the doctrine of transubstantiation arguably helped to nudge English Protestants towards a sacramentarian position, while their inveterate hostility to images may have contributed to the spirit of iconoclasm that was such a marked feature of the Edwardian Reformation.[45]

The impact of suffering and persecution on the sense of identity and commitment of Protestants who remained in England and survived the experience, and the effects on Protestants in exile with the reformed churches of Frankfurt, Strasbourg, Zürich and Geneva, is the starting point for the study of those who, in the reign of Elizabeth, saw themselves as the „godly" but were often stigmatized by their detractors as „precisians" or „puritans". Their efforts to achieve a more thoroughgoing reformation than the settlement of 1559 allowed have been much studied, as also, more recently, have the social processes whereby a small group of „godly" clergy and lay people (at first mainly of high social status) gradually expanded to include by the early seventeenth century substantial sections of the gentry and of „middling groups" (yeomen and the substantial husbandmen, craftsmen and traders) in London, in many provincial towns, and eventually also in rural parishes. While the genuinely religious appeal of „godly" devotion must not be discounted, many historians have argued that puritanism also attracted these groups because it offered an ideology of social discipline that sanctioned moral reform programmes or „reformation of manners".[46]

Equally closely studied have been committed Catholics in Elizabethan and early Stuart England, especially „recusants": their uncompromising stance laid them open to the financial and, in some cases, physical penalties of the law; on the other hand, the experience of persecution and awareness of a separate religious identity helped to form powerful bonds of community. Haigh is undoubtedly right to stress, against the views of John Bossy, that the late Elizabethan recusant community was rooted firmly in Catholic survivalism of the 1560s and 1570s. However, the community could hardly have emerged as strongly as it did without the stiffening impact and subsequent

---

[45] *Diarmaid MacCulloch*, England, in: Andrew Pettegree (Ed.), The Early Reformation in Europe. Cambridge 1992, 172-177; *Ryrie*, Gospel and Henry VIII (note 43), 232-237.
[46] *Patrick Collinson*, The Elizabethan Puritan Movement. London 1967; *idem*, Godly People. Essays on English Protestantism and Puritanism. London 1983; *Martin Ingram*, Religion, Communities and Moral Discipline in Late Sixteenth- and Early Seventeenth-Century England: Case Studies, in: Kaspar von Greyerz (Ed.), Religion and Society in Early Modern Europe, 1500-1800. London 1984, 177-193; *David Underdown*, Fire from Heaven. The Life of an English Town in the Seventeenth Century. London 1992; *Robert von Friedeburg*, Sündenzucht und sozialer Wandel. Earls Colne (England), Ipswich und Springfield (Neuengland) c.1524-1690 im Vergleich. Stuttgart 1993; *Patrick Collinson/ John Craig* (Eds.), The Reformation in English Towns 1500-1640. Basingstoke 1998; *John Craig*, Reformation, Politics and Polemics. The Growth of Protestantism in East Anglian Market Towns, 1500-1610. Aldershot 2001; *Keith Wrightson/David Levine*, Poverty and Piety in an English Village. Terling, 1525-1700. 2nd Ed. Oxford 1995.

support of the seminary priests and Jesuit missionaries from Catholic Europe. As it was, committed Catholics were reduced to a tiny and embattled minority in most areas by 1600; and, though there was some growth in Catholic numbers in the early seventeenth century, in London and elsewhere, in absolute terms the increase was small.[47] The numbers and significance of so-called „church papists", who were willing to attend the services of the national Church while harbouring in their minds a commitment to Catholicism, are matters of greater uncertainty. Their willingness to compromise and dissimulate aroused the concern not only of the die-hard Catholic leadership but also of the government, fearful of a fifth column of unknown dimensions. On the other hand, Protestant zealots were apt to stigmatize conforming members of the Church of England who adopted a less intolerant view of ritual and ceremony as „church papists". „Church papists" thus abound in the polemical literature of the late sixteenth and early seventeenth centuries; whether they did so in reality by the turn of the century is doubtful.[48]

The issue is related to the broader question of the religious beliefs and behaviour of people who fell between the extremes of Catholic recusancy and Protestant godliness: the „unspectacular orthodoxy" of those who simply conformed to the national Church. In that such people constituted the great majority of the population, their importance is self-evident; but their very quiescence has made them a singularly elusive quarry, and interpretations of what conformity represented have been sharply divided. For the reasons already implied, Alexandra Walsham is inclined to recruit some of them into the ranks of church papists, though she offers no means of distinguishing them in practice from genuine conformists. Christopher Haigh, on the other hand, has identified groups of „parish anglicans", or, in a less than happy phrase, the „spiritual leftovers of Elizabethan England" – „those (or the children of those) who had reluctantly surrendered Catholic ritual in the 1560s [and] now expected from their ministers as much ceremony as the Church of England would sanction". Certainly some were vociferous in their support for the words and rituals of the Book of Common Prayer and insistent that their clergy should not depart from them, whether from mere neglect or in a spirit of zeal for further reformation. But Judith Maltby interprets this in a much more positive light than Haigh, rejecting the residual, backward-looking implications of his categories and viewing the people concerned as

---

[47] *John Bossy*, The English Catholic Community, 1570–1850. London 1975; *Christopher Haigh*, The Continuity of Catholicism in the English Reformation, in: Past and Present 93, 1981, 37–69; *idem*, From Monopoly to Minority: Catholicism in Early Modern England, in: Transactions of the Royal Historical Society, 5th Series 31, 1981, 129–147.
[48] *Alexandra Walsham*, Church Papists. Catholicism, Conformity and Confessional Polemic in Early Modern England. Woodbridge 1993.

"Prayer Book Protestants". Yet this argument too is open to question. Maltby assumes that commitment to the Prayer Book reflected genuine religious sentiment. But it may be that its attraction in this intensely legalistic society lay primarily in the fact that it was established by law: those who took their stand on the Prayer Book were by definition in a strong position against those who did not.[49]

A more detailed and realistic picture may be substituted for these broad-brush characterizations through study of the visitatorial and disciplinary activities of the ecclesiastical authorities. The English church courts have emerged from recent work with a much enhanced reputation. Before the Reformation they appear to have been, for the most part, well organized and efficient, serving a variety of useful social functions and helping to maintain conformity and high standards of religious observance by firm yet flexible action. As noted earlier, they did suffer some loss of business from about 1490 onwards, but this did not affect their core functions. Undoubtedly they were severely destabilized by successive changes of the official Reformation: levels of business collapsed in many areas and the courts were savagely attacked by puritan polemicists.[50] But from about 1570 the courts revived and were successfully modified to suit the needs and aspirations of the new Church of England. The conditions in which they at first had to work – religious dislocation and tides of catholic survivalism that only slowly ebbed away – were certainly difficult, and the impact of the courts on the parishes was always limited by the fact that they were operated by relatively remote authorities whose local knowledge was often imperfect. Moreover they could employ only spiritual sanctions, while the canon law ethos that informed the courts' working inclined them to mitigate rigour with mercy. Seen through unsympathetic eyes, this could make them look inefficient. Their greatest asset was the *persistent pressure* that they were able to exert, in visitation after visitation, generation after generation, in an undramatic but by no means ineffectual war of attrition. By this means they were able, not only to do solid work in combating sexual transgression and other forms of immorality, but

---

[49] *Walsham*, Church Papists (note 48); *eadem*, The Parochial Roots of Laudianism Revisited: Catholics, Anti-Calvinists and „Parish Anglicans" in Early Stuart England, in: Journal of Ecclesiastical History 49, 1998, 620–651; *Christopher Haigh*, The Church of England, the Catholics and the People, in: idem (Ed.), The Reign of Elizabeth I. Basingstoke 1984, 195–219; *Judith Maltby*, Prayer Book and People in Elizabethan and Early Stuart England. Cambridge 1998.
[50] *Brian L. Woodcock*, Medieval Ecclesiastical Courts in the Diocese of Canterbury. London 1952; *Ralph Houlbrooke*, The Decline of Ecclesiastical Jurisdiction under the Tudors, in: Rosemary O'Day/Felicity Heal (Ed.), Continuity and Change. Personnel and Administration of the Church of England, 1500–1642. Leicester 1976, 239–257, 284–286; *idem*, Church Courts and the People During the English Reformation, 1520–1570. Oxford 1979; *Richard M. Wunderli*, London Church Courts and Society on the Eve of the Reformation. Cambridge, Mass. 1981.

also to enforce at least minimum standards of religious observance and, in time, actually to raise such standards. In areas that have been studied in detail, it has been shown that church attendance, reception of the communion, and observance of Sunday by abstention from work had all improved by the early seventeenth century.[51] Independent quantitative evidence of such advances is hard to come by, but some of what exists is impressive. It might be thought that ritual conformity would be especially hard to enforce in the rapidly expanding metropolis, but it is clear that, where churchwardens and other local officers were meticulous in their efforts to secure compliance, a great deal could be achieved. Thus it has been shown that in St Saviour's parish in Southwark in the 1620s, over 90 per cent of the inhabitants received communion annually during the Easter season.[52]

Admittedly these figures may have been unusually high. More generally, the limits of parochial participation, and its ambiguous significance in relation to religious belief and commitment, must also be recognized. That the authorities had to keep up the pressure to enforce even the most basic of religious duties suggests an underlying reluctance. Indeed the very fact that certain religious duties were compulsory and defined by canons and statutes, in combination with the law-mindedness characteristic of the period, may have encouraged a minimalist approach to devotion which some erected into a virtual principle.[53] On the other hand, compliance cannot be understood simply in terms of coercion by the authorities. The reigns of Elizabeth and James I witnessed the implementation of a massive programme of Protestant education. The educational and professional standards of the clergy were rising rapidly, and a host of the more able and dedicated penned and published large numbers of didactic and devotional works designed to communicate the essentials of Protestantism and nourish the faith of lay people. Notable among these works were large numbers of catechisms of varying degrees of sophistication. No doubt the clergy often faced difficulties when they tried to employ these teaching aids at the parish level; but even Haigh concedes that they had some effect.[54] The impact of the Protestant liturgy itself, which by

---

[51] *Ronald A. Marchant*, The Church under the Law. Justice, Administration and Discipline in the Diocese of York, 1560–1640. Cambridge 1969; *Martin Ingram*, Church Courts, Sex and Marriage in England, 1570–1640. Cambridge 1987; *idem*, Puritans and the Church Courts, 1560–1640, in: Christopher Durston/Jacqueline Eales (Eds.), The Culture of English Puritanism, 1560–1700. Basingstoke 1996, 58–91, 268f., 288–295.

[52] *Jeremy Boulton*, The Limits of Formal Religion. The Administration of Holy Communion in Late Elizabethan and Early Stuart London, in: London Journal 10, 1984, 135–154.

[53] *Martin Ingram*, From Reformation to Toleration. Popular Religious Cultures in England, 1540–1690, in: Tim Harris (Ed.), Popular Culture in England, c. 1500–1850. Basingstoke 1995, 114–118.

[54] *Patrick Collinson*, The Religion of Protestants. The Church in English Society, 1559–1625. Oxford 1982, 92–100; *Ian Green*, The Christian's ABC. Catechisms and Cate-

the end of Elizabeth's reign had gained the dignity of long continuance, must not be underestimated. Duffy emphasises the extent to which the pre-Reformation liturgy was the source from which the religious beliefs and paradigms of the people were drawn, and seems to recognize that the same principle applied later: „Cranmer's somberly magnificent prose, read week by week, entered and possessed their minds, and became the fabric of their prayer, the utterance of their most solemn and their most vulnerable moments". In the same way the words and images of the English Bible seeped into, and eventually saturated, religious mentalities. Nor should the attractions of communal singing of metrical psalms, a key feature of post-Reformation congregational worship, be ignored. Sophisticated observers found the standard Sternhold and Hopkins version execrable, but nonetheless testified to its popularity. Sermons, too, could have a wide popular appeal, if they were pitched at the right level.[55]

Attachment to the church and its services must also be seen in the context of the central role that ecclesiastical institutions played in social life. In the sixteenth and seventeenth centuries the parish became increasingly important as a unit of administration for secular as well as ecclesiastical administration. Crucially it was primarily via the parish that the poor laws, which were themselves to become a fundamental component of local society by the seventeenth century, were routinely administered. Moreover, it was actually in the church, churchyard and adjacent buildings that numerous forms of local business, such as the election of officers and the casting of accounts, were regularly transacted. Fire-fighting equipment and the parish armoury were often stored on church premises – a reflection of the church's role as a rallying-point in times of crisis. The church bells were rung to signal alarms and to celebrate events of national rejoicing, and ordinarily one of them was rung „for curfew and day". There was often a school of some sort associated with the church or minister. Rhymes and lampoons against whoremasters, whores, cuckolds and other local ne'er-do-wells were sometimes pinned up on the church door – a reflection of the church's status as the moral centre of the community.[56]

For individuals as for the parish as a whole, participation in the services of the church was intimately associated with local identity, respectability and status. This emerges most vividly from arrangements for seating in church. Households and individuals were assigned particular places, some of which

---

chizing in England c.1530–1740. Oxford 1996; *idem*, Print and Protestantism in Early Modern England. Oxford 2000; *Haigh*, Success and Failure in the English Reformation (note 40), 41–49.

[55] *Duffy*, Stripping of the Altars (note 7), 2, 51f., 593; *Ingram*, From Reformation to Toleration (note 53), 98, 112.

[56] *D. M. Palliser*, Introduction: the Parish in Perspective, in: Wright (Ed.), Parish, Church and People (note 11), 5–28; *Paul Slack*, Poverty and Policy in Tudor and Stuart England. London/New York 1988; *Ingram*, From Reformation to Toleration (note 53), 112f.

were attached by right to certain holdings or properties. Broadly speaking the seats in the church were arranged in order of social importance. Better and more elaborate „rooms" at the front were allotted to gentry and other leading parishioners (the best had high panels for protection against draughts, curtains, cushions, and other conveniences); the poor were assigned to mean benches at the back; in the middle were a variety of intermediate sittings. Often there were other divisions – between „men's seats" and „women's seats", and between accommodation for the householders of the parish and subsidiary provision for servants, apprentices and other youngsters. Such arrangements were designed to give symbolic expression to the parish hierarchy – a conservative vision of a well-ordered community, meeting in the presence of God, in which everyone knew his or her place. In practice there were sporadic scuffles as individuals contested particular seats or tried to claim „better" ones; while sooner or later the effects of social mobility, movement in and out of the parish, and other demographic changes would make necessary a total reallocation of seats – often presaged by general grumbling if not contention. While such disputes may reflect badly on the devotion and Christian charity of the people concerned, the very fierceness with which places were cherished indicates how important these matters of status were, and how far the aspirations of parishioners locked them into the system of corporate worship.[57]

The strength of such attachment may well have varied with social status. Probably it was the middling ranks of society upwards – those who monopolised local offices and who contributed most to the upkeep of the church and the well-being of the parish through the payment of church and poor rates and through contributions to local voluntary charities – for whom the forms of religion were of greatest social importance. However, a number of recent studies caution against supposing that the appeal of church membership was necessarily much weaker lower down the social scale. Many „honest householders" of the poorer sort, who had a definite, albeit modest, stake in the community as payers of some local rates with a right to a place in church, may plausibly be supposed to have shared similar values. Nor should one assume any kind of simple contrast between town and country. Local attachment to the church has been documented for rural parishes in Wiltshire, Norfolk and elsewhere. But it certainly existed also in urban parishes, in London, Chester and other provincial towns.[58]

---

[57] *David Underdown*, Revel, Riot, and Rebellion. Popular Politics and Culture in England, 1603–1660. Oxford 1985, 30–33; *Ingram*, Church Courts, Sex and Marriage (note 51), 111f.; *Susan Dwyer Amussen*, An Ordered Society. Gender and Class in Early Modern England. Oxford 1988, 137–144.
[58] *Nick Alldridge*, Loyalty and Identity in Chester Parishes 1540–1640, in: Wright (Ed.), Parish, Church and People (note 11), 85–124; *Ian W. Archer*, The Pursuit of Stability. Social Relations in Elizabethan London. Cambridge 1991, 82–92.

Popular commitment to the church, and the development of a Protestant identity, must also be seen in broader political and social context. For centuries religious orthodoxy had been linked with political loyalty, and the reliance of civil society on religious sanctions was reflected in the remarkable and growing frequency with which oath-taking was used both in the judicial system and in the processes of parish, borough, city and national government. More fundamentally, as many historians have remarked, obedience to the crown was a central feature of Henry VIII's religious vision. In the religiously divided realm that Elizabeth inherited, conformity with the established Church was yet more firmly associated with political obedience. Of crucial importance were the series of plots sanctioned by the papal bull of excommunication against Elizabeth in 1570, and the long wars with Spain after 1585. Aided by government propaganda, but rooted also in popular practice (such as the custom that developed in many communities of celebrating 17 November, Queen Elizabeth's Accession Day, with bell-ringing and bonfires), these threats to queen and realm served to forge a powerful sense of Protestant patriotism. The other side of the coin was anti-popery. Insistently the Papacy was identified with the Antichrist, and Roman Catholicism was associated with England's enemies and remorselessly linked with tyranny, oppression and persecution. Such messages were reiterated not only in books – of which John Foxe's massive and often luridly illustrated „Actes and Monuments" or „Book of Martyrs" is the most famous – but also in sermons, pageants, plays and ballads, hence reaching a mass audience including the illiterate. Anti-Catholic sentiment became grafted onto traditional English xenophobia and by the early seventeenth century was fully absorbed into popular culture. The point to emphasize here is that in Elizabeth's reign the chief effect was to bolster royal authority and promote peace within England. In the context of defensive wars against a dangerous external enemy, rebellion was further discredited as a means of political action. In this way what had begun as a top-down Reformation was consolidated by popular, traditional conservatism.[59]

Anti-Catholicism was related to the idea that in some sense England had succeeded Israel as God's chosen nation, and with a pervasive (though often latent) millenarianism: the belief that this was the „last age" of the

---

[59] *Catto*, Religious Change under Henry V (note 21), 97, 115; *Richard Rex*, The Crisis of Obedience: God's Word and Henry's Reformation, in: Historical Journal 39, 1996, 863–894; *David Cressy*, Bonfires and Bells. National Memory and the Protestant Calendar in Elizabethan and Stuart England. London 1989, 50–57, 67–74; *Hutton*, Rise and Fall (note 12), 146–151; *Carol Z. Wiener*, The Beleaguered Isle: A Study of Elizabethan and Early Jacobean Anti-Catholicism, in: Past and Present 51, 1971, 27–62; *Peter Lake*, Anti-Popery: the Structure of a Prejudice, in: Richard Cust/Ann Hughes (Eds.), Conflict in Early Stuart England. Studies in Religion and Politics, 1603–1642. London/New York 1989, 72–106.

world, and that the hoped for defeat of Antichrist would usher in the Second Coming of Christ.[60] This in turn was one element of a much broader set of providential beliefs: the idea that God, far from being a remote presence, intervened actively in the world to bless, warn and chastise His people. Providential ideas were not confined to Protestants and had, indeed, been widely current before the Reformation. But the Calvinist stress on the power and sovereignty of God, and the utter weakness and sinfulness of mankind, intensified them. In their strongest and most pervasive form, providential beliefs were characteristic of the „godly", both clerical and lay, in late Elizabethan and early Stuart England, and it has sometimes been thought that they were uncongenial to the bulk of the population. But it is now clear that they did in fact have a much wider appeal. One kind of proof is found in wills, which conventionally voiced thanks for „the wordly goods that it hath pleased God to bestow", and expressed a routine resignation to his will: „after it shall please God to call me". Another is the printed literature of the period. Peter Lake's work on murder pamphlets designed for popular audiences indicates that the writers – some of whom were „godly" clergymen appropriating the genre for pastoral purposes – commonly appealed to providential beliefs among their readers. A similar point has been elaborated in extraordinary detail by Alexandra Walsham. She shows how providential ideas expressed in sermons, pamphlets, ballads, and collections of cautionary stories – of which Thomas Beard's „Theatre of God's Judgements" is the most famous – constituted a kind of „cultural cement" which was crucial in creating „a collective Protestant consciousness, a sense of confessional identity which fused anti-Catholicism and patriotic feeling" uniting all ranks of society.[61] Walsham's argument has affinities with the work of Tessa Watt on the religious ballads, chapbooks and other forms of cheap literature (some of them illustrated with woodcuts) that both proliferated in this period and, it is clear, were very widely available and consumed across a wide social spectrum throughout England. While not necessarily „Protestant" in a strict doctrinal sense, the content was characteristically „post-Reformation".[62]

---

[60] *Patrick Collinson*, The Birthpangs of Protestant England. Religious and Cultural Change in the Sixteenth and Seventeenth Centuries. Basingstoke 1988, 3–27.
[61] *Keith Thomas*, Religion and the Decline of Magic. Studies in Popular Beliefs in Sixteenth and Seventeenth Century England. London 1971, 78–112; *Keith Wrightson/David Levine*, Death in Whickham, in: John Walter/Roger Schofield (Eds.), Famine, Disease and Social Order in Early Modern Society. Cambridge 1989, 161f.; *Peter Lake*, Deeds against Nature: Cheap Print, Protestantism and Murder in Early Seventeenth Century England, in: Kevin Sharpe/Peter Lake (Eds.), Culture and Politics in Early Stuart England. Basingstoke 1994, 257–283; *Alexandra Walsham*, Providence in Early Modern England. Oxford 1999, 5.
[62] *Tessa Watt*, Cheap Print and Popular Piety 1550–1640. Cambridge 1991.

V.

The period witnessed some broader cultural changes, that indeed altered understandings of religion itself. John Bossy has pointed out that usage of the term „religion" underwent important developments between the late fifteenth and the early eighteenth centuries. At first it meant a „religious" rule or order and those who followed it, and thus related more to action than belief. In the fifteenth century humanists revived the classical meaning of a worshipful attitude to God and a respect for holy things. In the context of sharpening divisions among the churches of Europe in the sixteenth century, „religion" came to refer to particular variants of Christian belief and practice and the communities associated with them. By about 1700 the word „religion" was coming to acquire a more abstract sense of a system of beliefs. Associated with these shifts, it may be suggested, was a very profound change whereby the collective and individual consciousness of „religion" was sharpened and enhanced. Before the Reformation, religion was a medium in which the world swam. Amid the fierce debates over doctrine and pious practice that were unleashed from the 1520s onwards, „religion" ceased to be something that could be taken for granted. More and more it came to be identified as a matter of choice and commitment, and hence diversity and potential conflict, in personal, social and political life. As a corollary religious *division* came to be seen as a fact of life that had in some way to be accommodated if it could not be eliminated.[63]

In this context two themes are particularly noteworthy. One is the contemporary recognition that religious difference entailed a threat to political unity and social harmony. At the core of the idea of religion as it had emerged from the late classical world and developed during the middle ages was a sense of „the ties that bind", and it is plain that this integrative element was highly valued in itself, irrespective of doctrinal issues. A marked feature of royal policy in the successive phases of the English Reformation was a stress on order and unity and an insistence that they should be preserved against the encroachments of religious disagreements. Thus Henry VIII constantly strove for „good unity and concord", „to establish Christian quietness and unity", to abolish „diversity in opinions", and maintain „a firm union among all his subjects". In the reign of Edward VI, the „Book of Common Prayer" was issued „to the intent a uniform, quiet and godly order should be had". Queen Mary, though later she was to enforce Catholic belief and practice with unprecedented rigour, began her reign by commanding her subjects „to live together in quiet sort and Christian charity, leaving those new-found devilish terms of papist or heretic". Her successor Elizabeth elaborated the point:

---

[63] *John Bossy*, Christianity in the West 1400–1700. Oxford/New York 1985, 170f.; *Ingram*, From Reformation to Toleration (note 53), 99f.

"Because in all alterations, and specially in rites and ceremonies, there happeneth discord amongst the people and thereupon slanderous words and railings whereby charity, the knot of all Christian society, is loosed: the Queen's majesty being most desirous of all other earthly things that her people should live in charity both towards God and man [...] willeth and straightly commandeth all manner her subjects to forbear all vain and contentious disputations in matters of religion, and not to use in despite or rebuke of any person these contentious words: papist, or papistical heretic, schismatic, or sacramentary, or any such like words of reproach."

This was the basis of a Church settlement that was designed to accommodate as many shades of opinion as possible, without (as Bacon famously expressed it) „making windows into men's souls". In other words, outward conformity rather than confessional commitment was made the touchstone of loyalty and obedience.[64]

Norman Jones has recently explored how, in a less explicit way, a modus vivendi based on concord or at least co-existence was sought in society at large. Many families included among their members differences (sometimes sharp ones) of religious opinion. Family interests, including the accumulation and transmission of property, dictated that such differences should as far as possible be downplayed or otherwise accommodated. It was the same at a more public level. Accommodation was most difficult in institutions, such as colleges at the universities, that were close to the heart of the religious establishment and whose members were subject to strong official pressure to conform. Nonetheless collegiality sometimes overrode confessional divisions or mitigated their consequences. It was somewhat easier in the inns of court, since confessional issues were not so central to legal discourse; and also in livery companies and city and borough councils, which could concentrate on their core functions and push religious divisions to the margins. Of course, in time the ethos of all these institutions was profoundly altered by the new Protestant context; but in the short term the potential social costs of religious change were mitigated.[65] More generally, a number of historians have noticed that in Elizabethan England popular intolerance of religious dissent was often muted, even in the case of groups like the Family of Love, whose views were well beyond the mainstream and, in theory at least, viewed by the authorities with the gravest suspicion. It would seem that a kind of de facto toleration sometimes operated at the local level, especially among neighbours who knew each other well and among colleagues in small institutions and corporate bodies.[66]

---

[64] *Bernard*, Making of Religious Policy (note 15), 325, 345; *Williams* (Ed.), English Historical Documents, 1485–1558 (note 1), 849; *Paul L. Hughes/James F. Larkin* (Eds.), Tudor Royal Proclamations. 2 Vols. New Haven/London 1969, Vol. 2, 6, 128.
[65] *Jones*, English Reformation (note 41); *Robert Tittler*, The Reformation and the Towns in England. Politics and Political Culture, c. 1540–1640. Oxford 1998, 9, 127.
[66] *Christopher W. Marsh*, The Family of Love in English Society, 1550–1630. Cambridge 1994; *Jones*, English Reformation (note 41), 147–149.

The second theme arising from the increasing self-consciousness of religion is related: this was a tendency to distinguish between religious and non-religious matters. Before the Reformation religious ideas permeated all aspects of society to such an extraordinary extent as to discourage such distinctions. But the reformers explicitly sought to restore „true religion" and purge it of „idolatry, superstition, hypocrisy, with such other errors and abuses". In so doing they desacralized many times (such as the abrogated feast days), places (such as abbeys and other monasteries), and objects (such as relics and religious images) that had hitherto been accepted as holy. Among the many consequences, an issue that has attracted particular historical attention is the fierce determination of contemporary reformers to distinguish more sharply between „religion" and „magic". In European perspective it can be seen that this was a feature of both Catholic and Protestant reform, but Protestants denounced as „magical" or „superstitious" not only popular notions and practices that pre-Reformation churchmen had long viewed with more or less disquiet, but also doctrines, symbols and rituals that were central to Catholic religion.[67]

This redrawing of the boundaries of the sacred in turn had profound and far-reaching, but very various, effects. The most dramatic was the unleashing of a legal campaign against supposed witches (mostly poor women) for „maleficium" against persons and property, and against „cunning men" and „wise women" for various forms of „white" magic. It would seem that in the reign of Elizabeth persecution was most intense in areas – the county of Essex in south-east England is the outstanding example – where Protestantism was preached with particular zeal with the result, it may be supposed, that religious anxieties were particularly aroused. On the other hand, witchcraft accusations were rarely the vehicle for attacks by Protestants on Catholic neighbours and vice versa.[68] Another consequence was a sustained attempt by churchmen to eliminate the many allegedly „superstitious", „magical", or „pagan" practices that had previously been woven into the fabric of the Church's liturgical year. However, as Hutton has argued, the impact of this campaign was mitigated to the extent that such practices were not altogether destroyed. Though subject to constant attrition in the late sixteenth and early seventeenth centuries, some continued to exist as elements of popular calendar festivities.[69]

There were many related developments. For example, the proscription of intercessory prayer, and the abolition of institutions associated with it, made it necessary to draw a line between gilds dedicated to prayers for the dead

---

[67] *Peter Burke*, Popular Culture in Early Modern Europe. London 1978, 209–212.
[68] *Thomas*, Religion and the Decline of Magic (note 61); *Alan Macfarlane*, Witchcraft in Tudor and Stuart England. A Regional and Comparative Study. London 1970; *James Sharpe*, Instruments of Darkness. Witchcraft in England 1550–1750. London 1996.
[69] *Hutton*, Rise and Fall of Merry England (note 12), ch. 4–5.

and those that existed for the regulation and protection of crafts and trades, and, more generally, between endowments for „superstitious" activities and those devoted to social objectives such as education and poor relief. Notoriously this proved extremely difficult to do. An even trickier distinction was between remembering the dead for the purposes of intercessory prayer and simple memorialization of the great and the good, particularly of benefactors to institutions such as livery companies, colleges, schools and hospitals. In the short term, the expedients and compromises that had to be resorted to in making these distinctions may have eased the transition from Catholic to Protestant culture, by perpetuating established customs in a new guise.[70] But in the longer term the effect was surely to change people's notions of the religious, and to alter the scope of some important related concepts. Most notably, the meaning of „charity" narrowed to denote efforts to relieve the poor, with a primary though not exclusive emphasis on their physical, educational and medical needs. It is tempting to describe these changes as a process of gradual secularization. Arguably this is misleading to the extent that, throughout the sixteenth and seventeenth centuries, Christian doctrine was not merely one among a number of available philosophies but remained the dominant framework for understanding the world and the place of mankind within it: all other discourses – those of the law, medicine and „natural philosophy", for example – were subordinate to it. But it is the case that in certain areas of life religion began to recede from the foreground of consciousness. This change helped to identify means whereby certain forms of behaviour that had hitherto been morally unacceptable, such as the taking of interest on loans, could within defined limits be regarded as licit. It also contributed to shifts in thought that eventually favoured religious toleration. In the shorter term, in the reigns of Elizabeth and James I, it perhaps helped their subjects to avoid the worst excesses of religious strife.[71]

A related cultural development is of interest. There was a long tradition of writings on the subject of „courtesy", the appropriate forms of behaviour, especially in formal settings such as feasts, in aristocratic households and princely courts. The publication of Erasmus's „De civilitate morum puerilium" (1530; English translation 1532) inaugurated a European-wide process of transformation by which concepts of „civility" were endlessly elaborated. „Civility" did not refer merely to the niceties of polite behaviour among the aristocracy; in some of its usages it could apply to any rank of society and re-

---

[70] *Jones*, English Reformation (note 41), ch. 4; *Ian W. Archer*, The Arts and Acts of Memorialization in Early Modern London, in: J. F. Merritt (Ed.), Imagining Early Modern London. Perceptions and Portrayals of the City from Stow to Strype, 1598–1720. Cambridge 2001, 89–113.
[71] *Bossy*, Christianity in the West (note 63), 168; *C. John Sommerville*, The Secularization of Early Modern England. From Religious Culture to Religious Faith. Oxford/New York 1992; *Ingram*, From Reformation to Toleration (note 53), 99f.

ferred to qualities that a later age would term respectability, propriety and decency. It thus had a hard moral edge. The language of civility, absorbed into the popular consciousness in England from the late sixteenth century, offered a complementary basis for moral conduct, an ethic consistent with Christian morality but based in social rather than religious bonds. Such an ethic, it may be suggested, had a particular utility in a society threatened by religious divisions: the idea of „civility" provided the means to re-establish some common ground.[72]

VI.

From the seventeenth-century perspective, the limits of such arguments are obvious. It was not until 1689 that even a limited toleration was established by statute. The 1640s witnessed civil war and the „Puritan revolution". Before that, religious tensions had often run high: Collinson has suggested that clashes between the „godly" and their opponents in some communities – conflicts over what, in retrospect, might seem to be such trivial issues as maypoles, cakes and ale – should be seen as England's „street wars of religion".[73] Even for Elizabeth's reign, an emphasis on a peaceful outcome of religious change depends in part on taking a narrowly English view. An Irish perspective changes the picture. Ireland was part of the English polity, in the early sixteenth century a lordship deriving from Papal grant, a dependent kingdom from 1541. The attempts of the crown, partly for security reasons, to extend English power in Ireland eventually developed into a policy of conquest and colonization that was all the more politically disruptive because it was spasmodic, inadequately financed, and undermined by feud and faction. Its progress was made even more problematic by its association with what was, by comparison with its English counterpart, a failed attempt at Protestant Reformation. At the level of official action, things seemed to go reasonably well at first. The royal supremacy was enforced by Henry VIII. But the Anglo-Irish aristocracy, the gentry of the English-controlled territory called the Pale, and the leading townsmen, tended to remain Catholic. Since these groups had traditionally been upholders of the English interest in Ireland, this yawning division between their religion and their political loyalties was ominous. There was more overt resistance from Gaelic Irish lords, rendered

---

[72] *Dilwyn Knox*, Erasmus' *De Civilitate* and the Religious Origins of Civility in Protestant Europe, in: Archiv für Reformationsgeschichte 86, 1995, 7-55; *Anna Bryson*, From Courtesy to Civility. Changing Codes of Conduct in Early Modern England. Oxford 1998; *Martin Ingram*, Sexual Manners: The Other Face of Civility in Early Modern England, in: Peter Burke/Brian Harrison/Paul Slack (Eds.), Civil Histories. Essays Presented to Keith Thomas. Oxford 2000, 87–109.

[73] *Collinson*, Birthpangs of Protestant England (note 60), 136–155.

yet more dangerous by the strategic importance of Ireland in the 1580s and 1590s as a potential back door for Spanish invasion. The upshot was Tyrone's rebellion, which broadened into the Nine Years War (1594-1603). By 1600 English power in Ireland had been reduced to almost nothing, and a small Spanish force managed to land at Kinsale in 1601. It is true that the English were eventually able to neutralize, if not totally destroy, the earl of Tyrone and his confederates. But it was only at the cost of large-scale military intervention and the expenditure of huge sums of money. Moreover, deep tensions and profound religious divisions remained in Irish society.[74] It is beyond the scope of this paper to pursue the story in either Ireland or England into the seventeenth century. Suffice to say that, when English Protestantism had split into bitter conflict between Calvinists and anti-Calvinists in the reign of Charles I (1625-1649), renewed rebellion in Ireland was one of the most important catalysts for an escalation of political and religious conflict in England. The muted tensions and small-scale street wars of the period before 1640 gave way to strife on an immeasurably greater scale of intensity and destructiveness – to what has sometimes been seen, indeed, as England's long delayed „wars of religion".[75]

---

[74] *Henry A. Jefferies*, The Early Tudor Reformation in the Irish Pale, in: Journal of Ecclesiastical History 52, 2001, 34–62; *Karl S. Bottigheimer/Ute Lotz-Heumann*, The Irish Reformation in European Perspective, in: Archiv für Reformationsgeschichte 89, 1998, 268–309; *Hiram Morgan*, Tyrone's Rebellion. The Outbreak of the Nine Years War in Tudor Ireland. Woodbridge 1993.
[75] *John Morrill*, The Religious Context of the English Civil War, in: Transactions of the Royal Historical Society, 5th Series 34, 1984, 155–178.

Bibliographical Update

By

Ralph Houlbrooke and *Martin Ingram*

Several important books have appeared since the submission of the preceding critical reviews three years ago. Ian Forrest has explored the detection of heresy in pre-Reformation England, in the process shedding light on the antecedents of royal control of the Church.[1] On religious policy during Henry VIII's reign, George Bernard has developed and substantiated his earlier claims for the king's fundamental consistency.[2] John Schofield, in disagreement with Bernard, argues that Henry was for a time tempted to follow a Lutheran path.[3] Peter Marshall analyses „the complex web of overlapping and competing religious identities" assumed by Henry's conservative and evangelical subjects during years of unprecedented and unpredictable change.[4] Different aspects of the Marian restoration are discussed in two collections of essays. One, edited by John Edwards and Ronald Truman, focuses on the special contribution of a member of Philip's Spanish entourage, Bartolomé Carranza.[5] The other, edited by Eamon Duffy and David Loades, achieves the most comprehensive assessment of the theology, pastoral practice and ecclesiastical administration of Mary Tudor's Church yet published, concluding, cautiously, that it „had more features of strength than it has been generally given credit for".[6] In an important study of long-term developments that contributed to the triumph of Protestantism in England and Scotland in 1558–60, Clare Kellar emphasizes the links between some leading evangelicals and their shared vision of a reformed Britain.[7] Elizabethan notions of *adiaphora* are discussed in contributions by Louise Campbell and Ethan Shagan to a collection of essays about „moderate voices" in the Reformation. Alain Tallon in the same volume, and Luc Racaut in a separate article, compare the „Anglican" and Gallican Churches.[8] The considerations that in-

---

[1] *Ian Forrest,* The Detection of Heresy in Late Medieval England. Oxford 2005.
[2] *George W. Bernard,* The King's Reformation: Henry VIII and the Remaking of the English Church. New Haven, CT/London 2005.
[3] *John Schofield,* Philip Melanchthon and the English Reformation. Aldershot 2006.
[4] *Peter Marshall,* Religious Identities in Henry VIII's England. Aldershot 2006.
[5] *John Edwards/Ronald Truman* (Eds.), Reforming Catholicism in the England of Mary Tudor: the Achievement of Friar Bartolomé Carranza. Aldershot 2005.
[6] *Eamon Duffy/David Loades* (Eds.), The Church of Mary Tudor. Aldershot 2006, xvii.
[7] *Clare Kellar,* Scotland, England, and the Reformation, 1534–1561. Oxford 2003.
[8] *Luc Racaut/Alec Ryrie* (Eds.), Moderate Voices in the European Reformation. Aldershot 2005; *Luc Racaut,* Anglicanism and Gallicanism: between Rome and Geneva?, in: Archiv für Reformationsgeschichte 96, 2005, 198–220.

fluenced appointments to the early Elizabethan episcopal bench are analysed by Brett Usher.[9] Gary W. Jenkins exposes fundamental inconsistencies in the anti-Roman polemic of John Jewel, the best-known early defender of the Elizabethan Church.[10] The emergence of a Roman Catholic minority in England and government responses to this development are important themes of Michael Questier's study of the Brownes, a leading Catholic noble family, and of essays contributed by Questier, along with Ethan H. Shagan, Peter Marshall, and Thomas McCoog to a collection on English Catholics and the „Protestant Nation".[11] Alexandra Walsham explores issues of tolerance and intolerance, arguing that „to situate 'persecution' and „toleration" at opposite ends of the intellectual and political spectrum is deeply misleading".[12] Note finally that a special number of the journal *Historical Research* was in 2004 devoted to assessments of the work of Geoffrey Dickens, one of Britain's foremost historians of the Reformation, by a group of English and German scholars.[13]

---

[9] *Brett Usher*, William Cecil and Episcopacy, 1559–1577. Aldershot 2003.
[10] *Gary W. Jenkins*, John Jewel and the English National Church: the Dilemmas of an Erastian Reformer. Aldershot 2005.
[11] *Michael C. Questier*, Catholicism and Community in Early Modern England: Politics, Aristocratic Patronage and Religion, c. 1550–1640. Cambridge 2006; *Ethan H. Shagan* (Ed.), Catholics and the 'Protestant Nation': Religious Politics and Identity in Early Modern England. Manchester 2005.
[12] *Alexandra Walsham*, Charitable Hatred. Tolerance and Intolerance in England, 1500–1700. Manchester/New York 2006.
[13] Historical Research 77:195, 2004.

Autorenverzeichnis

Prof. Dr. *Robert von Friedeburg*, Hoogleraar Geschiedenis, Faculteit der Historischen en Kunstwetenschappen, Erasmus Universiteit Rotterdam, Postbus 1738, 3000 DR Rotterdam; wichtige Publikationen: Widerstandsrecht und Konfessionskonflikt: Gemeiner Mann und Notwehr im deutsch-britischen Vergleich, 1530-1669. Berlin 1999; Self-Defence and Religious Strife in Early Modern Europe. Aldershot 2002; Europa in der frühen Neuzeit. Frankfurt am Main 2006.

Prof. Dr. *Mark Greengrass*, University of Sheffield, Humanities Research Institute, Arts Tower, Floor 14, Sheffield S10 2TN; wichtige Publikationen: The French Reformation. Oxford 1987; The Longman Companion to the European Reformation 1500-1618. London 1998; French Wars of Religion 1559-1589. London 2005.

Prof. Dr. *Ralph Houlbrooke*, University of Reading, Early Modern Research Centre, Faculty of Arts and Humanities, School of History, Whiteknights, Reading, Berkshire RG6 6AA; wichtige Publikationen: The English Family 1450-1700. Harlow 1984; English Family Life, 1576-1716: an Anthology from Diaries. Oxford 1988; Death, Religion and the Family in England, 1480-1750. Oxford 1998.

Dr. *Martin Ingram*, University of Oxford, Brasenose College, Faculty of History, Broad Street, Oxford OX1 3BD; wichtige Publikationen: Church Courts, Sex and Marriage in England, 1570-1640. Cambridge 1987; Reformation of Manners in Early Modern England, in: P. Griffiths/A. Fox/S. Hindle (Eds.), The Experience of Authority in Early Modern England. Basingstoke 1996, 47-88.

Prof. Dr. *Luise Schorn-Schütte*, Historisches Seminar der Johann Wolfgang Goethe-Universität, Neuere Allgemeine Geschichte unter besonderer Berücksichtigung der Frühen Neuzeit, Grüneburgplatz 1, 60323 Frankfurt am Main; wichtige Publikationen: Die Reformation. Vorgeschichte, Verlauf, Wirkungen. München 1996, 4. überarb. Aufl. 2006; Evangelische Geistlichkeit in der Frühneuzeit. Deren Anteil an der Entfaltung frühmoderner Staatlichkeit und Gesellschaft. Dargestellt am Beispiel des Fürstentums Braunschweig-Wolfenbüttel, der Landgrafschaft Hessen-Kassel und der Stadt Braunschweig (16.-18. Jahrhundert). (Quellen und Forschungen zur Reformationsgeschichte, Bd. 63.) Gütersloh 1996; Historische Politikforschung. Eine Einführung. München 2006.

www.ingramcontent.com/pod-product-compliance
Lightning Source LLC
Chambersburg PA
CBHW050908300426
44111CB00010B/1437